The Politics of American English, 1776–1850

The Politics
of American English,
1776-1850

DAVID SIMPSON

New York   Oxford
OXFORD UNIVERSITY PRESS
1986

OXFORD UNIVERSITY PRESS

Oxford New York Toronto
Delhi Bombay Calcutta Madras Karachi
Kuala Lumpur Singapore Hong Kong Tokyo
Nairobi Dar es Salaam Cape Town
Melbourne Auckland

and associated companies in
Beirut Berlin Ibadan Nicosia

Published by Oxford University Press, Inc.,
200 Madison Avenue, New York, New York 10016

Library of Congress Cataloging-in-Publication Data
Simpson, David, 1951-
The politics of American English, 1776-1850.
Bibliography: p. Includes index.
1. English language—United States—History.
2. American literature—History and criticism. I. Title.
PE2809.S56 1986   420′.973   85-13601
ISBN 0-19-503724-3

Printing (last digit): 9 8 7 6 5 4 3 2 1

Printed in the United States of America

To my brother Richard, with love

Acknowledgments

It gives me great pleasure to thank the following institutions for support during the years in which I was gathering material for this study: The British Academy, for a travel grant (1979) and a research stipend (1981); Harvard University, for access to the Widener Library and for generous hospitality; the Huntington Library, for a short-term research fellowship (1979); and, most of all, the John Simon Guggenheim Foundation, for a full-year fellowship (1983–84). Acceptance of these various grants was made possible thanks to the generous sabbatical policies of King's College, Cambridge, and Northwestern University.

I respectfully acknowledge the precedents established by, and the information gathered from, the writings of two scholars in particular: H. L. Mencken and Allen Walker Read. I have also depended on the fruits of the research done by James Franklin Beard and his team of editors on the SUNY Cooper edition.

As a nonspecialist in American studies, I have benefited more than usual from the advice and assistance of various people. Harrison Hayford has been a constant source of encouragement and information. I thank also John Barrell, Wally Douglas, Robert Gundlach, Robert and Mary K. Madison, Russell Maylone, Randolph Quirk, Tony Tanner, John Troy, and Jack Wilson. Philip Gura and the reader for Oxford University Press read the manuscript carefully, and offered valuable advice. Bill Sisler has been a most cooperative editor; and no one could hope for better informed or more helpful booksellers than Truman Metzel and Jeff Rice of *Great Expectations*. "Wot larks."

Evanston, Illinois   D.S.
June 1985

Contents

Abbreviations

The following abbreviations have been used:

DA   *Dictionary of Americanisms,* ed. Mathews (1951)
DAE   *Dictionary of American English,* eds. Craigie and
       Hulbert (1938)
NAR   *North American Review*
OED   *Oxford English Dictionary*

Most references in the text are by author and date of publication;
the Bibliography should be consulted for precise details.

The Politics of American English, 1776–1850

Introduction:
A Language Still Becoming

This study is an account of the development of American English between the Declaration of Independence and the middle of the nineteenth century. Part of its purpose is documentary; it shows that by the time Melville and Hawthorne sat down to write their novels, there was already in existence a language significantly, if not substantially, different from that being written by their British peers. Thanks to the efforts of two generations of linguistic pioneers, Noah Webster foremost among them, and to the spectacular rise in national self-confidence, America had, by about 1850, a version of English that was recognizably its own.

Much more interesting than the mere existence of this new kind of English, however, is the range of arguments that surrounded its coming into being. Many of these arguments continue to be heard today, though usually in the contexts of specialized debates about education and ethnicity. In the first half century of nationhood they were heard much more loudly and widely, for they were seen to entail great consequences for the process of unification that had only begun in 1776. Many, like Webster, believed that the establishment of a common language on national principles would be the greatest possible single contribution to political and cultural solidarity among the citizens of the new republic. Because such commentators were talking about this language as a prospect rather than assuming it as an entity already in existence, they undertook also an analysis of all that might stand in the way of the achievement of a common language—the social, political, and ethnic differences that characterized an unhomogenized population.

Arguments about the language were always, in this way, political and social arguments. When, for example, "dialect" is discussed, it is not just the aesthetic propriety of certain words and phrases that is at stake but also (and much more urgently) the interests and rights of those who speak those words and phrases. To exclude intonations and items of vocabulary from designation as "proper" is to exclude also those who are preconditioned to utter them.

Modern America is not much more homogeneous than was the America of the early nationalist period, but it has lost, for the most part, the discourse once available to describe its differences and tensions. As a result, politicians and public figures now find it all too easy to speak of "the people" as if it were a body composed of individuals with identical interests and equal opportunities for pursuing them. The beginnings of this change in the rhetoric of political argument also occur during the period of this study, around the election of 1840. When we observe it, we must realize that the pervasive model of exemplary subjectivity that is at the center of so many images of the national personality and the national society has not always been as dominant as it seems to be today. As well as describing the achievement of an American English, then, I have found myself describing also what was arguably lost or forgotten in that achievement. Arguments about the language coming into being were explicitly political and overtly conscious of all the tensions that would have to be adjusted in the consolidation of anything that might propose itself as "common"; when an achieved language is taken for granted, it is all too easy to forget or ignore the continuing presence of those individuals and interests that remain outside it. We tend to be aware of these "political" implications when we compare—as we continue to do—American with British English; we are usually aware that British and American English emanate from two different cultures and can project two different systems of values. The familiar quip about "two nations divided by a common language" applies to more than just having different words to describe identical objects. At the same time—and with the aid of the standardized representations offered by the media and, all too often, by the political parties—we are quick to assume an internal unity to the nation, a metaphysical identity shared by all Americans, or one to which all would-be Americans should by definition aspire. It is all the harder to see behind this facade when the language and discourse available to describe it has itself been depleted. The symptoms and consequences of this loss are the subject of the last part of this book.

Even if we do not go so far as to assert, with some linguists and philosophers, that language is the single organizing principle in human experience, there is yet no doubt that it is a very important one. This importance is experienced individually, in the life of every speaker, and also collectively, as a historical constituent in our wider cultural situation. Language above all instances the besetting predicament of so much individual behavior; that, as we spontaneously articulate our inmost and most immediate thoughts, we reproduce also (even as we deviate from them) the collective patterns of speech that have developed and go on developing through the generations. However we may choose to define culture, language must be recognized as an important part of it.

I mention two experiences of my own, not because they are "mine" but because they demonstrate the element of generality within particular experience, and because they embody many of the themes of this study. First, at the age of eight or nine years, a pupil at a rural school in England, I was enjoined to recite a poem for a tape recording to be sent to our companion school in the United States. The poem contained the word *kite* which, in my hitherto unmodified Norfolk accent, came out something like *koite*. I was forced by the teacher to say this word over and over again (seemingly for hours!) in hopes of getting rid of the illicit dipthong. No one laughed, for my shame was a communal shame—every other child in the class was on trial for the same offense. This memory, lost for years, came back to me as I was finishing this book. It is my first memory of the war between regional and received pronunciation that continues to exercise all British children, and to terrify many. In turning *koite* to *kite,* all evidence of regionalism was being erased from the tape. Those children in America, wherever they were, were being fooled about the English language in Britain, and were perhaps at the same time (though I doubt as vigorously) being fooled about the nature of their own language. The struggle of languages was on.

It is a struggle in which it is hard to be sure of a distinction between the oppressors and the oppressed. The teacher who thus disciplined my speech undoubtedly thought he was doing me a favor. And he had reason to think so, living as he did in a society that still accords an irrational respect to those who are "well spoken" (a telling phrase!), and still supports a significant class of teachers of elocution. My second memory dates from more recent times. I was asked to speak on a local (British) radio show, and a tape of my contribution was played back to me for final approval. I had not heard myself on tape before, as an adult, and I was very surprised. Side by side, as if in the voice of another person, I could hear three quite separate linguistic strata, clear as a slice out of the Grand Canyon. First, there were the trained sounds acquired by several years of life within the university, vowels and stresses that would have suited the career of a BBC newsreader. Second, lurking around them, were the undoctored East Anglian diphthongs, still there after all those years; *i* still tended toward and at times became *oi*. Third, there was something new: a series of Americanisms, racy, Whitmanesque idioms and expressions that came over as having the appeal of brevity, classlessness, and sociological anonymity (itself of course another form of typing).

In the case of both of these memories, what appeared on paper gave no hint of what came out on the tapes. The tension between the spoken and the written will be addressed in detail in this study, and in historical terms. Further, and also in detail, the history of those Americanisms, to which I resorted with such unconscious relief, will be explored. Of course, their availability as vehicles of release is restricted to the British speaker, for whom they appeal as an alternative to the local rules of the game. This I am sure contributes to the still common disdain that some British speakers have for American English, often cast as, precisely, vulgar—for it is always "vulgar" to challenge the rules of the game. For the American speaker, conversely, these words and phrases are either unremarked, or they function within a different interactive context, that of the United States itself.

These questions are perennial, and it is almost irresistible to take up all sorts of quite appropriate modern contexts; but the focus of this study is historical. In the newly established United States, between 1776 and about 1850, the issue of language in fact excited some of the contentiousness that it has continued to have in Britain to this day, where it arises every time a Glaswegian gets off the train in London, and on most occasions when a politician or a member of the managerial class talks to or at the people. Such basic, everyday social exchanges serve to remind the community of language users that they are disunited and divided, whether by interest, aspiration, or opportunity. This situation is *relatively* less common in the United States today, though it can be perceived in the interactions between northerners and southerners, and between members of different races. But, during most of the period I shall be discussing, language was more "loaded" in the sociological and political sense than it (mostly) is now. By about 1850, democracy had become the dominant American ideology or self-image, so that, in the continuing development of a self-declared pluralistic culture, a struggle of languages has been the harder to perceive where it does exist.

The writings of James Fenimore Cooper, especially, can serve as an uncomfortable reminder of the questions that were laid aside in the acceptance of the democratic culture as something no longer needing to be questioned. For the image to survive, certain interests had to be excluded or coopted. Cooper's novels transcribe the languages of the Dutch, the Germans, the Irish, and various other ethnic minorities, most obviously the Native Americans. In the 1980s the debate continues—over Black English, over the teaching of Spanish as a first or second language, over the role of Native American languages in the reservation schools. The first two generations of Americans might have more readily seen these issues for what they still are—struggles of weighty cultural, political, and economic importance. It may be our loss, and a result of a lost sense of how we came to be what we are, that causes us to express surprise or outrage (or an equally unmeditated approval) at the attempts of others to challenge the linguistic contract. But the old Enlightenment assumption, that they are thereby challenging society in the widest sense, has not entirely disappeared.

Any comprehensive study of the American language in this period must also be a study of American culture and American litera-

ture. I have chosen to end the book with some rather tendentious
judgments about the implications and effects of Transcendentalist
theories of language and identity. More than any other group of
writings, these have contributed to the very definition of American
literature, the American language, and the American self. For many
readers and critics, that which is distinctively American appears for
the first time around 1850, and everything that has happened since
is measured against it. Thus, when we think of dialect in the novel,
we think of Twain; the historical novel brings Hawthorne to mind;
and when we think of novels of the sea, we instantly recall Melville.
When we need a philosophical correlative to any of these, we turn
to Emerson or Thoreau. All these writers thus become significant
"originals."

   The following study does not attend to these writers (Emerson
excepted), and I do not intend to demean them, or to expose them
in some trivial sense as less original than they are often thought to
be. I do suggest, however, that a close study of the language and
literature of the early nationalist and Jacksonian periods can provide a quite alternative idea of what the American experience was.
Quentin Anderson has opened this topic in pointing out the "profound extra-social commitment" (1971, p. viii) of Emerson and
his kind; and he has looked to Emerson's authoritative presence as
a way of understanding how we have ignored "the actual character
of our negation of the social bonds as it was imagined in the nineteenth century" (p. 5). For in the nineteenth century, at least, there
are two American literatures, one that reproduces this negation as
its first principle and another that explores the awkward predicament of man in society.

   The very spirit of the differences between these two traditions
can be perceived by attending to the representation of the American
language. Ideas about the nature and uses of language have always
been highly sensitive indices of the social and political tensions of
the times in which they come into being. In the seventy-five years
after independence there was ceaseless argument, on both sides of
the Atlantic, about what American English was, about what it might
become, and about what it ought to be. These arguments respond
both to the strains between Britain and America, around the Revolutionary War, the War of 1812, the copyright war, and the wider

war for mental independence (as Cooper called it), and also to the crises within the new nation itself. Arguments about dialect, about ethnic vocabularies, and about the presence or absence of a common language, reveal the existence of a discourse and presumably an experience of struggle and difference. The name of the nation spoke unity, but the evidence does not bear out its assertion.

This study then concentrates on a period in American history, and a tradition in American literature and language, that are (relatively) ignored, perhaps because they image forth an America that many believe no longer exists. My aim is thus partly to rehabilitate a series of ignored writers, to whom renewed attentiveness is more than appropriate. I make no claims on the grounds of greatness or minority, though such could indeed be made; nor do I mean to place Cooper, for example, in competition with Melville as a literary founding father. My purpose is rather to make what I think is a new kind of *sense* of Cooper and his generation. We do not have to establish one writer's significance at the expense of another, but a serious scrutiny of one writer may tell us things about another that we might otherwise have passed over. Thus, studying Emerson in isolation produces a different version of his writings from that obtainable by knowing what Cooper was writing about during the same period. Moreover, we are by such juxtaposition also likely to become more aware of the inherited or intuitive priorities and prejudices in our own readings than we would be by reading authors on their own terms. That so much of the critical literature on Melville has focused on questions of consciousness and of aesthetic sufficiency has to do, I think, with the common location of his work within an Emersonian tradition. To read him as a successor to Cooper produces a different set of questions also verifiably pertinent to Melville's fiction.

If we choose to remain within the terms of an aesthetic valuation, it is of course the case that Cooper is less agile and complex than, for example, Melville. The Shakespearean prototype that was for Melville something of a liberation into a dramatically allusive diction was always for Cooper an obviously ungainly legacy. It is hard not to wince or smirk as Cooper's Tamenund echoes Lear—"Take you the wampum, and our love" (1983, p. 313)—whereas we tend to respond positively to the thematic complexity of Ahab's echoes of the same figure. Only Cooper could seem to intend no irony in describing his heroine's dog as having "an intelligence but little inferior to that which beamed in her own lovely countenance" (1980, p. 287), though many of these infelicities were in fact the results of printers' errors rather than authorial intentions. The inner lives of Cooper's characters are seldom developed, his plots are often contrived, and they often move with a glacial pace. It can almost always be said of his tales that "much less time was consumed in the occurrence of these events, than in their narration" (1980, p. 272). The famous demolition of Cooper that Twain published in 1895 was right to claim that he was "not a word-musician," and that his "word-sense was singularly dull"; Conrad similarly opined that Cooper wrote "before the great American language was born" (Dekker and McWilliams, 1973, pp. 286, 288).

But Conrad's "great American language," I shall argue, is no more metaphysically American than what came before it; and what is really being expressed here is a lack of interest in the themes and arguments that Cooper's language addresses. He does not indeed transcribe the "spermatic, man-making words" that Emerson will recommend and Ahab speak out, but that may be because the issues he is dealing with do not call them forth. Too many readers who know Twain's essay better than they know Cooper have deceived themselves into thinking that a point made about *style* is a point made about quality, originality, or essential meaning. The refusal of an aesthetic satisfaction inhibits all further inquiry. Perry Miller, who wrote very intelligently indeed about the literature of the Jacksonian period (1967, pp. 197–207), claimed also that *Huckleberry Finn* was "the originating point for modern American literature because of its mastery of language" (p. 229). Twain did indeed *master* the medium in a way that Cooper did not; but for Cooper the ambiguities of mastery itself, whether of language or of the world, were much more prominent and perplexing. In a similar spirit, Larzer Ziff organizes a recent study of the literary independence of America around Poe, Emerson, Hawthorne, Thoreau, Whitman, and Melville. For him, these are writers of the "first rank" (1982, p. x), while Cooper is merely a conservative follower of "English literary models" (p. ix). This position depends once again on taking for granted the very priorities that Cooper questioned so severely. Here is Ziff again:

> The new nationalism was an essential condition for the new litera-
> ture because it provided a positive, dynamic sense of American
> identity, however much the artists were to criticize the naked
> avarice it revealed. The generation we have been observing grew up
> in a country that had an ebullient sense of its national self—Irving
> and Cooper did not (p. 301).

The assumption here is that a vital literature can only come from a
culture with a zestfully positive self-image. The proposition thus becomes a tautology: ebullient nationalism produces ebullient literature. But it is quite another thing to suggest, as Ziff does, that this
is the essence of what is "greatly" American. The critic's case simply reproduces the very assumption it ought to be questioning.

Perhaps I am laboring the point. I mean simply to say that for
the critic, the historian, and the literary theorist (interested in canon
formation and the ideology of reading) a closer attention to the
years between 1776 and 1850 can only be salutary. A number of
recent studies indeed suggest that there may be a renewing interest
in the literature and culture of the early national period. Such general accounts as those of Joseph Ellis (1979), Benjamin Lease
(1981), Linden Peach (1982), and Emory Elliott (1982) focus
on, among others, precisely the writers I am discussing here. Additionally, the more thematically specific studies of Jay Fleigelman
(1982) and Robert Ferguson (1984) have added immeasurably to
our sense of the intellectual and historical complexity of these same
writers. My study will, I hope, prove companionable with these recent efforts at illuminating the relations between literature, language,
and society in the years following the Declaration of Independence.

The materials of this period are especially rich for the historian
of the American language and the student of the debates surrounding that language. American English as we recognize it today had
been essentially established by 1850. That is, its major deviations
from British English had by that time both been proposed in theory
(mostly by Noah Webster) and adopted into relatively common
(though not uncontested) practice. Charles Astor Bristed spitefully
argued that this was merely a result of Webster's dictionaries having "unfortunately happened to become a matter of commercial
speculation" (1855, p. 76). But there is more to say about this, as
we shall see. For many readers of the time there was also, by 1850,
an American literature, despite the fact that later critics were to in-

vent it as springing forth fully armed at exactly that time, as the expression of a quite different notion of what was American. Rufus Griswold's anthology, *The Poets and Poetry of America* (1842), was in its eighth edition by 1847, the year in which the companion volume, *The Prose Writers of America,* was published. For Griswold, we might note, Cooper had "contributed more than any of his contemporaries to the formation of a really national literature" (1847, p. 30).

We should, however, beware of making ourselves the prisoners of dates and the prophets of completion. This study ends around 1850, a date that itself suggests an imposing symmetry. Sometimes, births and deaths do occur at self-evidently "significant" times— Dryden died in 1700, Wordsworth in 1850, Yeats in 1939. It is tempting to turn these coincidences into argumentative devices. But Cooper died in 1851, and the changes that were responsible for bringing about the alternative concept of American literature from which he has been excluded were certainly starting to occur in the late 1830s, if not earlier. The date 1850, then, is convenient chiefly because it excludes the writings of the 1850s that have been canonized as constituting the "American renaissance."

As a way of further qualifying the rhetoric of completion, let me say that I mean my title seriously: a language still becoming. There have, of course, been significantly new developments in the debates between American and British English, and between the various options open to American English intrinsically considered. Readers familiar with the more recent literature on these questions may well be surprised, however, to discover from an account of the earlier material how very similar the basic issues are, and how traditional the terms of the responses to them can seem to be. T. S. Eliot complained of H. L. Mencken in exactly the way that others had complained of Webster a hundred and fifty years before, grumbling that he seemed "to be issuing a kind of linguistic Declaration of Independence, an act of emancipation of American from English" (1953, p. 11). In 1882, Twain was still asserting the differences between New England speech and that of the rest of America, as Webster's earlier opponents had done. Ten years later, Brander Matthews still sensed the need to turn the tables against the British, just as Webster had done, by ridiculing the "inward and spiritual belief that the Londoner is the sole guardian and trustee of the English language" (1892, p. 13). *Blackwood's Magazine* had previously chimed in in the same spirit, praising America for "dipping more deeply" than Britain into the true Anglo-Saxon core of the common language, that part of it which is "simple, homely, strong, solemn, poetical, passionate, and Saxon" (Anon., 1867, pp. 417, 399–400).

And so on. The question of language has also remained, as it always was, a question implicated very directly in social and political preferences and decisions. Literacy itself is a debatable entity, as Robert Pattison has recently pointed out:

> Literacy is an ambiguous word in our society. On the one hand it implies a rational application of the mind to the problems of language, an exalted cultural achievement. On the other it means the acquisition of mechanical skills in reading and writing, an important but not usually noble attainment. The ambiguity of the term allows for a pretense of egalitarianism in our culture while in fact we maintain a highly structured social hierarchy. Almost all Americans can read and write. Thus we seem to be equal. But very few Americans possess discipline in the habits of language necessary for its advantageous use, and those few who do effectively control the many who do not (1984, p. 181).

Pattison's eloquent formulation was as apposite in 1800 as it is today, in the face of the computer revolution and other new circumstances. As late as 1889, N. A. Campbell was still calling for an American Academy: "No other means will so effectually secure unity, prevent sectionalism, and abolish dialects" (1889, p. 127). He got no further with his suggestions than had John Adams a century earlier and numerous fellow spirits in the years since. A history of the attitudes and practices of the National Council of Teachers of English (in America) tells us that British received pronunciation was still the standard up to about 1930; that an alternative colloquialism became positively approved in the period 1930–35; and that many of the words that were then disputed as Americanisms were in fact survivals rather than coinages (McDavid, 1965, pp. 8–10, 18, 25). The same arguments and transitions can be found in the nineteenth century between, for example, the language of a Boston federalist of 1800 and that of a Kentucky tall talker of 1835. There is, in the simple sense, no evolution and no real "progress" in these debates; they continue to express the social tensions that indeed take different forms at different times but often continue to use the same polemical touchstones. Chaucer's Parson is both proud and defensive about his political and linguistic identity when he tells us, in the prologue to his tale, that

> . . . I am a Southren man,
> I kan nat geeste 'rum, raf, ruf', by lettre,
> Ne, God woot, rym holde I litel bettre.

Already, in this tension between the Norman French and the Saxon legacies, we can see the emergence of a theme that will be of central importance in Webster's career, as of many others. There is a continuing polemical tradition connecting Chaucer's Parson with the author of a study reported in the London *Sunday Times* (December 19, 1982), who argues that teaching Latin to working-class children would be "a blow for social and educational equality because class divisions in England are based on two different languages."

The relation between language and culture again became important in the reception of Chomsky's writings in the 1970s. Writing after a decade of unrest in the universities, and mounting a "liberal" attack on Chomsky's posited logical fusion of linguistic and political arguments, Geoffrey Sampson offered the unctuously concerned observation that such a fusion was taken seriously not only by those whom he termed "witless troublemakers" but also by "the serious, thoughtful students from among whom the society of tomorrow must draw its leaders" (1979, p. 11). Comical as such self-dramatization might seem with the privilege of hindsight ("scholar saves society from fatal error"), the urgency of the expressed relation between language and something like "civilization" is obvious and not untypical. To give another and more serious example, the problems facing the founding fathers of the United States and their successors in the sphere of language were faced also by Lenin in his meditations on a potential Russian revolution. He argued for linguistic pluralism, for tolerance of all ethnic and national minorities:

> People whose conditions of life and work make it necessary for them to know the Russian language will learn it without being forced to do so. But coercion (the cudgel) will have only one result: it will hinder the great and mighty Russian language from

spreading in other national groups, and, most important of all, it
will sharpen antagonism, cause friction in a million new forms, increase resentment, mutual misunderstanding, and so on. (Lenin,
1970, p. 96).

I recall reading somewhere of the Highland regiment that defended
itself to the death against fellow Scotsmen rather than be incorporated into a Lowland regiment wherein the speaking of Gaelic and
the wearing of the kilt would be forbidden. Like Webster, Lenin
did not so much applaud the existence of these different identities
as foresee their inevitable and easeful disappearance. Both were
wrong.

What I have said so far will explain some of the pretensions of this
study; I must also express some shortcomings and reservations.
What follows is complete neither as an account of the growth of
the language, nor of the literature in which it appeared. For reasons
of space and competence I have had to be somewhat selective, and
have chosen to concentrate on exemplary issues and the particular
texts in which they appear most dramatically. I would have liked
to do more than merely mention the linguistic features of the works
of such writers as William Gilmore Simms, John Pendleton Ken-
nedy, and Augustus Baldwin Longstreet. I have claimed an exemplary status for James Fenimore Cooper because I think that he
responds to my approach in fuller and more sophisticated ways than
any of his contemporaries, and therefore provides a new vocabulary
for looking again at those contemporaries. In this respect, I must
declare myself open to whatever qualifications the researches of
others might subsequently bring to light.

Looking at the writers of the period from the specific point of
view of language and diction results in some peculiar deflections.
Poe and Irving have, I believe, rather little to offer such analysis,
but this does not make them lesser writers, nor even necessarily less
"patriotic" ones. Bryant is similarly displaced from the center of
my attentions, as is Hawthorne, who was writing and publishing in
the 1820s, but who chose not to address himself in any major way
to the question of a national language. It must also be made clear
that some peculiar deflections may seem to occur in those writers I
do discuss in detail. From the particular perspective I have adopted,
it will appear as if, for example, Cooper is a more radical or so-

ciologically astute writer than Emerson; and from this particular
perspective, I believe that he was. But this does not mean that the
part can be assumed to stand for the whole, nor even that there is a
simple whole to be discovered. The more one reads and ponders,
the more it seems that the writers of these years shared a high degree of ideological confusion or irresolution. Cooper's sensitivity to
language was perhaps not something of which he was fully conscious, and it does not in any simple way accord with, for example,
his blindness about the slavery question. Nor does his undoubtedly
snobbish propensity for the life of a gentleman negate the sharply
critical analysis of British affectation and English upper-middle-
class society that his writings reveal. Similarly, one could easily discover a perspective from which Emerson would appear much more
conformable than Cooper with modern liberal expectations and
attitudes. Any attempt to decide on the complete historical and
ideological profiles of these and other writers is obviously beyond
the scope of this study. I can claim conviction only for the particular questions I am addressing, namely, those relating to the evolution of a national language.

Perhaps the major shortcomings of the following study, considered as a historical record of the language of Americans before
1850, is its almost complete silence on the subject of Black English.
There are a number of reasons for this. I am dealing with the literature of the white middle classes, within which the political implications of Black English are largely ignored or repressed. One may,
for example, congratulate or criticize Poe (in "The Gold Bug") for
the success or failure of his transcription of Jupiter's Gullah speech,
but that speech does not enter into political competition with that
of the narrator and protagonist. Jupiter's diction, like that of so
many of his peers in the novels of Poe's contemporaries, may indeed be 'realistic'; but it is contextualized as at best a source of
humor, at worst of condescension or parody. The Black American
plays the role of clown or scapegoat in all too many of these novels
and stories; his language is not represented as affecting the evolution of the hegemonic American English. The Native American is
dramatized, but only because he is posited as disappearing; he is
thus open for imaging within the terms of a tragical romanticism,
as the embodiment of values that are being *lost*. These values can
be safely lamented because they are thought to be vanishing; they

can never emerge as a credible challenge to the new nation. The Black American, one must assume, represented more of a threat to the hegemonic culture, especially as the sense of crisis mounted in the years before 1860. If so, it is not at all surprising that Black English is so often "wished away" or exploited for little more than colorful localism or comic relief.

One could, of course, research the slave narratives, and other written records. So important and complex is this task that I would rather not attempt it than fail to do it justice. When it has been investigated, it seems likely that our sense of the American language will be radically different. J. L. Dillard (1973, p. 4) claims with great credibility that "it has been assumed in our language histories and in our grammars that only the British-derived parts count." His study presents a powerful case for considering Plantation Creole as a separate language, with its own grammar, rather than as a mere dialect or pidgin—one that played a greater role in the formation of the 'national' standard than has been hitherto recognized. Dillard gives Cooper, for example, credit for the accurate transcription of this language, which he (Dillard) argues to have been that of the Black community at large, and not just a literary convention employed by white novelists. But Cooper's transcription does not register any social or political tensions in his fictional world of the sort that appear in his rendering of Native American speech. One can only speculate about the reasons for this. Perhaps the tensions were unapparent—which seems unlikely! More probably they were so threatening as to require complete and efficient repression. In much of the literature of this period, and in almost all the accounts of the progress of the American language, the place of the Black tradition can only be inferred from its absence or parodic inclusion. Literature, especially that of a dominant social faction, does not always reflect or represent the complexity of its times, either empirically or ideologically. The relative silence of this study on the matter of Black English is a reflection of the similar silence apparent in its subject matter. But any inquiry into the particulars of the language that might have been spoken in ordinary (as opposed to literary) exchange must take seriously the presence of Plantation Creole.

One final reservation. Given the focus on exemplary cases, I cannot hope to supplant the extraordinary research of H. L. Mencken, of the editors of the *Dictionary of American English* and the *Dictionary of Americanisms,* and of countless contributors to *American Speech.* I have made grateful use of all of these, as of other related studies, and if I have on occasion manifested a pedant's gleefulness in noticing something hitherto missed or misrepresented, then no mean spiritedness is intended. I have drawn widely on the studies of Brenni (1964), Krapp (1925; rpt. 1960), Laird (1972), Leonard (1929), Marckwardt (1980), Mathews (1931), Pyles (1954), Quirk (1972), and most of all from the wide range of essays published by Allen Walker Read. If I have still managed to miss a few facts that every schoolboy knows, the fault is mine.

Prologue: 1776

When in the course of human events it becomes necessary for one people to dissolve the political bands which have connected them with another, and to assume among the powers of the earth the separate & equal station to which the laws of nature and of nature's god entitle them, a decent respect to the opinions of mankind requires that they should declare the causes which impel them to the separation.[1]

Thus Thomas Jefferson introduces his famous list of truths that are self-evident, and begins the draft of the *Declaration of Independence*. The most and therefore least obvious aspect of this document is that it is in English. It is immediately intelligible to those against whom it is directed and from whom it declares itself disaffiliated. No act of translation is required. The *Declaration* speaks the language of the tyrant power, opposing from a common linguistic contract the "long train of abuses & usurpations" which that power had so often used the language to implement. At the same time, Jefferson's draft perhaps signals its common ground with the republican tradition that was thought to have brought about the most precious liberties of the British themselves. He was not the first English-speaker to react against the threats of an "absolute despotism."

But if Jefferson writes in English, it is a particular *kind* of En-

19

glish, one that appears to the modern reader as marked by inconsistent and even whimsical spellings. He uses the forms *-ising* and *-izing* without any apparent sense of contradiction (*organising, agonizing, naturalization*), and also alternates *-our* with *-or* (*honour, tenor, endeavored*), setting up options that still inform the distinctions between modern American and British English. Additionally, he proffers spellings we might regard as merely out of date (*compleat*), or as idiosyncratic (*paiment, wholsome, souldiers*), or as just plain slips of the pen (*unacknoleged*). He consistently prefers *independant* over *independent*.

In the published text of the *Declaration,* which does not include all of Jefferson's original sentences and adds some others, we are at once aware of changes in orthography.[2] All nouns are capitalized, in the standard eighteenth-century (but not nineteenth-century) way. Jefferson's *organising* becomes *organizing,* to conform with *Naturalization. Payment, wholesome,* and *unacknowledged* appear in their familiar forms, and *independent* is preferred throughout. But *compleat* stands as before, and some asymmetry remains in the relation of *-our* and *-or.* The printed text reads *endeavoured* (twice) and *neighbouring* but oddly changes Jefferson's *honour* to *Honor.*

Going back a year in time, and perhaps (in the eyes of the nation about to be) several centuries in political philosophy, we find one of Samuel Johnson's contributions to the American crisis: "Taxation No Tyranny; an Answer to the Resolutions and Address of the American Congress" went through four editions in 1775, and was, of course, conceived to preempt Jefferson's putting pen to paper some months later.[3] Johnson is eloquent in the defence of the status quo, speaking against "these lords of themselves, these kings of *Me,* these demigods of independence" (p. 429). By such independence "the whole fabrick of subordination is immediately destroyed, and the constitution sunk at once into a chaos" (p. 425). He yet hopes that the rebellious spirits of the colonies "may be subdued by terrour rather than by violence" (p. 452).

Johnson's spellings again are striking, and this time they are quite self-conscious, as Jefferson's presumably were not. The author of the great (though not the first) *Dictionary* was adamant in his preference for *-our* and *-ick* forms, and we shall see later that this preference is to be related to larger political and social convictions. Johnson aimed to tidy up the language, and to do so according to conscious procedures. But even Johnson's text is inconsistent. The spelling *governors* (p. 420) coexists with *governours* (p. 440), and *terrour* is answered by *error* (p. 441), against the *Dictionary*'s attempt to legislate for *-our* endings in each case. The slips are probably not Johnson's own, but those of a typesetter. Nevertheless, the suggestion is that the language is too undisciplined to be efficiently restrained, too devious and ambiguous for the ambitions of rational reform. Johnson himself says as much in his voice as author of "The Plan of a Dictionary of the English Language" in admitting that "language is the work of man, of a being from whom permanence and stability cannot be derived" (Johnson, 1957, p. 130).

It might seem ironic that the published text of the *Declaration* in fact does so much to conform Jefferson's spelling with Johnson's models, given that the two belong on opposite sides of the political fence. There are hints here of a pattern that will recur often in the period under study (and indeed beyond it): the most independent and patriotic sentiments in America may be published in a language that continues to be governed by the conventions and strictures of metropolitan London, even as the British Parliament has lost political control, and may indeed even be in political opposition. But at the same time we must note the final word of the text: *Honor,* not *honour.* Johnson loses this one. If we cannot suppose this to be a conscious victory for the American printer, it is nevertheless a prophecy of the American English to come.

The year 1776 was a momentous one in literary and philosophical terms, as well as in national politics. It saw the first publication of the great books of Adam Smith and Edward Gibbon, as well as of important works by Paine, Price, Campbell, and Bentham. Looking at some of these texts, we find that the same pattern of moderate chaos is repeated, one that seldom threatens understanding yet does startle the modern eye.

Paine's *Common Sense* both fav*ors* and fav*ours* independ*ance* (not independ*ence*). A comparison of the orthography of the first and the first revised edition reveals a range of inconsistencies. I have not checked every case, but from a brief examination it seems that the first edition uses consistent *-our* forms, whereas the second alternates quite frequently.[4] It also switches between *connexions* and *connections* (e.g., pp. 15, 17). Once again, as in the draft and printed version of the *Declaration,* the language of liberty is a somewhat scrambled one. Paine's book, printed in Philadelphia, does not reveal any striking differences from the spelling habits of Richard Price's *Observations on the Nature of Civil Liberty,* which was reprinted in the same city, though presumably from the London edition. In neither case does there seem to be any connection between spelling and political sentiment.

In the case of Adam Smith, whose *Wealth of Nations* (another book not unconnected with the political crisis) also appeared for the first time in 1776, the question of language is further complicated by the fact that he was a Scotsman. Most of the quarrels over the Scots language in the eighteenth century had to do with pronunciation and dialect; the claims of Gaelic or Lallans to separate status were not much attended to in metropolitan culture, as they are not to this day. Nevertheless, Hume had felt himself obliged to delete the Scotticisms from his *History of England,* for the question of the Scots language and diction was a definite point of contention in the general task of subjugating and incorporating Scotland after the Act of Union in 1707.[5] As so often occurs, and as in the case of the United States in 1776 (though less dramatically here), this was a union only in name. The two Jacobite rebellions were the most spectacular instances of continuing discontent, but the Scottish problem was an enduring part of English political consciousness. Samuel Johnson, on his tour of the Highlands, noted:

> Of what they had before the late conquest of their country, there remain only their language and their poverty. Their language is attacked on every side. Schools are erected, in which *English* only is taught, and there were lately some who thought it reasonable to refuse them a version of the holy scriptures, that they might have no monument of their mother-tongue (1957, p. 701).

John Witherspoon, a Scotsman who emigrated to America, claimed to have coined the prophetic word *Americanism* from the analogy with *Scotticism* (1802, 4:460). Had Scotland remained independent, he remarks, no shame would have been attached to the term:

> But by the removal of the court to London, and especially by the union of the two kingdoms, the Scottish manner of speaking came to be considered as provincial barbarism; which, therefore, all scholars are now at the utmost pains to avoid (p. 461).

America will have a quite different fate, he predicts: "we shall find some centre or standard of our own, and not be subject to the inhabitants of that island, either in receiving new ways of speaking, or rejecting the old."

Adam Smith seems to have managed to put forth a largely acceptable "English" style, or so it would seem from a brief inspection. His orthographic habits are not dissimilar from those already encountered. The recent definitive edition of *The Wealth of Nations* (1976) lists (2:952f.) among its variants many of the words already familiar: *independent/-ant, compleat/-ete, public/-ick,* and so forth. A good sense of Smith's own habits, rather than those of printers or other hands, can be derived from a glance at the edition of the *Correspondence* (1977). The letters written during 1776 are especially fascinating, although the American crisis merits only the briefest mention. Smith is preoccupied with the affecting sight of his friend Hume dying, and with the resulting uncertainties over the publication of the notorious *Dialogues Concerning Natural Religion.* In those letters printed by the editors from holograph sources, Smith alternates *expell* and *expel* (p. 201), uses *Collonel* for *Colonel* (p. 203) and *dyed* for *died* (p. 203; but *die* on p. 206), and the forms *alledge* (p. 204), *antient* (p. 201), and *chearfulness* (pp. 206, 203). He seems to use *-our* consistently over *-or.*

The point has surely been made, though further examples could be adduced. Except for Samuel Johnson, no one in 1776, on either side of the ocean, seems to show much concern for a standard spelling practice, whether in personal drafts or printed texts. This view of the situation is not only supported but almost prescribed by a glance at the dictionaries. Nathan Bailey's *Dictionarium Britannicum,* published in London in 1730, Johnson's more famous successor, and John Entick's *New Spelling Dictionary* (first published in 1764, then edited by William Crakelt and reprinted in 1784 and 1791) cover between them most of the variable spellings seen so far, with the exception of obvious idiosyncrasies. Entick and Bailey give both *compleat* and *complete,* while Johnson decides for the second; Johnson has *allege* for Entick's and Bailey's *alledge,* and opts (with Bailey) for *honour* and *publick* (against Entick). Bailey does declare that *honorable* is "the truest Spelling" of the word he lists as *honourable,* and bravely tries to discriminate between *inferior* (as adjective) and *inferiour* (as noun). The diligent language

user of 1776 would, in other words, search in vain for complete
agreement among the authors of the dictionaries themselves. Noah
Webster, who produces what is arguably the first significant American dictionary in 1806 (though he will not use the title until 1828),
does not depart from the above options in his transcriptions of
these words.

Noah Webster is, however, a radical in the realm of language,
and is the first major challenger of the linguistic hegemony of the
British in general and of Johnson in particular. Although, as we
shall see, many of Webster's claims were made on conservative
grounds, so that putative Americanisms were consistently explained
as true English words defunct in the mother country, it is yet impossible, after Webster, to be unaware of the argument about language as a *national* argument. After Webster, inconsistencies cannot be assumed to imply the same apparent insouciance that marks
the language of 1776. They continue to occur, of course, and we
will encounter all the familiar ones and some new ones in the letters of James Fenimore Cooper, whose writings occupy a central
place in this study. But the context for these vagaries is different
after Webster, so that we must question whether Cooper might be
consciously or unconsciously ignoring the potential for a consistently American language in a way that no writer of 1776 would
have been. Later, I shall discuss various ways of accounting for
this, from the reductive explanation (which contains some truth)
suggesting that Cooper was so dependent on the British market that
he could not afford any belligerently American linguistic identity,
to the more substantial and complex one that involves an assess-
ment of Cooper's own politics and sociolinguistic insights.

As 1776 did not usher in a new language, so neither did it invent
a new literature or a new philosophy. It did, however, impose the
demand that these prospects be examined and worked for, and it
determined that the traditional Enlightenment preoccupations per-
sisting or arising in the early years of independence should take on
a consciously national resonance, whether for or against innovation
and novelty. Thus, although ambitions for changing, fixing, or analyzing to its roots the quixotic spirit of language had been commonplace in the eighteenth century, they become focused as part of
the *American* ideal after 1776. Not for the first time Webster an-
nounces:

Now is the time, and *this* the country, in which we may expect success, in attempting changes favorable to language, science and government (1790a, p. 80).

And he does so in various kinds of English. The preface to his *Collection of Essays and Fugitiv Writings,* also published in 1790,
advertises

Essays and Fugitiv Peeces, ritten at various times, and on different
occasions, az will appeer by their dates and subjects (1790b, p. ix).

That Webster's plan for a coherently innovating American English
ultimately had only a heavily modified success should not allow us
to underestimate the ramifications and implications of its claims.
And, three years later, William Thornton makes the nationalist
claim even more vociferously:

You have corrected the dangerous doctrines of European powers,
correct now the languages you have imported, for the oppressed of
various nations knock at your gates, and desire to be received as
your brethren. As you admit them facilitate your intercourse, and
you will mutually enjoy the benefits.—The AMERICAN LANGUAGE will
thus be as distinct as the government, free from all the follies of
unphilosophical fashion, and resting upon truth as its only regu-
lator (1793, pp. v–vii)

"I perceive no difficulties," says Thornton, continuing to address his
countrymen: "if you find any, I trust they are not without remedy."
Side by side with this preface, he gives the text entire in his reformed mode of spelling, beginning thus:

Iu hav korektid ᴲꓱ deend√ras doktrinz ov
Iuropiiꓱ∩ p◻u꓿rz . . .

There lie the difficulties! But if none of the schemes of which this
is an example came to anything, and if they seem intrinsically mad-
cap to us now, they yet had their place in a varied and widespread
argument about the prospects for an American English.

For by the middle of the nineteenth century such a linguistic
practice, if not quite a "language," had come into being. Its conventions were, as they still are, much less completely differentiated
from the British norms than many good patriots would have liked.
But they were at the same time somewhat too distinctive for the

Anglophiles, and for the British themselves. The arguments about the relative features and qualities of British and American English have not ceased, except that the boot is now often on the other foot; since the end of World War II, it is Great Britain that has felt the need to defend itself against the incursions of an American English. But however familiar these issues are to us now, they have certainly become much less obsessive than they were in the period from independence to the middle of the next century. During these years, the formative years of the new nation, it seems to have been impossible for any traveler to cross the Atlantic in either direction without weighing in on one side or the other of the language debate.

Returning to the *Declaration* of 1776, it is worth noting that not one word in the printed text or in Jefferson's draft could be thought of as an Americanism. The silence of the document in this respect is a good indication of the gravity of its message, as well as of the state of the language at the time it was written. Of course, few of the words that were to become the object of obsessive self-consciousness in the succeeding years—*bison, sleigh, creek, bluff,* and so forth—would have fitted into it anyway. A word like *caucus* would have been too innovative in a document of such historical weight; and, however much prior caucusing there might have been, the assembly did after all meet in *congress.* In this respect the *Declaration* is not prophetic, for very few written works of the following century or so were to escape scrutiny, supportive or otherwise, for the presence of Americanisms, and a great number of them produced such words.

Finally, by way of introduction, there is the matter of the American speech. What would Jefferson have sounded like, reading over the draft aloud to himself? Evidence on this subject is thin and contentious. It was and continued to be a nationalistic commonplace that there were no dialects in America, and that the Americans spoke a clearer and more uniform English than the British themselves. This was surely true, to a degree, and American English is still more uniform than the language spoken in Britain. Nevertheless, hints of qualification exist, and they are there from the early years of the new nation. Once again, Webster is informative. From his *Dissertations* (1789a, pp. 103–13) we can infer that Jefferson, as a Virginian, might have said *holpe* for *help* and *tote* for *carry* (though perhaps not in a public assembly!) and that he might have "almost" omitted "the sound of r as in *ware, there.*" If the Adams contingent, arriving in Philadelphia in 1776, had noticed and perhaps sneered at these or other speech habits, then Jefferson might have reciprocally registered the oddity of the men of Massachusetts saying *keow* for *cow,* and *marcy* for *mercy.* They might have shared with the local Philadelphians the habit of saying *wessel* for *vessel,* if not the tendency to pronounce *drop* as *drap* or *crop* as *crap.*

One might guess that all these features that Webster notices among "that class of people who do not travel" would have been either absent or considerably softened in the speech of the learned delegates. But Webster makes clear that dialects do exist; he even goes on, like a true son of the Enlightenment, to connect them with particular social configurations. Thus the "drawling nasal manner of speaking in New England" is deduced from the features of local government and the prevailing distribution of property. New England has no slaves and few "family distinctions," so that the speech patterns are consequently hesitant and diffident. No one must trespass on the rights of another, or imply that he might be anything less than an equal. So, for the New Englander, "Is it not best?" replaces "you must." Later we shall see that this feature of New England speech was not to be lost on Fenimore Cooper in his portrayals of the artful Yankee.

It must further be stressed that dialect in general is an important and highly contested ingredient of the American literary language well before Twain and his immediate precursors. When we see the same phenomena in British literature, we do not usually have to look very far to note its implications in class struggles and self-definitions. The issue is less emphatic in American literature, but it is still important, whatever level of comic celebration might enliven it. As America becomes a nation, or declares itself one, it is perhaps already *not* one nation, at least under the gods of speech. The working out of this question in, for example, Cooper's *The Pioneers,* produces a complex intensity with clear social and historical functions. At one extreme it is a matter of translation—from Delaware to English, from poetry to prose. At the other, less tragical pole it is a struggle for linguistic hegemony between a range of ethnic and special interest groups. Cooper's melting pot is one that is still a very long way from the liquefying temperature, and in the heating process the cracks already appear. The struggle he projects is one in which even silences are eloquent.

But Cooper writes his first novels almost fifty years after the *Declaration of Independence,* and he emerges from a tradition that is still insufficiently familiar to literary critics and historians. The coming into being of an American language and an American literature during this period was a considerably less self-confident process than that most commonly described as occurring in the 1850s. The following chapters are devoted to an account of this part of the birth process.

1

Founding Fathers and the Legacies of Language

Our solid and increasing establishments in America, where we need less dread the inundations of barbarians, promise a superior stability and duration to the English language (Hume, 1932, 2:171).

Thus wrote David Hume, in a letter of October 24, 1767, to Gibbon, who was himself to incorporate into the first chapter of his great history (published in 1776) a paragraph of sound advice (though not innocent of possible irony) against expanding the limits of empire beyond their natural boundaries. Hume was, of course, to be proven wrong about the solidness of these establishments, but in forecasting for the colonies a future free from invasion (military and linguistic) he was advancing an argument that would become very popular among the Americans themselves. In 1774, an anonymous correspondent addressed a letter "To the Literati of America" proposing the foundation of an American Society of Language:

The English language has been greatly improved in Britain within a century, but its highest perfection, with every other branch of human knowledge, is perhaps reserved for this LAND of light and freedom. As the people through this extensive country will speak English, their advantages for polishing their language will be great, and vastly superior to what the people in England ever enjoyed.[1]

The writer's prophecies fell on willing ears—including his own, if he was, as H. L. Mencken (1973, p. 11) suggests, John Adams.[2]

Four years after the Declaration of Independence Adams was in Amsterdam, from where he wrote to the President of Congress (September 5, 1780), arguing that just as forms of government have an influence on language, so "language in its turn influences not only the form of government, but the temper, the sentiments, and manners of the people" (Adams, 1852, 7:249). Language, in other words, is seen from the start as a potential element in constituting a political and cultural unity among the citizens of the new republic; or, if it goes wrong, a means of prescribing or perpetuating disorder. Noting that no extant dictionary or grammar "has the least public authority," Adams continues:

> The honor of forming the first public institution for refining, correcting, improving, and ascertaining the English language, I hope is reserved for congress; they have every motive that can possibly influence a public assembly to undertake it. It will have a happy effect upon the union of the States to have a public standard for all persons in every part of the continent to appeal to, both for the signification and pronunciation of the language. The constitutions of all the States in the Union are so democratical that eloquence will become the instrument for recommending men to their fellow-citizens, and the principal means of advancement through the various ranks and offices of society (pp. 249–50).

Adams argues for the foundation of an American Academy—academies were a traditionally contentious subject in Britain itself[3]—and forecasts the inevitable dominance of English as a world language: The British and the Americans together must "force their language into general use, in spite of all the obstacles that may be thrown in their way, if any such there should be" (p. 250).

Already, in these early nationalistic enthusiasms, there are hints of problems to come, and of the controversies, both practical and ethical, that will mark subsequent discussions of a uniform and "legislated" language. We might notice Adams' emphasis on the power of eloquence as the means of political advancement. John Quincy Adams was to make the same point in his *Lectures on Rhetoric and Oratory* (1810), in an even more emphatic voice:

> In the flourishing periods of Athens and Rome, eloquence was POWER. It was at once the instrument and the spur to ambition. The talent of public speaking was the key to the highest dignities; the passport to the supreme dominion of the state (1:19).

But by 1810, his audience was not so pliable. The review of his book in *The Port Folio* (n.s. 4, 1810, 122–36) complains of the garishness of the author's style, and of his tendency toward neologism: "such words as *relucts, idealized,* &c. are not to be tolerated, but held up and denounced as innovations upon the language" (p. 124). The persuasive power of eloquence could only be comfortably accepted in a society confident of its unanimity about basic issues and priorities. If it is hard to think of the America of 1780 as such a society, it is impossible to describe the America of 1810 in these terms. Eighteenth-century society in general had lost whatever was implied of primitive innocence in the second Adams' image of classical oratory, not only because of its identity as a print culture (which perhaps could be thought to entail a redeeming appeal to less impulsive emotions than those aroused by public speaking), but also because of the self-evident acerbity of its political divisions. What the Adamses admire as the power of eloquence was to be a frequent source of suspicion in other commentators, who saw in the power of words the potential for demagoguery and deceit that would emerge in one version as the tradition of the confidence man.

We might notice also, in John Adams' 1780 letter, the firm confidence in the ultimate hegemony of English as a worldwide language, its propensity to remove by "force" whatever obstacles might be put in its way. Most immediately, this promises to define the relation of English to the other languages still spoken inside the new republic—German, French, some Dutch, and a whole range of Native American languages, all of which would be displaced even as selected elements of them would be incorporated, with varying degrees of reluctance and romanticism, into American English. In the longer term, it forecasts the linguistic corollaries of an expanding commercial economy, exporting its goods and its language to other parts of the world.

But 1780 was not a time for doubt or cynicism over these prospects, even if they were to preoccupy (and to fail to preoccupy) later thinkers. What is most emphatic in Adams' letter to Congress is the implicit potential for an *American* English, and this theme was to prove both popular and controversial in the debates on language throughout the next thirty years and, indeed, beyond. It is probably apocryphal that anyone seriously recommended that the new nation adopt Hebrew or Greek as its language in order to heighten the political division between it and the parent culture; and even more so that Iroquois or Algonquin were seriously proposed for the same purpose.[4] But at the same time, ideas about the *kind* of English that might be spoken in the United States were quite clearly motivated by a sense of the newly achieved political distinctions. Jefferson, in 1779, comments on the potential for a simultaneous reform of politics and language by simplifying the language of politics and making it available to a wider audience:

> Will it not be better . . . while we are reforming the principles to reform also the language of treaties, which history alone and not grammar will justify? The articles may be rendered shorter and more conspicuous, by simplifying their stile and structure (Jefferson, 1950–, 7:476–77).

We may infer that along with such a simplification would go a demystification of the role of the patrician as executive and interpreter, and a consequent decline in the power of any special interest that might be embodied in a particular kind of linguistic competence. In a later letter to John Waldo (August 16, 1813), Jefferson reveals that he never lost his populist tendencies in the sphere of language. He argues for the priority and authority of "usage" over "grammar," and favors "neology" (itself a new word) because the diversity and novelty of American geography and culture must "call for new words, new phrases, and for the transfer of old words to new objects" (Jefferson, 1903, 13:339–40). Neither language nor government has any business proscribing innovation; it is the duty of both to follow where they are led by the popular will and the popular needs. By 1813, the political opponents of Jefferson and Jeffersonianism were very much in the habit of picking up on the political implications of statements about the national language.

The British Inheritance

Before pursuing our inquiry into the debate about the state of the language in the United States in the years after the Revolutionary War, it is worth making clear that the political and factional themes implicit and explicit in the writings of Jefferson and Adams on this subject were present also in similar writings in the British inheritance. These arguments were themselves, of course, part of the American tradition; it was to prove more difficult to declare independence from Samuel Johnson than it had been to reject George III. In each case, opinions about the kind of language a nation should speak, and how it should write it, tend to alert us to the suspicion that there was no such thing as a single nation, neither in language nor in terms of social and political affiliations. This is important not only in the arguments over the relation of dialect to metropolitan conventions (e.g., in the debate over Scotticisms), but also in the more apparently abstract theories of language put forward by the major philosophers. It would be absurdly reductive to suggest that these arguments should be read in exclusively political terms; but at the same time it is clear that the widespread philosophical obsession with the topics of the origin, identity, and progress of language can be situated within specific historical contexts that give some sense of urgency to their appearance.

It was presumably the English Civil War that sharpened Thomas Hobbes' sense of the connection between an ordered language and an ordered state. For Hobbes, this connection is much stronger than one of mere analogy. Words are all that we have, both to signify our turbulent passions and to consolidate the otherwise shapelessly fluent atomic sense data into shareable ideas of objects. Tending toward an extreme nominalism, Hobbes argues for language as the major organizing principle in human experience, and without it "there had been amongst men, neither Commonwealth, nor Society, nor Contract, nor Peace, no more than amongst Lyons, Bears, and Wolves" (1973, Part I, ch. 4, p. 12). Before Babel, all mankind spoke the same language, and the "oblivion of his former language" that was imposed on man afterwards was a punishment for his "rebellion" (p. 13). This word must have resounded loudly indeed for Hobbes and for his readers in 1651. The punishment for rebellion is the disintegration of language and the social contract that language *embodies,* rather than merely represents. Hobbes must have witnessed the instability of the terms of communication when fought over by warring factions:

> For one man calleth *Wisdome,* what another calleth *feare;* and one *cruelty,* what another *justice;* one *prodigality,* what another *magnanimity* . . . such names can never be true ground of any ratiocination (p. 18).

Indeed, and to try to make them so is to garble language and make it nothing more than the projection of special interests: those who supply the definitions of these unstable terms are those who rule the society and figure reality in their own image. One continuation of this way of seeing things leads to the case for absolutism, one authority being better than continual quarrels among rival factions producing only a perpetual instability. This is most necessary in those areas where language is most unstable. Another inference leads to an obligation to limit the claims of authentic language, and to make clear the few things that can be properly said and trusted. Hence metaphor, which is perfectly appropriate to literature, where it is indeed a mark of genius, is quite out of place in the language on which the social contract should be based. In any discourse that does not confess its own untruthfulness (as literature does), the function of metaphor can only be to "deceive others" (p. 13). Hence

> Metaphors, and senselesse and ambiguous words, are like ignes fatui; and reasoning upon them, is wandering amongst innumerable absurdities; and their end, contention, or sedition, and contempt (Part I, ch. 5, p. 22).

The metaphoric union links together things that are properly kept apart, in an act of renomination or refiguring. Thus, it is the perfect vehicle for those who would reorder our perceptions after their own images. For Hobbes, metaphoric figures were associated with the spread of ignorance and superstition (and, some concluded, of religion); because of their tendency to stimulate arguments over what is figurative and what is literal or real, they were also, as we see in the above passage, liable to persuade their users into "sedition." Either we will conduct these arguments and hence pass into contention; or, even worse, we will fail to see the need for an argument at all, and simply accept their modifications of our perceptions as the single available reality. In both cases, the users of language have ceased to be able to reason from shared principles, and civil strife must result.

Hobbes was no great influence on eighteenth-century readers, perhaps because of his reputation as an atheist, and perhaps also for the boldness and clarity with which he accounts for the relationship between social and linguistic discord. Otherwise, were it not for the dangers of an infamous coalition, we might speculate that the opponents of Jeffersonian republicanism might have found some support in the writings of the translator of Thucydides. For Hobbes does confront explicitly the sorts of issues that Locke, who *was* frequently consulted by eighteenth-century readers interested in matters of language, prefers to ignore or avoid. The evasiveness of Locke's *Essay* in this respect has been analyzed and made central to an important recent interpretation of the British eighteenth-century language debate by John Barrell (1983), so that the case need not be expounded at any length here.[5] Barrell argues convincingly that Locke and a large number of his followers fail to specify the exact identity of what they call "common usage," which they cite as the authority to be followed; he suggests that any closer definition of this entity would dramatize in an embarrassing way the degree to which what is called common is in fact something rather more exclusive. The rhetoric of the "common language" thus functions as a sort of populist placebo in treatises on language that are in various ways covertly authoritarian. What is held to be "common" can therefore exclude what is held to be "vulgar," and so forth. Additionally, as we shall see, the tendency of this kind of problem, once exposed, to encourage the sense of a *divided* society, would have further persuaded commentators working within an Enlightenment vocabulary to ignore it. Locke tried very hard, as did Adam Smith in the economic ideal described in *The Wealth of Nations,* to avoid admitting that there were or need be any divisions of interest or inequalities of opportunity within the class of "general nature." Locke in fact seems to wander somewhat on this question. At one point he admits that

> common Use, being but a very uncertain Rule, which reduces it self at last to the *Ideas* of particular Men, proves often but a very variable standard (Locke, 1979, p. 522).

Previously, however, he has shown himself much more impatient, in focusing exactly the tension between individual and collective rights that was to preoccupy the first generation of Americans, both politically and linguistically. In this passage from Book III, ch. 11 of the *Essay,* "common use" is used as an argument to inhibit change:

For Words, especially of Languages already framed, being no Man's private possession, but the common measure of Commerce and Communication, 'tis not for any one, at pleasure, to change the Stamp they are current in; nor alter the *Ideas* they are affixed to; or at least when there is a necessity to do so, he is bound to give notice of it (p. 514).

The images of words as coins, as stable elements in a system of commerce whose exchange value is assured by the image stamped on them, is a telling one, and one that recurs frequently in the rhetoric of the language debate. Locke does try to come clean about where the limits of this common usage might be set, and who might change it:

The proper signification and use of Terms is best to be learned from those, who in their Writings and Discourses, appear to have had the clearest Notions, and apply'd to them their Terms with the exactest choice and fitness (p. 514).

But if we then ask who these writers might be, and how we might know them, we are reduced either to a circular argument (those who embody the common language) or to a further level of analysis that Locke does not anticipate, unless very vaguely in the model of scientific writing or that of ostensive definitions. The format of the *Essay* itself, whereby the same issues are explored and illuminated from different angles at different times, seems to enable Locke to avoid confronting the incongruent elements in his own argument. He observes that

the great *Augustus* himself, in the Possession of that Power which ruled the World, acknowledged, he could not make a new Latin Word: which was as much as to say, that he could not arbitrarily appoint, what *Idea* any Sound should be a Sign of, in the Mouths and common Language of his Subjects (p. 408).

We may take the force of the argument against absolutist legislation, though it could be challenged as an example of disingenuous humility. But the ethic of commonality that is invoked to support this argument can itself only subsist as long as it goes unanalyzed.

It seems that Locke is generally suspicious of neologism, though he cannot allow himself the illiberal gesture of saying so explicitly. We need not trace here the various responses to and echoes of

Locke's formulation, from Swift's faith in legislation by means of an academy, to the more latitudinarian options favored by his successors. George Campbell, for example, in *The Philosophy of Rhetoric* (first published in 1776), seems to anticipate Jefferson's faith in usage giving the law to grammar, rather than grammar to usage; but when the logical question is called, he too gives the final authority to "authors of reputation" (1850, p. 144). He does at least mean *reputation,* rather than the more evasive "quality," as he argues in utilitarian terms that it is not up to any grammarian to try to outface fashion; and yet disputatious adjectives do creep in as he refers to "reputable, national, and present use" as his yardstick (p. 215). As for the difference between honest simplicity and mere vulgarity, we are supposed to know it when we see it, just as we are to know the honest and deserving poor from the rogues and dissemblers:

> True ease in composition, accompanied with purity, differs as much from that homely manner which affects the familiarity of low phrases and vulgar idioms, as the appearance of a woman that is plainly but neatly dressed, differs from that of a slattern (p. 199).

Like many eighteenth-century patricians, Campbell likes his poor people and his women to show forth for exactly what they are, never hiding behind the dangerous homogeneity of fashion. The odd word may be ennobled, just as the odd deserving members of the lower orders may be raised in life; but vulgarity, in words as in people, will always show forth its "vile and despicable origin" (p. 169).

Two other figures must be invoked before we can rejoin the subject of the English language in America: Samuel Johnson and Edmund Burke. Johnson was unquestionably the best known and most frequently invoked of all the eighteenth-century commentators on language, although he wrote neither the first dictionary nor the first grammar. Johnson too declared an avowed faith in the customary, sometimes with an apparently democratic enthusiasm, and sometimes with a melancholy resignation over the inevitability of change. (See Barrell, 1983, pp. 144–75, for an excellent account of this.) Johnson was never quite the Frenchified follower of fashion that his American critics—for their own reasons, as we shall see—made him out to be. But his pronouncements on the language do have political affiliations and implications. This may be demonstrated by comparing his arguments in *The Plan of a Dictionary of the English Language* (1747) with those produced almost fifty years later by Burke in the *Reflections on the Revolution in France* (1790). Each casts himself as a well-meaning superintendent over processes (respectively in the progress of language and of civil society) that are in themselves ultimately ungovernable, and each claims to be doing the best he can, becoming thereby a sort of rearguard tragic hero. Johnson sees in the language an entity "without dependence, and without relation" (1957, p. 128), which is exactly what Burke feared in the social contract. The English language, like Burke's idea of the constitution (much lampooned by Paine), is the product of mingled initiatives, "composed of dissimilar parts, thrown together by negligence, by affectation, by learning, or by ignorance" (p. 130). Its syntax, like Burke's model of human nature and thus of executive protocol, is "too inconstant to be reduced to rules," and can only be passed on by "special precedents" (p. 131). Precisely the same rhetoric informs the preface to the *English Dictionary* in its fourth (1773) edition, the last to receive the author's revisions. The product of "time and fashion" (1957, p. 301), language embodies "the boundless chaos of a living speech" (p. 307), and if they are to find a way through it, lexicographers cannot be bound by rules; rather, they must navigate by a mixture of "experience and analogy" (p. 302). If innovation must come, then it had better come from those "who have much leisure to think" (p. 320). Best of all, it should not come at all, for people should not disturb

> upon narrow views, or for minute propriety, the orthography of their fathers. . . . Change, says *Hooker,* is not made without inconvenience, even from worse to better. There is in constancy and stability a general and lasting advantage, which will always overbalance the slow improvements of gradual correction (p. 304).

Let alone the more chaotic modifications of immediate revolution! To turn to Burke's highly influential work of 1790 is to become aware of a remarkable symmetry of rhetoric and argument between these two great eighteenth-century conservative thinkers. Burke also casts himself as one trying to assess the "strong principle" of the "spirit of liberty" (1899, 3:241), and sees a chain of events being determined by a "strange chaos of levity and ferocity"

(p. 244). Like Johnson ("the orthography of our fathers"), Burke is obliged to defend a tradition of continuity he must recognize to be full of gaps and leaps, and he similarly argues that "a revolution will be the very last resort of the thinking and the good" (p. 271), for by such action "the whole chain and continuity of the commonwealth would be broken" (p. 357). Like Johnson, Burke seeks a way of excluding novelty without appearing to advocate the restriction of "power, authority, and distinction to blood, and names, and titles" (p. 297). But, if the "evils of inconstancy and versatility" are indeed "ten thousand times" worse than those of "obstinacy and the blindest prejudice" (p. 358), then we are clearly being persuaded to think of an ideally unchanging order, or one that changes so slowly that nothing is felt or noticed, thanks to a "slow, but well-sustained progress" (p. 457).

We should not force this comparison to the point of a conscious and complete identity. Burke's rhetoric is indeed far more manic and energetic than Johnson's, as one would expect given the nature of his subject and his historical predicament. Burke's images of father and family, and of the organic body of the state, are much more intense than anything in Johnson, for whom irony and hyperbole are commonly available as a form of self-distancing. Burke is, after all, reacting to world historical events, which Johnson's analysis of the state of the language only images or forecasts at the most implicit levels: threats to property and to public credit in the form of spuriously created paper money, as well as to the more general overturning of the social order. Coining new words and redirecting the applications of old ones may intimate such a crisis (and we shall see that Burke also was aware of this), but for Johnson at least it did not appear along with a revolution.

Despite the differences of time and occasion, however, the arguments of the two men are remarkably close. As Johnson finds things simply too confusing for the establishment of fixed rules, so Burke also begs leave "to throw out my thoughts, and express my feelings, just as they arise in my mind, with very little attention to formal method" (p. 243). This is a more flagrant assertion of argumentative opportunism than Johnson's recourse to "experience and analogy"—"experience, which practice and observation were continually increasing; and analogy, which, though in some words obscure, was evident in others" (1957, p. 302). But in the final analysis both writers are asserting the basic credo of patrician politics: that it never be made to commit itself to publicly avowed rules of procedure that might then come back to accuse their compiler. Johnson himself was to upbraid the Methodists for their avoidance of such rules! But for Johnson in the sphere of language and for Burke in that of politics, the attribution of chaos and confusion functions to legitimate the legislator's own freedom of maneuver and to preserve his own unaccountability. These, precisely, were the terms in which Paine challenged Burke in analyzing the nature of his much-vaunted "constitution."

The Debate in America

I shall return to both Burke and Johnson in later contexts. For the moment, it is enough to have established the point that, if the explicit connections made by Hobbes between the disordering of language and the collapse of civil society were not postulated so thoroughly by any of his successors, they yet underlie and inform, at various levels of avoidance and allusion, much eighteenth-century writing on the subject of language. This context in turn gives an enhanced significance, I would argue, to those seemingly more off-handed comments of Jefferson and Adams on the nature and prospects of an American language, or a new kind of English. They were not approaching the question out of a vacuum, nor with any merely theoretical or naively patriotic impulse.

At the same time, we should not imagine Jefferson, Adams, Hamilton, and the other founding fathers haranguing each other very regularly over the state of the language. Benjamin Franklin did write to Noah Webster, in 1789, complaining about the New England neologisms in his native language, about the passing of the habit of capitalizing important nouns, and about the increasing use of "the round s instead of the long one" (Franklin, 1806, 2:351–57). But this, like his proposal for spelling reform, was but a small part of his career as a politician and man of science. Similarly, Jefferson himself was something of an innovator in the realm of language. He coined the noun *breadstuffs* and the verb *to belittle,* supported the authority of *lengthy* (by using it), proposed new names for the coinage system, and tried unsuccessfully to popularize *monocrat* (see Mencken, 1973, pp. 5, 50, 129, 130, 135, 229). His political opponents were not slow to make connections between his political and his linguistic habits. At the same time, with Jefferson as with Franklin, though to a lesser degree, we should not assume that the reform of the language was a consistent or an obsessive priority. The notable point is perhaps that the politicians were interested at all in the question of language; and they surely were, as we shall see again.

Neither Jefferson nor Adams seems to have been much preoccupied with the campaign to rename the nation itself, though others were. William Tudor, in 1799, wanted to establish the name *Columbia,* since the term *America* was too general and risked "confounding a brave, intelligent and free people, occupying a distinct territory, with every species of inhabitants which the new world has bred." Samuel Latham Mitchill preferred *Fredonia,* to be peopled by *Fredes* who would speak *Fredish* or *Fredonian.* The whole subject went too far for John Quincy Adams, who wrote a satire for *The Monthly Anthology,* presenting this orgy of renaming (associated also by this time with the Lewis and Clark expedition) as the delusory result of a bout of drunkenness:

> While all our heads are swimming,
> We'll dash the bottle on the wall
> And name (the thing's agreed on)
> Our first-rate-ship United States
> The flying frigate *Fredon.*[6]

For the most part, the issues that engaged the editors and readers of the magazines were less ambitious in their apparent significance, although there was no lack of intensity about the debate. It began politely enough, indeed, but during the turbulent years around the election of 1800, when the first drastic change of administrations was taking place, the argument about the American language became especially passionate. John Witherspoon's essays in *The Druid,* first published in 1781, are unprophetically modest in seeing as "unsettled" the larger question of whether the standard of good English will continue to be set by Britain or come to reside in America.[7] The mobility of the "vulgar" in the United States means that they are less prone than their British counterparts to settle into "local peculiarities, either in accent or phraseology" (p. 459); but,

while the British governing class observes all the proprieties in its
public language, whatever it may do in private, the public speech
of the American is much more marked by vulgarisms. Witherspoon,
who claims to be the coiner of the term *Americanism,* by analogy
with *Scotticism* (p. 460), sees linguistic vices and virtues on both
sides of the Atlantic. His major complaint about Johnson's *Dictionary* has nothing to do with its legislative ambitions; rather, he
objects to the sanctification of errors committed by major authors,
often in a spirit of irony that Johnson fails to detect in his appetite
for citation (pp. 472–73). There is an implicitly democratic point
here—Johnson is blinded by his uncritical respect for the great men
of literature. But it is no more than implicit.

Most of the magazine literature of the early national period is
marked by regular references to the state of literature and language
in the United States. Much of this is evenhanded, as we might expect from the divided allegiances in American society on the question of the general relation to the parent culture. The intensity with
which this topic is pursued seems to increase when the subject of
language becomes an element in the argument between the Jeffersonian and Federalist factions, rather than between the nation as a
whole and the British. Jefferson was elected to the presidency in
1800, and by this time also the challenging views of Noah Webster
and others on the subject of the national language were becoming
well known. The appropriately self-styled "Oliver Oldschool," alias
Joseph Dennie, includes in the first issue of *The Port Folio,* after
an attack on Tom Paine, a tirade against American English. The
word *lengthy,* already at the time of writing (1801) a notorious
Americanism, is dismissed as "undoubtedly the growth of the wigwam."[8] Dennie alludes here to the vocabulary and practices of the
Tammany Society, a democratic club first formed on anti-British
principles and continuing throughout the 1790s to profess egalitarian and Gallican sentiments. Its members dressed as Indians and
elected "sachems" and "sagamores" as their executive officers (see
Mushkat, 1971, chs. 1 & 2). Dennie's point is thus not about the
language in an abstract way, but about the politics of language. The
linguistic cudgels are employed very frequently in the early issues
of *The Port Folio,* and in exactly this spirit. Nor is "Oldschool"
content that the political point of his remarks remain merely implicit:

The French Revolution has given rise to many novelties of speech and writing, that have been admired and embraced by their partizans, but no man of good sense or good feelings can expect any thing pure or elegant, from that polluted source. Their language, like their actions, of late years, has been barbarous in the extreme (vol. I, n. 49, p. 306).

This reference to the French Revolution would have been a telling one. Because of the common late Enlightenment assumption of an organic connection between language and civilization, the evidence of imminent social disorder could be seen in language with somewhat more conviction than might seem appropriate to a modern observer. Hobbes, as we have seen, had expressed similar concerns in his analysis of the effects of the English civil war on the social contract, which was for him above all a contract in language, an agreement to share certain fundamental significations. This connection between language and the social contract was made urgent once again for those anxious spirits in Britain and America who were observing the progress of the French Revolution. The revolutionary Convention in France had indeed committed itself to renaming the months as well as a host of other things of more direct political import, so that any modification of the language would have been associated very closely with the mechanisms of a more general revolution. America had declared and indeed enacted its political independence, but it had not had a true revolution, in the manner of the French. Its internal constitution and its traditional social organization had not been completely overturned, because they had not yet come into being as distinctively *national* entities. By the mid-1790s, however, political life within the United States had become sufficiently contentious and procedures sufficiently well established (or at least clearly proposed) for the prospects of a French-style revolution to begin to worry some people. Or, at the very least, they found it in their interest to claim such a concern.

In fact, the evidence presented by some of the most influential historians of the period suggests that the early republic experienced a much higher degree of political instability than one might assume from perusing merely the more famous pronouncements of 1776. There was a tradition of crowd action, just as there was in eighteenth-century England (the Wilkesite and Gordon riots are two famous examples), which, even if it tended to be generated as a last resort, was nevertheless always in the background as a potential medium of political expression. To describe this phenomenon as mob violence is itself a political nomination, since some historians have argued that such behavior was consciously coordinated, very well-organized, and concerned to present itself as "theater" rather than being an outburst of uncontrollable energy. At whatever level of emblematic self-awareness, we must certainly conclude that the presence of a crowd must have served as a reminder of both the claims and the sheer presence of particular interests and factions (see Hoerder, 1977).

And factions there were. Gordon S. Wood, in his detailed study of the period, makes clear that concerns about divisions of interest within the state were absolutely central to American political rhetoric and to the experience it described. The *Federalist Papers* are full of such concerns, as are the writings of John Adams. Arguments about bicameralism raised the specter of class divisions between the interests thus represented, as did the fights over the constitution itself. Fears of demogoguery and rioting were widespread and vocal. The whole effect of Wood's account is to suggest that very little must have seemed stable or predictable to the founding fathers and to the people they governed, or for whom they governed.[9]

Additionally, both Wood and (in greater detail) Bernard Bailyn (1967) suggest that the American Revolution was a highly "literate" phenomenon, accompanied and stimulated by a deluge of pamphlet literature. This might of itself have created a strong association between the written word and historical events of the greatest magnitude; further, within this literature the arguments often seem to have been of a distinctly linguistic species. There was, for example, an obsession with the definition and description of the "constitution" (Bailyn, p. 175f.; Wood, pp. 128–32), perhaps itself part of the tradition on which Tom Paine draws in attacking Burke's use of the term in the 1790s. Another very common term, defined and debated in all its varieties, seems to have been *conspiracy* (see Bailyn, p. 144f.). Words could indeed do wonders.

If the political atmosphere of the United States in the 1780s was indeed already unstable, for some of the reasons suggested above, then it could only have become more so with the outbreak of the French Revolution. There was, as has been said, a close connection between political and linguistic reform in France itself after 1789. While we may rightly distrust as merely fashionable any idea that to revolutionize a language is at once and wholly to revolutionize a society, there is at the same time no doubt that the strong mid-twentieth-century correlations between language and power have produced much evidence for the historical importance of the written word and of the contemporary reactions to it.[10] In the English-speaking world, the relation between political and linguistic innovation was famously advanced by Burke, who saw in the French Revolution not only an attack on the propriety of property and public credit, but also on that of language. In his "Preface to the Address of M. Brissot" (1794), he objects that

> Things are never called by their common names. Massacre is sometimes *agitation,* sometimes *effervescence,* sometimes *excess;* sometimes too continued an excercise of a *revolutionary power* (Burke, 1899, 5:81).[11]

Here is Hobbes' concern restated for the audience of the 1790s, trying as it was to come to terms with the experience of the Terror. For Burke, as Brissot and his like were reducing the state to confusion, so they were also coining a new and indecipherable language:

> There are some passages, too, in which his language requires to be first translated into French,—at least into such French as the Academy would in former times have tolerated. He writes with great force and vivacity; but the language, like everything else in his country, has undergone a revolution (p. 91).

No one much read William Blake, but if they had they might have registered the declaration of stylistic independence prefacing the first chapter of *Jerusalem,* and culminating in the credo that "Poetry Fetter'd Fetters the Human Race," in a similarly politicized context (see Blake, 1982, p. 146). Blake was an English Brissot with no audience.

Partly for reasons of geography, and partly perhaps because they felt that they had already had their revolution, the fear of contamination by the French example was not as great among the citizens of the United States as it was in Great Britain. Nevertheless, such a fear did figure significantly in the rhetoric of the debate between the Federalists and their political opponents. Citizen Genêt, the

ambassador of the new French republic, received a hero's welcome
when he arrived in the new world, one accompanied with enough
elements of disorder and carnival to disquiet many Americans. And
Jefferson's first address to Congress in 1801, which began with the
words "Fellow Citizens," was controversial enough to persuade him
to preface the next twenty-five messages with the blander term
"Gentlemen."[12]

This context helps explain why Joseph Dennie and others like
him might have been so sensitive on the subject of words that
seemed to them the products of the "wigwam." Dennie is not reacting principally to the question of the rights and wrongs of deviating from the practice of the parent culture in Great Britain. We
should certainly not underestimate the extent of the schism that the
process of independence introduced into American minds about
their residual allegiance, if any, to all things British, whether cultural, economic, or simply emotional. A large number of colonists
did after all elect to leave the newly united states. Whether America
and Britain could or should continue to have a special relationship
was an urgent question, and the status of the common language was
clearly part of this question. But, as the precedents of Hobbes and
(more immediately) Burke might suggest, the most passionate en-
gagement with the language question in this period (though not always in later periods) seems to have occurred when the discussion
embodied or alluded to the internal political debate. Those who are
sensitive about new words and new concepts are often so because
they are concerned about what they see happening around them,
rather than with the more distant prospects for the relationship between American and British English. Discouraging the coining of
new words and the extended applications of old ones, by the traditionally licentious procedures of metaphor and association, was for
many writers not just a way of preserving some abstract propriety;
it was a way of expressing the desire to slow down social and political change and to inhibit the claims of various factions and interests
to alter the language—a language not only representing American
society but also capable of redetermining it. Burke had supported
the American cause, because he saw it as a movement quite in line
with the central theses of a traditional political rhetoric; it was not,
as the French Revolution was, a new language.

We can now see why there were many, aside from the committed

Anglophiles who would sanction no deviation from the rules set down in London, who were open to the prospect of some particularly American modification of the language, but who were at the same time uncomfortable about making a completely new beginning. Sheer common sense obviously must have supported this option, given the undeniable existence of strong cultural and linguistic continuities not to be done away with by mere political fiat. But we must add to this the suggestion that to have set out to build up the language from a completely new beginning, or anything close to it, would also have involved some clear recognition of the claims of various interests in American society to be a part of this language. Language reform almost inevitably raises the question of divided interests of the sort that Locke and others had sought to gloss over in their use of the image of a common language.

It is not then surprising that the most popular policy among American men of letters is the policy of gradual change: modification as and when called for, rather than revolution. Charles Brockden Brown's *American Review* (1801–2), in its notice of Caleb Alexander's *Columbian Dictionary,* argues that, as political change should be in the hands of the patricians, so literary change should be in the hands of the great writers:

> To create language must be considered as the prerogative of those only who have acquired such an established reputation in the literary world as to stamp their opinions with something like the weight of authority. And even they must proceed in the exercise of their power with timid and cautious step, or they will find that the republic of letters will rebel (Brockden Brown, 1801–2, 1:220).

This is an interesting passage: one might for example question whether the rebellion that the author most fears is really the one that would be limited to the republic of letters, itself composed of an elite. But taking at face value this program of supervised innovation, as many wished to do, it then necessarily calls up the further question of whether there *was* such a class of literary men in America. This prospectus seems to depend on a senatorial class of men of letters that (many thought) had not yet come into being; and which, in order to come into being, might well require a homogeneous national culture to be already in place! If language can only be legislated by a literary class and a tradition of "polite" let-

ters, might that tradition not require an existing national language
if it is to develop as a national entity in the first place?

The Federalist wits were not slow to see the usefulness of this
apparent paradox in putting forward the case for a complete subservience to the language as it stood. The editors of *The Monthly
Anthology* (6, 1809, p. 5) declared in their own voices that

> American literature is not a tract where we expect any regular an-
> nual product, or where we are sure of constant improvements from
> the hand of well directed industry; but it is rather a kind of half
> cleared and half cultivated country, where you may travel till you
> are out of breath, without starting any rare game, and be obliged to
> sit down day after day to the same coarse, insipid fare.

For Oliver Oldschool and *The Port Folio,* the prospect of an American English is all the more threatening because there is no buffer
against the ravages of populism, no class of authoritative American
writers. Hence the dangers of the "growth of the wigwam" and of
the "vicious, fugitive, scoundrel and True American word" *lengthy*
(vol. I, no. 31, p. 247). In a similar spirit, Theodore Dehon (1807)
commented, probably with consciously Johnsonian spellings, on the
value of a great literature to its society:

> The barbarity of savage nature is softened, heroism is cherished,
> vice loses at least its boldness and its grossness, publick spirit is
> purified, and love is refined, wherever the influence of correct lit-
> erature is felt (Dehon, 1807, p. 466).

Consequently, given his awareness of the lack of patronage and his
distaste for the national obsession with financial and political self-
advancement, Dehon is concerned that "the *republick* of letters
may have its dignity and prosperity endangered by sliding inadver-
tently into a *democracy*" (p. 472); and this democracy might then
extend to other elements of social life. Given the absence either of
an academy (which Adams had proposed back in 1780) or of a
commonly recognized literary class, it must have seemed to many
observers of the linguistic situation that there was little alternative
to absolute chaos on the one hand and complete subservience to
British standards on the other.

The special place of Noah Webster's writings in this debate will
be accounted for in the next chapter; Webster is both the most important and the most complex figure in the national language argu-

ment. For the moment, we must take note of the other grammarians and compilers of dictionaries who were his rivals in the struggle for the custodianship of American English. Samuel Johnson Jr.'s *A School Dictionary* (1798) does not pretend to be complete, authoritative, or innovatory. It lists only common words (4150 of them) and shows no interest in Americanisms. Johnson's image of common speech might surprise the modern reader, including as it does such words as *shog, tosspot, tweag, tweedle,* and *perdue;* but every one of these words persists in Webster's 1858 dictionary, with reputable authorities, and their presence here does not seem to be at all polemical. Johnson's very name might indeed be thought to intimate no very radical instinct for change. The follow-up volume published by Johnson and John Elliott in 1800 similarly pretends to nothing more challenging than the education of youth in a "free republic" (p. 5), but it did enough to produce a stinging review in Brockden Brown's *American Review,* which declared that whatever was new in the book was bad because it was a departure from Walker, "the best standard for correct and elegant pronunciation" (1801–2, 1:211). The volume did include the word *foutra,* "for the first and last time in a dictionary of English" (Friend, 1967, p. 11), but even this was apparently an uncensored borrowing from Ash. It also listed borrowings from Native American languages, and American place names.

Among those who tried their hands at dictionaries before Webster, it was Caleb Alexander who seems to have ruffled the most feathers. He presumably began to do so with his very title, *The Columbian Dictionary of the English Language* (1800). The title page indeed promises "many new words, peculiar to the United States," and takes on the united forces of *"prejudice, ignorance, malice* and *pedantry,* four powerful enemies" (p. iii). Although Alexander's bark seems to have been much more nationalistic or democratic than his bite, he does include words like *Congressional, lengthy,* and *Yanky* [*sic*]. And he did enough to inspire both spite and sarcasm from Dennie in *The Port Folio* (1801). First the spite:

> This work, a disgrace to letters, is a disgusting collection of every vicious word, and phrase, chosen by the absurd misapprehension, or coined by the presumptuous ignorance of the boors of each local jurisdiction in the United States. It is a record of our imbecility (vol. I, no. 31, p. 247).

Possessing Samuel Johnson (senior) for energy and elegance of vocabulary, and Walker for "accurate and courtly pronunciation," we have no need for the "sectary Alexander" and his "wigwam words." Here now is the sarcasm:

> If we can once become unintelligible to foreigners, one great source of corruption will be dried up. . . . To coin new words, or to use them in a new sense, is, incontrovertibly, one of the unalienable rights of freemen; and whoever disputes this right, is the friend of civil tyranny, and an enemy to liberty and equality (vol. I, no. 41, p. 325)

The verdict of *The American Review* (1:217–28), though hostile enough, is modest by comparison.

Dennie's mention of Johnson and Walker is fairly representative of "polite" preferences in the period. Walker especially had his rivals, Sheridan and Entick among them, but they too were British. James Carrol's American contribution (1795) made little headway.

In the realm of grammars, Lindley Murray came into the field in 1795—a field in which Webster had already staked his claim—and conquered it.[13] Murray's gift, perhaps predictable in one who had traded profitably with the royalists during the war, was one of compromise. American-born, his book was heavily based on his British predecessor Robert Lowth, and he published it in London, and imported it from there into the United States. Disdaining absolutism of any kind, Murray trades heavily in the ideology of common sense. In matters of language, perfection is impossible and confusion reigns, so that Samuel Johnson is chosen as the standard not because of a declared respect for his convictions but because any standard is better than none. Innovation of any kind only adds to this tendency toward confusion, so it is better not to try it (1823, pp. 23–25). Ancient usage should not be proposed as a guide to present usage, since even the polemically charged Anglo-Saxons were innovators in their time (pp. 134–35). But, at the same time, Latinate and other foreign constructions are not to be recommended either, since we have a "plain, native style" already perfectly sufficient for our needs (pp. 294–95). With more diplomacy than most of the contemporary diplomats, Murray guides the ship of language with perfect poise between the Scylla of Jacobinism and the Charybdis of Federalist extremism. The plain style, as he describes it, is neither the language of the vulgar nor that of the elite. His *Grammar* is the perfect panacea for a troubled generation—a generation in which at least one concerned Federalist could lament that "even the nursery is not exempt from the unremitting efforts of these disturbers of the human race" (the Jacobins), who are seeking "to corrupt the minds of the Rising Generation, to make them imbibe, with their very milk, as it were, the poison of atheism and disaffection."[14] Murray's popularity must have been at least partly related to his skill in presenting a model of linguistic propriety in which all controversial traces have been suppressed or sublimated.

But it is, of course, the career of Noah Webster that is most central to the debate about the national language. No one worked harder for it, and no one aroused deeper passions among readers and reviewers; and ultimately, I shall suggest, no one demonstrates such radical tensions and contradictions in his writings. To look closely at Webster is to raise once again all the issues and controversies that Murray seeks to avoid. Whether by belligerent reference or indeed by omission, Webster's ongoing analysis of language is politically charged from start to finish. We must now turn to an examination of the first twenty years or so of Webster's career.

2

Noah Webster

There are many Noah Websters, and in this chapter I shall not even be concerned with his most famous persona, that of the author of *An American Dictionary of the English Language,* published in two volumes in 1828 and deservedly acknowledged as the first major American dictionary. This work will be discussed in its place later in my argument. The range and energy of Webster's publications and addresses have led one of his biographers and interpreters to give him the title of "Schoolmaster to America."[1] Indeed, there is seemingly no department of educational policy or practice that Webster does not touch upon: he wrote spelling books, grammars, theoretical treatises, and dictionaries, as well as a less well-known but almost as energetic series of reflections on political and commercial questions. Looking at his bewilderingly large and varied output, it is often tempting to conclude that coherence is simply not to be found, and to cast Webster as a mere opportunist, prepared to publish with or against the times in whatever ways might have seemed to him immediately profitable.

This case is worth taking seriously, because *The Monthly Anthology* (8, 1810, 147–48) makes the very same accusation in the context of Webster's campaign for an American orthography. Benjamin D. Perkins, writing under the pseudonym of "Steady Habits" (as opposed, one supposes, to populist instabilities), claims that

Webster's primary purpose is to establish the need for American imprints of everything published in English; if Webster's scheme were to be adopted, every book would have to be "translated" into American spellings for the American market. There is no doubt that Webster was not blind to the possibility of turning a penny, nor was he alone in this attitude to the American market. Even the Englishman Herbert Croft, self-styled successor to Samuel Johnson, had planned to title his great work (which he never finished) the "English and American Dictionary," in hopes of attracting the American reader (see Allen Walker Read, 1937b, p. 202). But to rest with mere self-interest as an explanation of Webster's strategy does not do justice to the nature and contexts of his ambitions. In fact, Webster had confessed, some twenty years before Perkins wags his finger, that the stimulation of an American book trade was one of the principal purposes behind the proposed spelling reform. In the *Dissertations* (1789) he had predicted a future in which "posterity, being taught a different spelling, would prefer the American orthography." There are indeed some comically penny-pinching aspects to this argument, such as the following (with which no modern bibliophile would disagree!):

> Such a reform would diminish the number of letters about one sixteenth or eighteenth. This would save a page in eighteen; and a saving of an eighteenth in the expense of books, is an advantage that should not be overlooked (Webster, 1789a, p. 397).

Before dismissing this as a hyperbolic example of Yankee thrift, we should remind ourselves once again that Webster thought and wrote within a society for which the circulation of information and opinion through print was held to be of the greatest importance. Godwin, publishing five years later, was to argue, presumably with some hope of credibility, that the increased circulation of printed matter alone might be enough to bring about the gradual progress toward social and political perfection that revolution itself could never produce. One of the arguments of the *Enquiry Concerning Political Justice* is that the truth need only be printed in order to spread of its own accord.

Such an idea must seem naive to us now, taking for granted as we do (and as some of Godwin's own contemporaries were begin-

ning to do) the force of vested interests and unconscious inclinations in constituting what we tend to denominate "truth." But, as
we shall see, there is much in Webster's early writings that identifies
him as a true son of the Enlightenment, a believer in the prospect of
rational universals and in the gradual supplanting of error and
superstition by truth and good feelings. These convictions are not
unchallenged, but they are there. Within this manner of thinking,
cheaper books would have meant a wider readership and thus an
enhancing of the opportunity for a unified nation.

Furthermore, such books would be *American* books, and thus
part of an American commerce and industry. Webster shared with
many of his fellow citizens a strong concern about the dependence
of the United States on manufactured goods imported from Britain.
At the very best, such goods would be necessities; at worst, luxuries
and superfluities, the centrality of which had been argued by Adam
Smith to be an inevitable and desirable result of a divided labor
situation. As division of labor increases efficiency, it produces a
surplus, which can be exchanged for what people desire rather than
simply what they need. For Smith, a British economist, this was an
essential stimulant to the recirculation of wealth: the rich would be
prevented from hoarding by the demon of fashion in their own
hearts and minds. This paradigm was, of course, just as theoretical
and idealistic in the late eighteenth century as similar ideas can
seem today, and a harsh view of Smith's argument might see it as
little more than a sophisticated apologia for the Whig economy,
one in which private vices were once again to be converted into
public virtues. We can see at the same time that such idealism
might have been more credible to a British than to an American
audience. The wealthier British citizens were, after all, purchasing
their own manufactures, whereas the Americans, as Webster himself argues,

> have no body of manufacturers to support by dissipation. All our
> superfluities are imported, and the consumption of them in this
> country enriches the merchants and supports the poor of Europe.
> . . . This is the pernicious, the fatal effect of our dependence on
> foreign nations for our manners (Webster, 1790b, p. 88).

We may notice that Webster accepts the Smithian argument for the
producing nation: the merchants *and* the poor are enriched in this

ideal pattern of continually circulating wealth. America, however, as a consumer, is impoverished by her own buying power. As long as she continues to feed the manufacturing economy of another country, that country is getting back more than it gives.

That Webster here pinpoints the power of "manners" takes us to the heart of his case against Anglophilia and, by extension, back to the question of the book trade. Americans who ape English manners will buy English goods to display their affiliations (much as many young people in Europe now wear jeans and drink Coca-Cola). Such tendencies might be corrected by rigid legislative intervention—as they had been by Lycurgus of Sparta (the usual eighteenth-century example), who prohibited all imports and exports, lest the surplus economy necessary to create them should bring corruption in its wake. But such a policy could hardly obtain in a nation like the United States, in which the ideology of commerce and freedom of trade was a founding doctrine, even as it was not completely uncontested. More practically, American manners must be influenced by persuasion, by convincing every citizen to behave in one way rather than another. The medium of persuasion for Webster's generation was the printed word: hence the urgency of providing cheap, American books for American readers. This would not only stimulate a native book trade, but would embody a native morality, politics, culture, and fashion. Additionally, for the early Webster, it would also publicize an American orthography.

We can now see why the book trade must have seemed a very important factor in the struggle for cultural independence. I have presented the argument in a more thoroughgoing and exhaustive way than Webster, as far as I know, ever presents it himself. But what I have said is not inconsistent with Webster's various comments on the subject, and does offer an explanation of their purpose and intrinsic coherence. Webster believed that the fight for true independence had only just begun:

A fundamental mistake of the Americans has been, that they considered the revolution as completed, when it was but just begun. Having raised the pillars of the building, they ceased to exert themselves, and seemed to forget that the whole superstructure was then to be erected. This country is independent in government; but totally dependent in manners, which are the basis of government (1790b, p. 84).

So much, then, for the case against Webster as a mere profiteer. Perhaps I have labored the point, but the point is important. Whatever degree of intuitive self-interest we might see behind Webster's public persona (and it should not be forgotten that such self-interest was a part of the mythology of the Yankee and thus an element of the rhetoric readily available to Webster's opponents), that same persona yet incorporates important historical and ideological coordinates. It is to such coordinates, as well as to the individual and biographical circumstances, that we must turn if we are to understand the trends and tensions that show up in Webster's writings. In this spirit we may now approach some of the thematic arguments in those writings.

The Spoken and the Written

The question of the relation between writing and speech has again become a popular academic concern. Much of this concern has focused around the reading of Jacques Derrida's *Of Grammatology,* translated into English in 1976; though, as always in such cases, we should be aware also that an audience for Derrida's arguments was already in existence. Derrida describes a tradition in post-Enlightenment thought for which the written word is mythologized as a debased form of the spoken: more ambiguous, less immediate, and (though Derrida travels lightly here) perhaps the image of a divided society. Describing an exemplary formulation (if not an origin) of this syndrome in Rousseau, Derrida analyzes its emergence or persistence in Lévi-Strauss, Saussure, and others. His account does not, for reasons of its own, expound the importance of the opposite tradition, in which the written is an advance over the spoken, in that it solidifies by publication what might otherwise remain merely reported and distorted, and in that it appeals coolly to the reason while the spoken, in its very immediacy, is all too prone to inflame the passions and the desires. Hence, for Hegel (to take one example), the superiority of the philosophic over the aesthetic and religious world views: the highest form of expression and communication is the most rational form of prose.

This question of the relation of the spoken and the written was also, in rather different ways, an urgent one for the eighteenth-

century mind. In the case of Webster and his audience in the new
republic, it was especially urgent. Webster's early writings are emphatic about the need to try to reduce the widening gap between
written words and spoken sounds. Hence his argument against
Johnson, a writer

> whose pedantry has corrupted the purity of our language, and
> whose principles would in time destroy all agreement between the
> spelling and pronunciation of words (1789a, p. ix).

Should Johnson's policies be accepted and pursued, there might in
the course of time be "as great a difference between our *written*
and *spoken* language, as there is between the pronunciation of the
present English and German" (p. 404). When Johnson spells *errour,* because of some reputed analogy with the French, from which
the English word might have been secondarily derived, but speaks
and pronounces it as *error,* he is not just being unnecessarily in-
genious but also socially divisive, as Webster points out in the preface to his *Compendious Dictionary:*

> The great body of a nation cannot possibly know the powers of
> letters in a foreign language; and the practice of introducing for-
> eign words in a foreign orthography, generates numerous diversities
> of pronunciation, and perplexes the mass of a nation. And the prac-
> tice is, I believe, peculiar to the English (1806, p. x).

It would be hard to refute, then as now, that the English do employ
the language to perplex the mass of the nation, though they are not
the only offenders in this respect. Johnson's academicism is, covertly,
a strategy tending to establish the hegemony of a class of educated
etymologists, or pseudo-etymologists, over the community of language users. (This could of course also take the comic form of
overtly personal or political word definitions, such as the famous
dictionary entries for *oats* and *pension,* a tactic reciprocated by
Webster in his definition of *Federal!*) At best, the Johnsonian protocol is pompously redundant, as in the list of learned citations
(from Knolles, Milton, and Berkeley) to elucidate the meaning of
the word *hand;* at worst, it is explicitly divisive.

Webster further argues that any attempt to *fix* the orthography
of a language (as Johnson's was) must be seen as an improper in-
hibition on subsequent changes in the spoken language. There is al-

ready a wide gap between the spoken and the written in Johnson's scheme, and this can only become wider with the passage of time:

> Every man of common reading knows that a living language must necessarily suffer gradual changes in its current words, in the signification of many words, and in pronunciation. The unavoidable consequence then of fixing the orthography of a living language, is to destroy the use of the alphabet. This effect has, in a degree, already taken place in our language; and letters, the most useful invention that ever blessed mankind, have lost and continue to lose a part of their value, by no longer being the representatives of the sounds originally annexed to them. Strange as it may seem, the fact is undeniable, that the present doctrin [sic] that no change must be made in writing words, is destroying the benefits of an alphabet, and reducing our language to the barbarism of Chinese characters instead of letters (1806, p. vi).

This is a rather radical notion of Webster's: that the great virtue of an alphabet, wherein letters and small groups of letters represent sounds, is that spellings can change as sounds do.[2] In this respect, the accusation against Johnson is a two-pronged one. First, he has tried to institute a gap between the spoken and the written, and, second, he has attempted to ensure that this gap will become greater through time. The political analogue (if not the inspiration) of this policy is obvious: language starts out as the province of an elite (because only they can cope with a complex writing-speech relation), and becomes more so through history. Language can be accurately deployed only by a mandarin class. This cannot be appropriate to an American English, which must cease to contain the linguistic traces of such classes as well as doing away with them in actuality, wherever they might appear:

> From the changes in civil policy, manners, arts of life and other circumstances attending the settlement of English colonies in America: most of the language of heraldry, hawking, hunting, and especially that of the old feudal and hierarchical esaablishments of England, will become utterly extinct in this country—much of it already forms a part of the neglected rubbish of antiquity (1806, p. xxii).

Webster was not alone in seeking to reduce the gap between the spoken and the written language in the cause of a more democratic English. In America, James Carrol's *American Criterion* (1795)

takes up the case, on behalf of children and foreigners, as does
William Thornton's *Cadmus* (1793), which also explicitly attacks
Johnson on these grounds (p. 23f.).[3] Thornton's answer was, as we
have seen, a wholly new system of spelling aimed at bringing together orthography and orthoepy, so that "the pronunciation of the
scholar, would, by reading alone, be perfectly attained by the peasant and the foreigner" (p. 38). Benjamin Franklin had also laid
plans for spelling reform (see 1806, 2:357–66), and like Thornton
he had suggested that the Spanish convention of placing a question
mark at the beginning of a sentence might be adopted into English,
so that we might know in advance what intonation to adopt (p. 355;
Thornton, 1793, p. 90). Thornton tried for a still more elusive
speech mark in calling for a "mark of irony"! In both these cases,
the aim is to bring the written into a more exact relation with the
spoken.

Johnson was no less unpopular on these and other related grounds
among his British readers, or some of them, and once again it is
helpful to see Webster's reactions in a transatlantic context, as a
way of pointing out what is common and what is distinct between
the two traditions. Archibald Campbell, the anonymous author of
Lexiphanes (1767) and an "old style" Tory in his opposition to
Whiggery and to the whole house of Hanover, takes on Johnson (a
more ambiguous and accommodating Tory) for his gaudy and bombastic style, full of hyperbole and circumlocution. In so doing, he
compares the British situation to that of the Romans "when their
licentious republick had degenerated into a most despotick tyranny,"
to the degree that their natural literary effusion was nothing more
than "a parcel of *Shiners,* and *Lexiphaneses,* and *Paradox-Mongers*"
(p. 164), all committed to vulgar display and to "a disease of hard
long-tailed words, drawn from the Greek and Latin languages"
(p. 87). Webster repeats this case in regarding Johnson as one
seeking to dazzle with "a glare of ornament" and by exploiting "the
music of the language" to gratify the ear at the expense of the understanding (1789, p. 34); and John Witherspoon fills in the logic
that both Campbell and Webster allow to remain implicit:

> Absolute monarchies, and the obsequious subjection introduced at
> the courts of princes, occasions a pompous swelling and compli-
> ment to be in request, different from the boldness and sometimes
> ferocity of republican states (1802, 3:531).

The question of the "real" or the "complete" Johnson is not at
issue here.[4] The very things that Webster and Campbell object to
were explained by Godwin, for example, as frequently the products
of a Johnsonian irony. There is no more "fervent anti-Whig and
anti-Gallican" than Godwin's Johnson, and much of the bombast
and the indulgence in paradoxes is to be attributed to an experiment
in "how far it was possible, by a grave and solemn air, to impose
upon the world the most contemptible mistakes" (Godwin, 1797,
pp. 379, 399). I do not mean to pursue this subject here; but I
would say that such an irony, or tendency to overstatement, is not
incompatible with a Johnson who might seriously hold the positions
thus expressed. Often the very appeal of irony is that it need neither affirm nor deny a simple attitude to what it reports on. Thus,
while Johnson's rotund affectation of dignity is surely at times to be
seen as tongue-in-cheek, there is yet no doubt that he does hold to
a linguistic protocol which, for all its talk of honest independence
and the common usage, is yet based on the exclusion of certain
members of the commonwealth. Thus, Thomas Spence, one of the
most radical of eighteenth-century Englishmen, argued that

> the darkest hieroglyphics, or most difficult cyphers, which the art
> of man has hitherto found out, were not better calculated to con-
> ceal the sentiments of those who used them, from all who had not
> the key, than the state of our spelling is, to conceal the true pro-
> nunciation from all, except a few well-educated natives (Spence,
> 1775, preface).[5]

Writing in his own system of spelling, Spence claimed to have discovered that "Nŏthing ŵoz ĭn 'Anărke bŭt Lăngwĭj ănd Polĭtĭks,"
and to have corrected them both by a new alphabet and a new constitution (1808, p. 70). Similarly, James Elphinston's *A Minniature
ov Inglish Orthoggraphy* (1795) complained that "evvery vowel
and evvery consonant ar almoast az often falsifiers az immages ov
dhe truith" (p. 2). Arguing that one symbol "must no more usurp
dhe office ov anoddher" (p. 12), Elphinston contends that

> our litterature haz hiddherto' no likenes ov our language; and haz
> continnued inaccessibel to' evvery native, az much az to' evvery
> strainger (p. 17).

The scope and intention of Webster's ambition of bringing together the spoken and the written can now be more fully appre-

ciated as part of a transatlantic tradition trying to make the language more democratic. Not only did Webster consider it a political and economic necessity that America should have its own language; he also thought it a real possibility. The new nation was imaged, as it has so often been since, as a new beginning: "Here men are prepared to receive improvements, which would be rejected by nations, whose habits have not been shaken by similar events." America can have "a *national language,* as well as a national government," but the moment must be seized, lest delay breed other habits and those habits then inhibit further change, resulting in "a national acquiescence in error" (1789a, p. 406). Because America will never be conquered by a nation speaking another language or experience other "violent" internal events of the sort that might change the one it has, there is no reason why "pronunciation and orthography cannot be rendered in a great measure permanent" (p. 35). This is sound Enlightenment doctrine. By "permanent," of course, Webster does not mean ossified; he has already argued for the alphabet as ideally able to record the *changes* in the spoken language. It is the *correspondence* of speech and writing that is to be preserved. Changes in speech will occur, and writing can follow and transcribe them in a regular and rational way, with the same letters representing the same sounds throughout.

Webster's actual orthographic innovations are well known: they are ably summarized in Shoemaker (1936, pp. 267–72). They were never as radical as those proposed by Thornton, Spence, or Elphinston, and they became even less radical as Webster grew older. Many of them have indeed made their way into the modern American language: *honor* for *honour, center* for *centre, defense* for *defence,* and a range of single consonants in verb forms where the British English still doubles (e.g., *traveled* for *travelled*). Webster's preference for *public* over Johnson's *publick* now prevails on both sides of the Atlantic. He did not achieve credibility over the omission of final silent vowels in a large number of words (e.g., *determin*), but did succeed with some (e.g., *ax*). Although the 1806 dictionary is full of apparently eccentric words that have not survived, so too are most other dictionaries of the period, British and American. (The question of Webster's Americanisms I shall pursue later). Despite the oddity of the spelling habits of the early publications, "ritten at various times . . . az will appeer by their dates and subjects" (1790b, p. ix), Webster's program was, as I have said, always more modest than those of some others. That the books he published did not always maintain consistency even within themselves is not an ultimately negating irony; like Samuel Johnson's, they should probably be seen as composite texts, in which Webster's own practice was modified by those of other hands and by simple typographic slips; thus the *Miscellaneous Papers* (1802) displays a range of Websterian initiatives—for example, *thot, brot,* and *altho* (pp. 88, 29, 45), for *thought, brought,* and *although*—at the same time letting through the Johnsonian *clamours* (pp. 48, 63) and *traffick* (p. 99).

Perhaps Webster's ideas aroused such strong passions precisely because their author could not be dismissed as merely a utopian or a madman, committed to an improbably complete restructuring of the language. What he argued for was always close enough to the possible, and even to the probable, to be genuinely threatening. His attempt to bring together the spoken and the written did have an evident democratic motive. A glance at the available pronouncing dictionaries reveals that the language really was in a state of chaos, at least as represented. Walker (1791) cites *errour* as pronounced *ĕr′rŭr* and *education as ĕd-jŭ-kā′shŭn,* and provides separate sections in his text dealing with the particular pronunciation problems of Irish, Welsh, Scots, and London speakers (pp. xii–xiii)! This last initiative (minus the Londoners) is found also in Sheridan (1780, 1:58–62), who gives *ĕr-rŭr* and *ed-ŭ-kāte* as the proper transcription of the sounds of the same two words. Spence (1775) offers ɪRIR for *error;* and so on. Making allowance for the overlaps that result from different schemas for representing the same sounds, we can still see that there was very little agreement on matters of stress and pronunciation. Next to such proposals as these, Webster's seem modest and simple—more effectively democratic than any, it might be argued, given that they could be understood without learning a new alphabet and a new system of marking quantities.

We must now try to explain how it was that Webster, in this role as a man of the people on the question of the relation of the spoken and the written, could also and at the same time have been a bona fide Federalist. Following this, we must also assess the terms in which he managed to offend the diehards within the Federalist party itself.

Federalism and the Common Man

Webster was a Federalist before he was a democrat, if indeed the second term should even be applied to him at all. In his *Sketches of American Policy* (1785) he begins conventionally enough with the notion that "The sovereign power is the whole body of the people collectively, and the people will never make laws oppressive to themselves" (p. 4). But when we move into the analysis of *how* these laws are made and executed, we encounter the same questions, here explicit, as we have seen to be implicit in the various British ideas of a common language that must yet be legislated by somebody. Webster's "representative democracy" (p. 11) includes a crucial role for the magistracy, without whom only a destructive and incoherent populism could prevail. Thus, Athens and Greece before the time of Solon and Lycurgus exemplified the dangers of a people who "being under no restraint, having no settled form of deliberation, and being at the same time illiterate and credulous, were generally at the command of some noisy demogogue"; in such a world, "freedom was licentiousness" (p. 14). Denying all notions of an original imperative toward civic virtue or "disinterested public spirit" (p. 24), Webster argues that self-interest is the principal motivation in human behavior. In a democracy this fact is redeemed because of the way in which each man must persuade his fellows that his particular interest would be positive if it were applied generally. Laws may be *made* by the many, but they should be executed by the few; analogously, Webster advances a strong argument for federal unity over the potentially chaotic practice of states' rights (p. 30f.).

As early as 1785, Webster's political theories thus seem to include a significant role for restraint and direction, the linguistic analogue of which might well seem to be a privileging of grammar over usage, rather than the other way round. But there are ways in which Webster avoids such a contradiction, or tries to. He maintains a real optimism about the future of the United States, which, instead of being shackled by a traditional and hierarchical culture, makes its start in "the most enlightened period of the world" (p. 23). Reli-

gious toleration and an equal distribution of property will ensure
that inflexible divisions of interest do not arise. Thus, there need be
no conflict of interest between the layman and the politician who
speaks for him. In another series of political writings in 1788–89,
published in the *American Magazine* under the pseudonym of
"Giles Hickory" (and republished in 1790b, pp. 45–80), Webster
pursues the question of the nature and obligations of representation.[6] Legislators must be independent of *particular* popular mandates, which are always going to embody local or specific interests.
To allow these to become codified into law would be to ossify the
political system and to render it unreceptive to *change*. This dy-
namically Burkean argument, wherein some of the people are invoked against others, is clearly analogous to the argument about
common usage in the debates over the language. On the one hand,
Webster says, the legislators can be trusted to be independent and
honest because they do embody the will of the people as a whole,
by whom they have been elected and by whom they might also be
removed. On the other hand, they are not to respond to the pres-
sures of any faction *within* the people. According to the needs of
the argument, the people is presented as either a unified or a
divided body.

The problem here revealed in Webster's political mandate is not,
however, simply duplicated in his writings on the national language.
Although America found itself speaking a language that had (unlike
its political principles, for the most part) been evolving elsewhere
for hundreds of years, it could yet expect to rediscover and preserve
what is most original and permanent within it. Webster is able to
convince himself that the factions whose incidence he seems to see
in the political forum need not occur in the realm of language. He
sees in language the evidence for the regular and rational habits of
mind which are, by implication, becoming harder to find in the
conduct of affairs of state. From one perspective, we might explore
this tension as a way of undercutting the integrity of Webster's analysis of the language; from another, we might see it as lending a special urgency to the preservation and encouragement of that sphere
of human action in which right reason might perhaps prevail.

Let us approach this model of right reason by further exploring
the implications of Webster's sense of the historical moment of the
American language. We have already seen some of the political and

economic reasons why he thought that America *should* have a language of its own:

> Customs, habits, and *language,* as well as government should be national. America should have her *own* distinct from all the world. Such is the policy of other nations, and such must be *our* policy, before the states can be either independent or respectable. To copy foreign manners implicitly, is to reverse the order of things, and begin our political existence with the corruptions and vices which have marked the declining glories of other republics (1789a, p. 179).

At the time of writing (1789), "an astonishing respect for the arts and literature of their parent country, and a blind imitation of its manners, are still prevalent among the Americans" (p. 398). Note Webster's reference to the "declining glories" of other nations. Like many men of his time, he believed that European society had been perfected at a certain point in history, after which it could only enter into a phase of decline. The model of the classical civilizations was frequently invoked as evidence of this tide in the affairs of men, suggesting that in the long view the whole process might be seen as cyclic. Priestley, of whom Webster sometimes approved, had made a similar point:

> The progress of human life in general is from poverty to riches, and from riches to luxury, and ruin. . . . Our very *dress* is at first plain and aukward, then easy and elegant, and lastly downright fantastical. Stages of a similar nature may be observed in the progress of all human arts; and language, being liable to the same influences, hath undergone the same changes (Priestley, 1762, p. 173).

Hence, for some critics, the gaudy bombast of Johnsonian diction. Britain was, on such evidence, clearly on the downward part of the cycle.

Not so America. The United States had the unique advantage of seeming to superimpose one part of the cycle on another, thus defeating the principle of repetition. It *begins* in a state of perfection, or incipient perfection, and because it has no *history,* it need not be assumed to be on the point of decline. There were, of course, many Americans who did see disaster immediately ahead, as we shall see shortly; but for Webster in his role as critic of the language America is expanding and moving toward a new and unprecedented peak even as it has the option of inheriting the best elements of the civilization it is supplanting.[7] American English will be the English of the future:

> In fifty years from this time, the *American-English* will be spoken by more people, than all the other dialects of the language, and in one hundred and thirty years, by more people than any other language on the globe, not excepting the Chinese (1806, pp. xxii–xxiii).

But what kind of English will it be? Here is where the ingenuity of Webster's argument comes into play. The *new* language will be an image of precisely what is original and permanent in the *old,* stripped of the false sophistications and excesses that result from the fact that British culture has itself for some time been in a pattern of decline. It will thus be a "radical" language to precisely the degree that it is conservative, on genuine principles. (At the same time it will, of course, also include new American words, though many of these are projected as traditional British ones.) In fact, to rediscover the linguistic zenith that has been passed in Britain, Webster does not seem to want to put the clock back very far:

> Our language was spoken in purity about eighty years ago; since which time, great numbers of faults have crept into practice about the theater and court of London. An affected and erroneous pronunciation has in many instances taken the place of the true; and new words or modes of speech have succeeded the ancient correct English phrases (1790b, p. 96).

This is in fact a very standard argument. Sheridan (1780) saw the reign of Queen Anne as a linguistic golden age, and Godwin, in the essay "Of English Style" published in *The Enquirer* (1797), notes that, while a few scholars have preferred the age of Elizabeth,

> the multitude of readers, for a long time, perhaps to this day, have pitched their tents, and taken up their rest, under the banners of Anne (p. 435).

Godwin goes on to imply that for most readers this was also a political preference; they were opting for a time just before the Whig hegemony and Sir Robert Walpole had come into the picture, along with the "general propensity" toward "commerce and gain" which it encouraged (p. 436). If the Whig supremacy was a very important *fact* of eighteenth-century English political life, it was perhaps even more important as a mythology. Tory writers, which is to say most British writers of the period, continually invoke the model of ancient British liberties (variously Saxon, Celtic, or Welsh) subverted by a new generation of greedy commercial aristocrats. And given that these writers were Tories, their "liberties" tended to include a good deal of what others might describe as retrograde or despotic: small, manageable communities with no social mobility or circulation (whether of wealth or of people), and a way of life wherein both political power and good taste would continue to reside in the country rather than the city, and in the land rather than the stock market.

However, if Webster is tapping this model of the good English style, we can hardly imagine him to have intended also an endorsement of the old Tory world order that was so often thought to have produced it. His expressed taste in prose does indeed privilege the likes of Bolingbroke, Swift, and Pope; but it finds room also for the likes of Price and Priestley (1789a, pp. 31–32), who were by no means of the "roast beef of old England" school. But Price and Priestley had defended the cause of the American colonists on the grounds of their preservation of "ancient liberties," so that even their radicalism came under the flag of tradition.

What we are witnessing here—and we shall see it again—is an instance of the complexity of the process whereby political mythologies were transferred from Britain to America in the eighteenth century, as well as an example of the degree to which they were modified merely by the passing of time. In the seventeenth century, the classical period of English republicanism, the "ancient liberties" argument had been invoked on behalf of the commonwealth (which was, of course, never common) against the tyranny of the crown.[8] When the Whigs came to power, as they did with the accession of George I in 1714, the very same rhetoric could become available to the Tory, agrarian opposition, who thus came to cast themselves as the guardians of the rights of the common man. The fact that the Whigs were increasingly seen to be turning into an aristocracy in their alliance with the monarchy meant that the speeches of Milton, Sidney, Harrington, and the rest could be turned against them. Webster, like other Americans of his time, is in turn in the happy position of being able to select whatever he wants from a hundred and fifty years of very confusing and volatile British political discourse. Thus, in the specific context of language, he can adopt as his ideal a culture which if it were examined too closely might prove highly undesirable as a model for American political life as a whole.

The ambiguities raised by Webster's eclecticism in this respect will be the subject of much of the rest of this chapter. For the moment, I would suggest that what was perhaps most immediate for Webster about the age of Anne was that it had no associations with the negative effects of a developing manufacturing capitalism—surplus, luxury, and hence decline—and that it was far enough removed in time not to be implicated in the recent tensions between Britain and America. On several occasions Webster related the corruptions in British speech and spelling to the "practice of the court and stage in London" (1789a, p. 24), which he saw to be subverting the *"general practice"* of the nation. He deplores the fashionable metropolitan pronunciations, which he transcribes as *edzhucation, natshure, keind, gyuide, shuperstition,* and so forth (1789a, p. 156f.; 1806, p. 36). Many Americans were to share this attitude, and perhaps Tom Paine did too, if he intended to be punning brilliantly in referring to George III as "his Madjesty" (Spiller, 1948, 1:139).

The case against "court and stage" was a powerful one in Webster's writings, and here too he had his British precursors and fellow spirits. Robert Lowth (1761, p. iii) blamed "the politest part of the nation" and the "most approved authors" for most of the corruptions in the language. In the same year, Sheridan in his *Dissertations* was applauding the guiding influence of "people of education at Court" in setting up the norms of speech and pronunciation (1761, p. 34). This is the class, unlike that of the "pedants," that has no vested interest in having things one way or the other (!); the language is so perfect that it would be wise to fix it now for all time, at least in the sphere of pronunciation (p. 35). The winds of political patronage seem to have been fickle, however, for by 1780 Sheridan was lamenting the access of the Hanoverians to the throne, and the accompanying linguistic contamination:

> From that time the regard formerly paid to pronunciation has been gradually declining; so that now the greatest improprieties in that point are to be found among people of fashion (1780, preface).

In taking over and adapting this rhetoric, Webster did not, of course, have to observe the tactics appropriate to a patronage system, and his contempt for the theatrical and the fashionable was reinforced by factors both economic (as we have seen) and traditionally religious. Not only did he have a natural disaffection for the English ruling class, but he inherited the traditional Puritan suspicion of ornament and affectation, and of everything theatrical (monarchy being but a larger form of theater). Additionally, the case against "court and stage" allows him to identify with an authentic English tradition existing intact before 1714, and now available to an American society that had not been corrupted by the Walpoles and the Johnsons. For Webster, it is that much vaunted entity the "yeoman" who embodies the linguistic and political alternative to court and stage, and who speaks for the true English language:

> On examining the language, and comparing the practice of speaking among the yeomanry of this country, with the stile of Shakespear and Addison, I am constrained to declare that the people of America, in particular the English descendants, speak the most *pure English* now known in the world (1789a, p. 288).

It is the British ruling class that has been led astray by "fashion" and "novelty," the products of their surplus economy, their luxurious tastes, and their proximity to other and similar nations, most particularly the French. Conversely, the "well-educated yeomanry" are "governed by habits and not easily led astray" (pp. 129–30). In this respect the American yeoman is the ally and image of his British counterpart, with the difference that he is not under the thumb of any social superiors:

> the common unadulterated pronounciation of the New England gentlemen, is almost uniformly the pronunciation which prevailed in England, anterior to Sheridan's time, and which, I am answered by English gentlemen, is still the pronunciation of the body of the British nation: the pronunciation recommended by Sheridan and Walker being there called the London dialect, and considered as a corruption (1806, p. xvi).

Webster's yeoman is of course no mere horny-handed son of the soil:

> Let Englishmen take note that when I speak of the American yeo-
> manry, the latter are not to be compared to the illiterate peasantry
> of their own country. The yeomanry of this country consist of sub-
> stantial independent freeholders, masters of their own persons and
> lords of their own soil. These men have considerable education.
> . . . In the eastern states, there are public schools sufficient to in-
> struct every man's children, and most of the children are actually
> benefited by these institutions (1789a, pp. 288–89).

In Webster's representation of the linguistic democracy, no authority
is accorded to a lower or "peasant" class; his argument would be
that America does not have such a class, given the plentiful supply
of land for everyone. This would make it all the more inappropriate
to import from Britain a language that has grown up to register precisely such social divisions. At best, it would be out of place; at
worst, it might encourage America to emulate Britain in this respect.

Because Webster, like many others, was able to envisage a future
for the United States in which land would continue to be more
important that manufacturing, he was also able to imagine that a
laboring class—hence a class system in general—need never develop
along the lines of that which existed in Britain. The evil effects of
the division of labor will thus not pertain in the new nation. Here
he takes up and paraphrases an important argument from Smith's
Wealth of Nations:

> A man who makes heads of pins or springs of watches, spends his
> days in that manufacture and never looks beyond it. This manner
> of fabricating things for the use and convenience of life is the
> means of perfecting the arts; but it cramps the human mind, by
> confining all its faculties to a point. In countries thinly inhabited,
> or where people live principally by agriculture, as in America,
> every man is in some measure an artist—he makes a variety of
> utensils, rough indeed, but such as will answer his purpose—he is a
> husbandman in summer and a mechanic in winter—he travels about
> the country—he converses with a variety of professions—he reads
> public papers—he has access to a parish library and thus becomes
> acquainted with history and politics, and every man in New En-
> gland is a theologian. This will always be the case in America, so
> long as there is a vast tract of fertile land to be cultivated, which
> will occasion emigration from the states already settled (Webster,
> 1785, p. 29).[9]

As there is no urban laboring class, dulled by the alienated nature of its daily employment to a state of passivity or unnatural excitement (its answering tendency, as Wordsworth argued), so there is no rural peasantry, as long as each man can own his own land and work for himself. And an undivided nation does not require a divided language.

We can see here that the westward migration that was to become an increasingly important fact of American life in the nineteenth century here becomes a moral necessity as well as a natural inclination. Only in an economy of subsistence and polymorphous labor can the mental and moral health of *homo americanus* be preserved. We can also see how Webster can reasonably adopt a model of linguistic purity and originality whose identity in the parent culture had been decidedly *anti*-commercial, at the same time as he was expounding a prospectus for the commercial development of the new nation, in the true Federalist style. Not only is the commerce of the United States not likely to be heavily dependent on a manufacturing industry, with all the social ills it can produce (as opposed, for example, to commerce based on a carrying trade or on an agrarian economy), but the United States is also a commercial *republic,* rather than an aristocracy. Every man thus has the same opportunities as another and can achieve the same results. Because of the absence of the discourse of a class system, Webster is able to ignore any potential contradiction between the ideal of subsistence and frugality and that of commercial development. Commerce in America can be a civilizing and egalitarian influence, because it remains at an early stage of evolution and will do so as long as there is land to clear in the west. Hence Webster does not destroy his case for the healthful presence of the American yeoman in arguing also that

> Commerce is the parent of civilization . . . the progress of illumination has been retarded by the ferocious, unsocial spirit, diffused over Europe by the feudal system, and the continual wars which it has engendered. But every where we see the mildness of manners, and the humanity of laws and institutions, are in direct proportion to the extent of commerce (1802, pp. 214–15).

Samuel Johnson, who was in many ways ambivalent on the subject of trade, had seen it as a threat to the integrity of the language:

> Commerce, however necessary, however lucrative, as it depraves the
> manners, corrupts the language; they that have frequent intercourse
> with strangers, to whom they endeavour to accommodate them-
> selves, must in time learn a mingled dialect. . . . This . . . will
> be communicated by degrees to other ranks of the people, and be at
> last incorporated with the current speech (Johnson, 1957, p. 320)[10]

Webster could afford to be more hopeful, given the distance between the United States and any of the nations with which it might
trade; such intercourse could never be too frequent nor too pervasive. With the major exception, of course, of trade with Britain.
When speech, politics, and the economy thus stand in a mutually
determining relation, it becomes once again crucial to see the issue
of national identity as a whole and to advance its cause at all levels
at once. It would not be an overstatement to describe Webster as
practicing here a political economy of language. The "polite"
(metropolitan) British English of the late eighteenth century was
widely held to be riddled with French words and locutions (we
shall see that this was satirized by Royall Tyler and others); so too
were the manners and morals of its speakers affected by French
affectations. Webster set out to discourage this trend in his own
society:

> All our ladies, even those of the most scanty fortune, must dress
> like a dutchess in London; every shop-keeper must be as great a
> rake as an English lord; while the *belles* and the *beaux,* with tastes
> too refined for a vulgar language, must in all their discourse, mingle
> a spice of *sans souci* and *je ne scai quoi* (1785, p. 47).

In so doing, they offend inherited Puritan values, corrupt the language, and disturb the organic solidarity of the community, and at
the same time unbalance its economy by spending money on unnecessary and imported trifles. Foreign books and foreign languages
go along with foreign fashions and a gradual impoverishing of the
nation's wealth.[11] Of course, the French connection was equally
undesirable as the socially divisive vocabulary of the *ancien régime*
and as the new lexicon of Jacobin liberties.

Something of the full range of motivations behind Webster's
prospectus for a federal English should now be becoming clear. It
has empirically economic implications (for the book trade), and

even more important diagnostic and prescriptive functions. As the language registers what *is* happening to society, so it can be redirected, or in Webster's case kept on course (the original purity being already apparent), in order to stop the society from developing in negative ways. This last momentum is perhaps only made to seem the more urgent when we realize that Webster's own positive sense of the role of commerce within American culture was *not* shared by all of his fellow countrymen. Even as the idea of "corruption" was principally associated with Britain by the colonists before 1776, with America being cast as the guardian of the true English constitution, there was also a strain of thought that explained the American revolution as the necessary and purgative result of a cycle of events *intrinsic* to colonial life.[12] According to this explanation, the revolution was the inevitable outgrowth of a process of decline, and its success was not so much a triumph as a rejection of recent trends in colonial history. The new order did offer a chance for change, but because it was the *result* of corruption the continuing dangers of corruption were all the greater. Thus some commentators (John Adams among them) took a quite different view of the likely effects of commerce in the new republic, and even predicted disaster (see Wood, 1972, pp. 413–29). William Cowper's famous description of the ills of British society was then one that would have found a willing audience among some American readers as a warning of the possible fate of their own:

> The course of human things from good to ill,
> From ill to worse, is fatal, never fails
> Increase of pow'r begets increase of wealth;
> Wealth luxury, and luxury excess;
> Excess, the scrophulous and itchy plague
> That seizes first the opulent, descends
> To the next rank contagious, and in time
> Taints downward all the graduated scale
> Of order, from the chariot to the plough.
> The rich, and they that have an arm to check
> The license of the lowest in degree,
> Desert their office; and themselves, intent
> On pleasure, haunt the capital, and thus
> To all the violence of lawless hands
> Resign the scenes their presence might protect.
>   (Cowper, 1787, 2:166–67)

These lines from *The Task* (Bk. IV, 578–92) are of course shot through with specifically British concerns—robbery and disorder in the countryside, and the stability of the social order—but the analysis of the corrupting effects of wealth and commerce is general enough to have seemed significant even in a more democratic climate; and, of course, by no means all Americans believed that the climate should remain quite so democratic. This element in the English Tory rhetoric could only have served to make the demon of fashion even more dangerous, and to stress the need for a pure and national language.

After what might seem to have been a rather long detour into the political economy of the early republic, we can now return to Webster's idea of the common language and its speaker, and the place of right reason in that idea. We have seen that the national language exists in the American yeomanry in a state of *preservation;* they are not innovators but guardians of the authentic element of English speech. Thus, when Webster argues for the authority of usage over grammar, he is making an essentially conservative argument. Priestley had written that "it is in vain to pretend that any person may not attempt to introduce whatever he thinks to be an improvement" (1762, p. 184). People will always assert their freedom to do so, and others will decide whether or not to follow them. Webster, even when he appears to be making a similar point, is saying something different: that innovation will contain within itself the *true* grammar (i.e., in the speech of the yeomanry), because it will evolve on the principles of rational analogy. Usage can thus dominate grammar because it is *more* grammatical than most professional grammarians, with recent British prescriptions in this realm being merely the short-lived effusions of an affected metropolitan habit.

Webster's idea of the common practice is not, as it was for Johnson and others, built out of a belief in the chaos of circumstantial details and conflicting paradigms too devious to allow us to rely on anything but special precedent. On the contrary, it is, "even among the unlearned . . . generally defensible on the principles of analogy" (1789a, p. viii). All languages have "a certain principle of analogy running through the whole" (p. 27), according to which a general uniformity in spelling, accentuation, and pronunciation is preserved. These traditions are "like the common laws of a land":

everyone is obliged to submit to them, and should do so of his or her own "natural" inclination. It is "fashion" that is "the child of caprice and the being of a day"; the true "principles of propriety" remain unchanged (p. 29). As the yeoman is the bearer of the true political and economic identity, so he is also the true lexicon of the language. He is a rational and rational*izing* being; he will tend to provide order where it does not exist already. In his more extreme statements, Webster extends this faculty even to the unlearned, not usually part of the yeoman class:

> The tendency of unlettered men is to *uniformity*—to *analogy;* and so strong is this disposition, that the common people have actually converted some of our irregular verbs into regular ones. . . . This popular tendency is not to be contemned and disregarded, as some of the learned affect to do, for it is governed by the natural, primary principles of all languages (Webster, 1807a, pp. 119–20).

Language may originate in relatively contingent and casual ways, and include therein some unadjusted elements. But gradually "certain analogies of sound and construction" are introduced, "from a natural or habitual inclination of man towards uniformity" (1798a, p. 5). Natural man is, in other words, *rational* man. This process begins in language use well before speech is transcribed into writing, and even longer before anyone takes it into his head to write a grammar. The first grammarians thus took their rules from the spoken practice:

> The writer does not frame the analogy—that exists independent of him, and perhaps has existed two thousand years—he only searches out and reduces to order, those principles which practice had previously established (1798a, p. 6).

So too should all other grammarians, lest their strictures be totally spurious.

Given this faith—a true Enlightenment faith—in the naturally rational instincts of the common man (even the Native American is included in this category), Webster can resolve (at least in his own terms) the tension between tolerance and authority that we have seen in Locke's idea of the common language. As in the *ideal* model of the relation between the people and its elected officials in the *Sketches of American Policy* (1785), Webster can assume that coercive legislation is unnecessary. The task of the grammarian can only be to codify and explain what is already there. There is no doubt that we could regard this model of Webster's as in practice a coercive one, if we wished to do so; but the class of speakers that would come in for such coercion is, for Webster, not just that composed of the speakers of dialect (who do not, as we have seen, meet with his endorsement), but also and most emphatically that of the "polite," and of the authors of books aimed at a polite readership, in late eighteenth-century terms. Authentic language can never be found in this class; they are precisely the people who pervert it.

In maintaining that books were not of seminal importance in the development of a rationally organized language, and in claiming further that many recent books have in fact done a great deal to destroy such a language, Webster is once again explicitly at odds with Dr. Johnson. In *A Journey to the Western Isles of Scotland* (1775) Johnson had described the "Earse" language as the "rude speech of a barbarous people" (1957, p. 748), and this barbarism results from its never having been a *written* language. For Johnson, writing introduces order into what is otherwise chaotic and primitive:

> When a language begins to teem with books, it is tending to refinement . . . speech becomes embodied and permanent; different modes and phrases are compared, and the best obtains an establishment. By degrees one age improves upon another. Exactness is first obtained, and afterwards elegance. But diction, merely vocal, is always in its childhood. . . . There may possibly be books without a polished language, but there can be no polished language without books (p. 749).

The written word is for Johnson the repository of the best efforts of the best minds, and it retains the materials required for each generation to improve upon the last; for Webster, all this has proved to be but an education in error. The Johnsonian author introduces order into chaos, while Webster accuses him of destroying the order that is already there.[13]

The idea of a rational principle at work in the common language enables Webster not only to chastise the affectations of the fashionable authors, but also, as I have said, to avoid the political difficulties tending to result from any attempt to adjudicate the rights and wrongs of dialect. I shall deal with the question of dialect in the next chapter; here it is enough to note that, in Webster's view, dialect must tend to disappear *of itself,* being out of step with the naturally rationalizing energy of the language. No coercion is therefore called for. We have seen already that Webster recognized perfectly well that some dialect traditions did exist in the United States in 1789. But, like so many language critics, he can claim to be speaking for the rights of the common man against the common man himself in seeking to "separate *local* or *partial* practice from the *general custom* of speaking" (1789a, p. ix). The provincial rustic is no more welcome in Webster's linguistic commonwealth than is the metropolitan dandy, even as the authority invoked against him is never allowed to appear politically charged or motivated.

Webster is thus, by virtue of his deployment of the Enlightenment argument for the naturally rational disposition in the human mind, very much a man in the middle in terms of the eighteenth-century debate about the politics of language. On the one hand, he is fiercely and intelligently patriotic, standing against the British for a series of mutually implicated reasons all entailed by a coherent theory of the nature of national virtue. On the other hand, he is certainly no celebrator of Brother Jonathan's more colorful speech habits, and certainly no exponent of linguistic pluralism within the new republic. The democratic cast of Webster's rhetoric thus needs always to be carefully contextualized, and understood within the limits he himself lays down. In this respect, it would seem that there is nothing in Webster's proposals that is essentially at odds with his public position as a defender of the Federalist faith. In the early years of the republic, under the aegis of Washington, Webster could think with some confidence of a national language as a way to "reconcile the people of America to each other, and weaken the prejudices which oppose a cardinal union" (1789a, p. 36). By the late 1790s, however, the end of the Federalist period was in sight, and it was sealed with Jefferson's election in 1800. The French Revolution, as we have seen, caused real alarm in America, especially among the members of Webster's party. He himself warned against "that false philosophy which has been preached in the world by Rousseau, Condorcet, Godwin and other visionaries," which he dismissed as "the wild theories of crazy projectors" (1798b, pp. 13, 15). In the same year he writes to Joel Barlow, expressing a strong objection to the idea of a necessary friendship with France; and in 1800 he roundly rebukes the aging Joseph Priestley, the famous British friend of liberty now residing in America, for his conflation of American and French republicanism: "By French principles are now meant, principles of Atheism, irreligion, ambition, and Jacobinism."[14] By 1802, Jefferson is being taken to task not only for his politics but also for his language:

> What a jumble of words! In one line, administration is the antecedent to *its,* and in the next, to *theirs.* Then follow *they, who,* and *them,* involving the sentence in a disgraceful confusion. . . . Whatever talents you may possess, you seem, Sir, to be a most unfortunate man in the use of logic and metaphors (1802, pp. 19, 42).

Jefferson's oddities of speech and spelling were indeed proverbial; Webster is adding to the chorus by accusing him of betraying the sacred principles of rational subordination, and thus of revolutionizing the language, much as Burke had accused Brissot.

On the question of Jefferson's election and the tendencies in the national policy, Webster is fully in line with all but the most extreme among his fellow Federalists. We have seen also that his ideas about the language, as expounded so far, were not at odds with his political profile in general. It is at first somewhat puzzling, then, to turn to the reviews of his writings, which reveal a strong vocal rage directed against him by the Federalist critics themselves. Thus, *The Monthly Anthology,* appearing between 1803 and 1811, is emphatic in casting Webster as one of the destroyers of civilization, even though it too is an opposition journal. For its reviewers, Webster becomes a sort of literary Jacobin, one of a band of "conceited innovators" who aimed at reducing the language to a "Babylonish dialect . . . fit only for the lowest of the populace." The appearance of Webster's 1807 *Grammar* causes the reviewer to pour scorn on "the notion of an American tongue, or of gaining our idiom from the mouths of the illiterate, rather than from the pages of Milton, Dryden, Swift, Addison," and so forth. And the 1806 *Dictionary* is described as "insinuating suspicions of the definitions of Johnson, justifying ridiculous violations of grammar, and spreading hurtful innovations in orthography."[15] This lament continues:

Over the ORTHOGRAPHY of our language Mr. Webster, in his twenty years warfare, has triumphed more frequently than the many millions who have written it for nearly a century and a half. If we may recur to his former heresies, we should declare him the wildest innovator of an age of revolutions; but we feel some pleasure in informing the publick that he has abjured many of his first errours (p. 251).

The Johnsonian spellings are, of course, deliberate. Webster had indeed softened many of his positions by 1806, and was as a whole much less sanguine about the prospects of success in the sphere of spelling reforms. But he does not seem to have backed down far enough for "Steady Habits" and the editors of *The Monthly Anthology*. Even though the populist rhetoric of Webster's argument did not, as we have seen, amount to anything very threatening, it seems to have been unacceptable to some readers. Webster's anti-British position was never modified, and was certainly genuine, and this of itself might have been enough to alarm the Anglophile community in America. Such readers would have insisted on following Sheridan and Walker, and not the good old style as recommended by Webster. Thanks to them, the British *Eclectic Review* could opine rather glibly that

> The bonds of customs and language cannot be broken like those of political authority. It gives us pleasure to observe, that, notwithstanding the violent prejudices against us, which are absurdly cherished by our fellow countrymen beyond the Atlantic, they are wise enough to aim at preserving the use of our language with correctness and propriety (3, Pt. I, 1807, p. 82).

Moreover, times were hard for the opposition during Jefferson's administration, and their claims to see the bloody beast of revolution, French style, on the horizon, could only have exacerbated an already natural affection for all things British. Webster's rather modest extremism, his sense that between the mad theories of Rousseau, Godwin, and others "and the old corrupt establishments, there is a *mean,* which probably is the true point of freedom and national happiness" (1800, p. 21), might well have seemed like equivocation to some of his Federalist readers.

These conditions alone do not, however, explain the strength of

the reaction against Webster in the early 1800s. And there was indeed more at stake than I have so far implied. First, there was the
issue of neologisms. Although Webster is thought to have himself
coined only one word, the verb *to demoralize* (see Leavitt, 1947,
p. 33), and although he argues *against* many grammatical and syn-
tactic innovations that have since become part of American English—for example, "I am done" (for "have done"), "write him"
(for "write to him"), "is home" (for "is at home"), and so forth
(see 1790a, pp. 44, 45, 49), there is yet no doubt that Webster is
in favor of words existing in America that did not exist in Britain.
Of course, these words were almost always argued to be authentic
ones that had simply gone out of use in Britain. The 1806 *Dictionary* claims to add about five thousand words that are not in Entick
(whose text Webster takes as his primary source), and these are
"mostly collected from the best writers, during a course of several
years reading" (pp. xix–xx).[16] This is quite in line with the whole
tone of Webster's argument about the bad effects of court and
stage. At the same time, *The Monthly Anthology* is not attacking a
complete straw man. Webster does say that there must be an American English, and one that, as well as preserving what is essential
and authentic in the inherited language, *will* add new words of its
own:

> Some words are either new in the United States, or what is more
> usual, English words have received a new sense. Words of these
> kinds, when in general use in a state or number of states, or sanc-
> tioned by public authority in laws and judicial procedings, are ad-
> mitted into this work. When the usage is local, that circumstance is
> noted (1806, p. xxii).[17]

These new words are often scientific and technical terms (e.g.,
ferric acid, electrometer), legal and commercial terms (e.g., *duti-
able*), and geographical and political terms of American origin or
application.[18] There are some localisms (e.g., *dreen, swosh*), some
borrowings from Native American languages, and a considerable
number of adjectives formed from proper names (e.g., *Newtonian,
Parisian*). Webster's spellings are much less radically innovative
than they had been in 1789, and, apart from the omission of silent
vowels in words like *determin,* most of the major features of the
1806 orthography have (as we have said before) been adopted

into modern American English. It is hard to imagine that the policy on new words alone would have been enough to ruffle the Federalist feathers in the way that Webster seems to have done. Besides this policy, and the anti-British polemic, and the democratic rhetoric of the common language (which we have seen to be a very limited category), there was another and arguably more potent reason why Webster might have caused such reactions: his explicit allegiance to the etymological theories of John Horne Tooke.

Horne Tooke and the Saxon Yoke

As one of the prime movers in the short-lived Philological Society of New York, conceived in 1788 "for the purpose of ascertaining and improving the *American Tongue,*" Webster presumably took part in the procession of July 23 of that year, in which the Society's standard was carried aloft through New York as part of the celebration attending the adoption of the constitution.[19] The New York *Packet,* August 5, 1788, p. 3, describes this procession, including the following detail:

> Vice-president and librarian, the latter carrying Mr. Horne Tooke's treatise on language; as a mark of respect for the book which contains a new discovery, and a mark of respect for the author, whose zeal for the American cause, during the late war, subjected him to a prosecution (A. W. Read, 1934, p. 133).

The "new discovery" may well refer to Tooke's ideas about the nominal and verbal origins of all the passive parts of speech; or it may intend an allusion to his argument for the Anglo-Saxon as the original element and abiding center of the English language. Thus, the account continues, the arms of the Society displayed

> a pyramid, or rude monument, sculptured with Gothic, Hebrew, and Greek letters. The Gothic on the *light* side, indicating the *obvious* origin of the American language from the Gothic. The Hebrew and Greek, upon the reverse or *shade,* . . . expressing the remoteness and *obscurity* of the connection between those languages and the modern.

This might have seemed all very fine to the bystander of 1788. John Horne Tooke, one of the most colorful personalities of the late

eighteenth century, ordained priest and inveterate gambler, was in
and out of court throughout his life, whether as plaintiff or as de-
fendant. He did indeed seek to raise money for the American cause,
and in 1786 he had published the first volume of his *ΕΠΕΑ
ΠΤΕΡΟΕΝΤΑ; or the Diversions of Purley,* the summary of his
etymological researches (the second volume followed in 1806).
Never a Jacobin, nor even a Painite, he nevertheless stood trial for
his life in 1794, at a time when the tolerance of the British government for anything associated with freedom and civil rights was at a
very low ebb indeed. The result of this and of similar incidents was
that by the middle of the 1790s Tooke had become a hated figure
among conservative thinkers, among whom were the contributors
to *The Monthly Anthology.* Thus, Webster is therein accused of
trying to reduce the language to some "version of Saxon barbarism"; and 'Steady Habits' sneers at him for finding his "refiners of
language" among "the Saxons, the Goths, the Celts, the Teutons,
and the Mohawks." In this respect he is the follower of that "Baal
of democracy," the dreaded Horne Tooke:

> Horne Tooke has been from his cradle a jacobin in literature, and
> a jacobin in politicks. . . . The real object of Horne Tooke's writ-
> ings on language is believed by many intelligent persons to have
> been, merely to obtain a medium through which he might defame
> his government and his country; and his pages evince, that he
> labours more to ridicule these than the errours in language.[20]

The *Diversions of Purley* is a very odd book, and one extremely
popular in its time. Tooke's politics therein are not, by modern
standards, particularly strident, but they are evident enough, and
readers on both sides of the Atlantic would have seen the point of
his declaration (not much diffused by the use of the potentially
ambiguous dialogue form) that

> Truth, in my opinion, has been improperly imagined at the bottom
> of a well: it lies much nearer to the surface: though buried indeed
> at present under mountains of learned rubbish; in which there is
> nothing to admire but the amazing strength of those vast giants of
> literature who have been able thus to heap Pelion upon Ossa
> (Tooke, 1829, 1:10)

Politics aside (though not for long), Tooke's theoretical originality
lay in his privileging of nouns and verbs as the essential parts of

speech (1:45–46).[21] Thus, conjunctions are derived from verbs. *If* is a contraction of *give that* (1:103–4), for example. And prepositions are but the corrupted "names of *real objects*" (1:299), so that *from* is a derivation of the Saxon noun for *beginning,* just as *to* comes from the Gothic noun for *act* or *effect* (1:321–22, 329). Etymology rests on verbs and nouns—above all, on nouns—and all other words can be explained as derivatives. There is more than a hint of philosophical materialism and political populism in this argument, and the latter is reinforced by the constant priority accorded to the Anglo-Saxon as the core of authentic modern English. Tooke even goes so far as to argue that

> The bulk and foundation of the Latin language is Greek; but great part of the Latin is the language of our Northern ancestors, grafted upon the Greek. And to our Northern language the etymologist must go, for that part of the Latin which the Greek will not furnish (1829, 2:139).

The power of this opposition between the classical and the "Gothic" can hardly be overestimated for the eighteenth century.[22] And Tooke is here quite consciously suggesting that a good part of what we receive as the classical is in fact of Gothic origin. Among the many political allusions touched on here, we may note particularly that which emphasizes that the common man (again!) possesses the core of the language. It was undisputed that most of the common nouns and verbs in English were of Saxon origin, and these were the words available to everyone, learned or not. Moreover, the Saxons were typically mythologized as the founders and defenders of the original British political freedoms, which were eroded but never completely displaced by the aristocratic Norman invaders— and, of course, their Latinate language. I shall have more to say on this subject in a moment; the point to grasp here is that to stress the Saxon origin of the major part of the language is to speak out for the linguistic (and wider) authority of the common man against the learned class and, perhaps, their patrons, now cast as the usurpers of the rights of freeborn Englishmen.

Webster does indeed take over much of Tooke's argument, as the role of the first volume of the *Diversions* in the procession of 1788 would suggest. In Webster's *Dissertations* (1789), conjunctions are derived from verbs (p. viii), just as they are in Tooke, and nouns and verbs are similarly the primary elements in language (p. 181f.). Common speech also holds for Webster the keys to etymology. Thus he declares that

> *Since* is merely a participle of the old verb *seon,* to see. In ancient authors we find it variously written; as *sith, sithence, sin, sithen,* &c. and the common people in New England still pronounce it *sin, sen,* or *sence.* Of all these, *sin* or *sen,* which is so much ridiculed as vulgar, comes nearest to the original *seen* (p. 190).

Tooke is credited with the discovery that "the peculiar structure of our language is Saxon" (p. 38), and both the second part of the *Grammatical Institute* (1790c) and the later *Grammar* (1807a) begin with generous praise of Tooke's researches. Thornton (1793, p. 21) is also a disciple of Tooke.

As his career develops, Webster does modify his worship of Horne Tooke.[23] But he never loses his sense of the primary importance of the Anglo-Saxon language that Tooke had foregrounded. In 1789 it is explicitly a part of the mythology of the yeoman:

> It has been remarked that the common people, descendants of the Saxons, use principally words derived from the native language of their ancestors, with few derivatives of the foreign tongues, for which they have no occasion (1789a, p. 62).

The 1806 *Dictionary* comments in the same spirit on the common pronunciation of *ask* as *aks:*

> The latter is the true pronunciation of the original word; the Saxon verb being written *acsian* or *axian.* The transposition of letters which gives the present orthography and pronunciation is a modern innovation of writers; but it has not changed the primitive pronunciation among the body of our people, and it is doubtful whether a complete change can ever be effected (p. xvi).

Thus, although Webster never (as we have seen) codifies such arguments as this into a widespread defense of dialect speech, he does yet justify this particular dialect habit where it happens to be the true repository of the tradition, and this would have been inflammatory enough to a "polite" readership.

It is now obvious why 'Steady Habits' should have seen Webster as a worshipper of the "Baal of democracy"; the endorsement of Tooke and the Saxon tradition would have been easily identified with the outpouring of "wigwam words" from Tammany Hall, even as it actually emanated from the other side of the political fence. The association becomes yet clearer when we explore the implications of the Saxon allusion, which proved to be for Webster something of a Saxon yoke.

Christopher Hill's famous and seminal essay, from which I have adapted and inverted this term, makes it clear that there was no more popular and pliable mythology than that of the original integrity of the Anglo-Saxon commonwealth and the reciprocal corruption of the Norman conquerors.[24] Hill sums up the paradigm as follows:

> Before 1066 the Anglo-Saxon inhabitants of this country lived as free and equal citizens, governing themselves through representative institutions. The Norman Conquest deprived them of this liberty, and established the tyranny of an alien King and landlords (1958, p. 57).

He follows its twists and turns through three centuries of English political discourse, and the range and variety of the citations he has gathered make it clear that this image of the "Norman yoke" was at least as potent and evasive an explanatory device as the rise of the middle class or the process of secularization have sometimes tended to be. Elizabeth Elstob introduced her English-Saxon *Grammar* (1715) with a dedication to the Hanoverian succession and in particular to the Princess of Wales, "in whose Royal Offspring the *Saxon* Line is to be continued, with encrease of all Princely and Heroick Virtues." Ironically, for many others, the close alliance of king and parliament that the Whig supremacy established after 1714 was thought by many to be a subversion of precisely the spirit of this Saxon line. Indeed, it often seems from a perusal of eighteenth-century history that doctrines of original integrity were naturally more comfortable within the rhetoric of opposition: corruption and tyranny are most usually the prerogative of the party in power! It is not surprising that the Gothic or Saxon personality should then be available as a source of satire as well as commendation, given that one man's primitive integrity is another man's barbarism. A modern editor of Fielding's *Tom Jones* comments thus on the earthy exclamations of Squire Western, glossing the phrase "D——n un, what a sly B——ch 'tis":

This is the first display of Western's west-country dialect, a direct descendant of West Saxon, the language of King Alfred. Western's characteristic *un* for *him* remains in rural speech from *hine* (pronounced 'hinna'), the West Saxon objective form eventually displaced by *him*, the old dative, in the dialects around London. Western's *un* is thus older and, in a sense, more valid than *him* (Fielding, 1973, p. 142).

If Fielding intends us to register the Squire's linguistic primitivism, then it is hardly a matter for applause, since Western is always presented as a parodic and vicious reduction of the "country party" Tory, quite unable to offer a viable alternative social or political practice to the dangers of the extreme Whig personality as embodied in the Blifils. The true heritage of Alfred is thus to be found in a class of distinctly sublunary squires interested only in drinking and hunting. To fill the gap between the ignorant and boorish anti-Hanoverian posture of Western and the maliciously compromising self-interest of the Blifils, which must otherwise conquer all, Fielding devises the moderate new Toryism of Tom Jones, loyal to the succession but true at the same time to the traditions of the country house.

In fact, no true eighteenth-century Tory could be very comfortable deploying the rhetoric of the Saxon commonwealth, principally because of its being more naturally the property of the anti-monarchist republicans of the generations before. Sharon Turner, whose monumental *History of the Anglo-Saxons* was first published between 1799 and 1805, makes it clear that the Saxon archetype was always more at home within the Whig ideology (not, of course, to be assumed coincident with their practice). Nobility among the Saxons came from landed property as *distinct* from birth; it was thus in principle "attainable by everyone" (1852, 3:72). This was the qualification for membership of the parliament, the famous *witena-gemot*. Turner is in fact not excessive in his admiration for the Saxon commonwealth; he points out that it was based on slavery, and that slaves outnumbered freemen (3:84). Even with regard to the freemen themselves, he warns that "we must not let our minds expatiate on an ideal character which eloquence and hope have invested with charms almost magical" (3:75). On the particular subject of the *witena-gemot,* however, he does allow himself to launch into hyperbole, and this section of his account was expanded in the third edition of 1821, as a result of public demand (see 1852, 1:ix). Early Saxon kings were technically *elected,* not born (3:132); and the parliament, representing the interests of all the elements of society (except the slaves), was ideally responsive to changing needs and tensions. As such, Turner sees it as the only begetter of the present-day English parliament, which (and here he slips rhapsodically into the present tense) "is the nearest human imitation of a superintending Providence which our necessities or our sagacity have yet produced or devised" (3:158). It need hardly be said that such a sentiment would have been a long way from the radical platform in 1821!

Not everyone went as far as Turner in this respect. Scott's *Ivanhoe* (1819) seems anxious to expose the whole subject to the gaze of common sense. If Prince John, the Norman, is indeed vain and ruthless, then Cedric the Saxon is no apostle of a bright promise in the native stock. Stubborn, outmoded, and conservative, he reveals (as does the slothful Athelstane) the true demise of the ancient population—one cooperating in the process of its own disappearance. The figures of compromise—Ivanhoe, Locksley, Coeur de Lion—are as ever the heroes of Scott's novel, whether they be Saxon or Norman. Needless to say, Scott's reduction of the myth of Saxon integrity to something more mundane is itself a political message of immediate contemporary application, even as it gestures toward the *vraisemblable.*

If the British Tory opposition in the eighteenth century was unable to deploy any fully confident version of the "Norman yoke" theory of history, for the obvious reasons, then no such restrictions applied to the political situation in America, and there were significant elements of Saxonism in the debates leading up to and succeeding the war of independence. The anonymous *An Historical Essay on the English Constitution,* published in London in 1771, was explicitly written with the American crisis in mind (p. iii).[25] Commending the model of the annual Saxon parliament (a recommendation that was also to reappear in The Rights of Man), the author declares that "Whatever is of Saxon establishment, is truly constitutional; but whatever is Norman, is heterogeneous to it, and partakes of a tyrannical spirit" (pp. 9–10). He goes on to say that "the government, established for the internal police of our American provinces, is founded upon the same principles, as that which

our Saxon forefathers established, for the government of a shire"
(p. 18). Further, and yet more extravagantly, given the course of
subsequent events:

> This Saxon model of government, when reduced to its first princi-
> ples, has a strong resemblance to the natural state of things, under
> which mankind were found to live, at the discovery of the new
> world, by Columbus. And I make no doubt, but that our American
> tribes, of native Indians, would naturally fall into our way of gov-
> ernment, upon the Saxon principles, with a very little instruction
> (pp. 31–32).

This is the context within which Webster's comments on the
Saxon core of the language might have been received. Though he
never makes this case for the political profile of the Native Americans, we can see something of the process of association that might
have allowed 'Steady Habits' to invoke the specter of the "Mohawks" as the likely legislators of Webster's new American English.
This same essay was in fact adapted and republished by 'Demophilus', in 1776, in Philadelphia, under the title *The Genuine Principles of the Ancient Saxon, or English Constitution*. This text
brings the image of the Saxon prototype even more closely into line
with the arguments of Webster's *Dissertations* (1789). It emphasizes its usefulness as a model for governing an agrarian community
based on a society of independent owner-occupiers in small groups
(p. 4): exactly the pattern of the American yeomanry as described
by Webster. The people of Pennsylvania are told that "this ancient
and justly admired pattern, the old Saxon form of government, will
be the best model, that human wisdom, improved by experiences,
has left them to copy" (p. 17). This text has been argued to have
had an important influence on Thomas Jefferson, as well as on the
drafters of the Pennsylvania constitution.[26] Jefferson was indeed
something of a Saxonist, as the following remark makes clear:

> English liberties are not infringements merely of the king's preroga-
> tive, extorted from our princes by taking advantage of their weak-
> nesses; but a restitution of that antient constitution, of which our
> ancestors had been defrauded by the art and finess of the Norman
> Lawyers, rather than deprived by the force of the Norman arms
> (Jefferson, 1926, pp. 192–93).

He founded a professorship of Anglo-Saxon at the University of Virginia, and himself wrote (in 1798) an essay on the Saxon language (see 1903, 18:359–411). Here he agrees (implicitly) with Webster in declaring that "the pure Anglo-Saxon constitutes at this day the basis of our language" (p. 366), and recommends the compiling of a Saxon dictionary and grammar in order to renovate the living language as well as to correct the "neglect of its ancient constitution and dialect" (p. 391).

In the same year, Samuel Henshall produced such a grammar (Henshall, 1798), and various British writers besides Horne Tooke, among them L. D. Nelme and Samuel Pegge, had explored the Saxon or Gothic origins of the language. Jefferson's essay seems not to have been much known, but we can imagine Webster's discomfort had he been aware that he shared a platform with the very man whose election to the presidency was widely held to signal the end of classical Federalism. Even if Webster's use of the Saxon mythology, which would of course have been appealing for its suggestion of a connection between the Norman usurpation and the fashionable eighteenth-century enthusiasm for Frenchified locutions, never made him into a Jeffersonian democrat, or anything like it, we can see that all the associations did point that way. And it *was* truly a part of the polemic against "polite" speech which is undoubtedly there in Webster's writings. It would thus have been very easy for the careless reader to assume from the vindiction of the Saxon tradition that Webster's common man was more common that Webster actually meant him to be, especially when, as we have seen, Webster does wander into occasional justifications of dialect when it happens to embody the genuine principles of origin and analogy. Comments such as the following, from James Carrol, could well have been taken, and were so taken, as attacks on the "best" people:

> almost all common every day English words, are derived from the Saxon and Teutonic. . . . The uncommon words used by elegant speakers, and writers, on lofty, or grave subjects, are derived from the Latin and Greek languages (1795, p. 43).

If we want to gain a sense of how to navigate these controversial waters without troubling anyone in the potential readership, we can

turn once again to the artful Lindley Murray, whose account of the
blending of the Norman and Saxon languages into what we now
know as English is as defused as it could possibly be of offensive
bias (1823, 1:135–38). He notes condescendingly that

> Ancient usage is not the test by which the correctness of modern
> language is to be tried. The origin of things is certainly a proper and
> gratifying subject of inquiry; and it is particularly curious and pleas-
> ing to trace the words of our language to their remote sources. This
> pleasure should, however, be confined to speculation. It should not
> lead us to invert the proper order of things, and to determine the
> propriety of our present words and forms of expression, by the
> practice of distant, and comparatively rude ages (p. 135).

It is hard not to suspect, once again, that Murray's successful cap-
turing of the market had something to do with his ability (conscious or not) to avoid outraging his audience on this issue of the
ancient constitution, political and linguistic. Webster was of course
no disturber of "the proper order of things" in matters political, but
he did enough to unsettle that assumption in the realm of language
to cause considerable offense, especially to a generation very familiar with the idea of a close association between language and civilization in general. He tried to make the yeoman image something
other than the property of the agrarian south, with which it might
more naturally have seemed to be associated. As a Federalist seeking to adapt the rhetoric of the common man to his ideal of the
national language, we can see how it was that he antagonized the
extreme elements in his own party. Perhaps he himself never fully
understood the complexities and ambiguities of the traditions on
which he was drawing, and their likely repercussions. In many
ways, it seems to have mattered little to his readers that the case
for the common language was a case against dialect, and against
innovation, and that the American yeoman was in fact a translation of the English country squire, minus his loyal retainers. The
associations called up by the mention of Horne Tooke and the
Saxons seem to have outweighed these careful qualifications. In this
respect it would appear that Webster did indeed labor under the
Anglo-Saxon yoke.

3

The Liberties of Literature, 1776-1810

To turn from Webster's writings on the nature and prospects of an American English to the actual practice of the first generation of American authors is to witness at first sight something of a decline in the intensity and scope of the issues they seem to raise. It is indeed true that the large volume of political and patriotic poems written during the first thirty years of the republic, on whichever side of the political debate, and for or against closer ties with Britain, does not on a cursory inspection seem to embody any high degree of enthusiasm for a national language. There are exceptions, notably that of Joel Barlow, which I shall discuss below. And indeed the climate of opinion was such that even the slightest hint of an Americanism was pursued with great tenacity by the reviewers on both sides of the ocean, and on both sides of the debate. Despite these reservations, it does, however, remain generally the case that the language of polite literature in America before the war of 1812 (and often after it) was remarkably close to the language of the same "polite" literature being written in Britain, even when, as in the case of Freneau, it was rather impolitely stressing the political differences between the two nations.

But this is by no means the whole story. If we remain within the terms of the debate as they were laid down by Webster, then we shall miss what was most distinctive and provocative in the American literature being written around him. For Webster, as we have seen, had prided himself on belonging to a culture in which the eventual elimination of dialect was not only possible but probable. He recognized the existence of localisms, and even recorded some of them in the 1806 *Dictionary;* but their preservation was never Webster's ambition, unless they fulfilled the requirements of the good old style. One of the purposes of the simplified spelling project was in fact the elimination of local conventions. Webster's goal was always that of a standard American language, a received practice of writing and speaking that had the advantages of ubiquity without the disadvantages of being a socially divisive imposition from above, by a learned or privileged class. Though we have seen that this doctrine was not without its complications, this at least was Webster's conscious purpose.

On examining the writings of Royall Tyler and Hugh Henry Brackenridge, among others, we yet find that much of the vitality and indeed the message of their work depends on the representation of dialect as an index of the differences of interest and aspiration in early American society. Thus, they are in a way representing an America that does not correspond to Webster's *ideal* model or prognosis. This dialect tradition in early American literature seems from the first to stand in a disjunctive relation to the "higher" tradition of linguistic universality implicit in most of the poetry of the period. Fiction and drama seem for the most part more appropriate media for the portrayal of different conventions of language than does "high" poetry. And already in this early period we can see the emergence of a tradition that will continue to appear in Cooper's novels and yet more emphatically in those of Mark Twain. Somewhere between or outside these two alternatives, and operating in a new dimension of linguistic consciousness tied in with the naming or renaming of actual places, stand the journals of Lewis and Clark. But first I shall discuss the theme of linguistic nationalism in the American poetry of the period.

Poetry and Patriotism

Five years before the Declaration of Independence, the young Philip Freneau and Hugh Henry Brackenridge collaborated on *A Poem on the Rising Glory of America,* read as a commencement address at Princeton and published a year later (Philadelphia, 1772). The poem predicts a rosy future for the new world, thanks to the absence of precious metals and the consequent likelihood of the preservation of civic virtue: gold is to be replaced by the more fruitful "golden commerce" (p. 16). Among other things the poem rehearses the Carthaginian theory of the origin of the Native Americans (pp. 7–8), and concludes with a long passage on the millenarian implications of the new world civilization. It is not at all explicit about any future difference of identity or purpose between America and Britain, nor is its language marked by any traces of an incipient national diction. The text of the first edition is much disfigured by typesetter's errors, but the familiar eighteenth-century inconsistencies remain evident, as we have seen them elsewhere. Even the words that have since become awkward or archaic, such as *skulking* and *disembogues* (pp. 12, 18), were not so at the time, and can be found in both Johnson and Bailey.

Brackenridge turned to prose and to politics, whereas Freneau went on to become one of the most nationalistic and indeed republican of all the early American poets. The vocabulary of his two volume 1809 edition of poems has been analyzed in some detail by Hustvedt (1928–29), whose conclusion is that while words of specifically American origin or application do occur, especially in the poems dealing with common life, there is yet not much evidence of any consciously belligerent Americanism in Freneau's language. Many of the words Hustvedt cites (e.g., *whipperwill, pone, backwoods, pine barren*) are indeed descriptive of things that would not exist in the experience of the British reader, and are thus examples of precisely the class of new words that commentators like Jefferson and Webster would have sanctioned. Freneau's "To a Katydid" apparently marks the first use of that noun in poetry (see Krapp, 1960, 1:104). Hustvedt's list of such items is actually quite a long one, but they do not seem to be invoked by Freneau with any clear intention of drawing attention to themselves. Thus Hustvedt concludes that

> Not even when . . . he complains about the general intellectual domination of England, does he so much as hint at an independent American language. Thus the most violent political enemy of England was in reality a friend of English letters and of English speech (1928–29, p. 18).

This indeed could serve as a description of much of the rest of the poetry written during the period. Freneau himself did not much approve of the writings of the "aristocratic, speculating faction at Hartford,"[1] the so-called "Connecticut Wits" who were for the most part on the other side of the political debate. Some of their poems are little more than versified Federalism, but even here some significant innovations are apparent, and in the context of a linguistic patriotism poets like Dwight and Humphreys are no less American than Freneau himself, even though they are generally in favor of maintaining closer ties with the parent culture than Freneau ever was.

David Humphreys' *Miscellaneous Works* (1804) includes an explicit declaration in favor of such a rapprochement:

> Albion! Columbia! soon forget the past!
> In friendly intercourse your int'rests blend!
> From common sires your gallant sons descend;
> From free-born sires in toils of empire brave—
> 'Tis yours to heal the mutual wounds ye gave;
> Let those be friends whom kindred blood allies,
> With language, laws', religion's holiest ties (p. 40).

Such doctrines do not call for any strident linguistic nationalism, least of all in a context wherein the fiercely anti-British Freneau is writing something very close to the King's English. Laughing Ceres now appears in the shape of the "lofty maize" rather than the nodding wheat, and the rivers all have new (usually Native American) names, but otherwise we remain well within the conventions of eighteenth-century British landscape poetry. Humphreys' main concerns about his style and vocabulary seem to be that, having been abroad on diplomatic service for so long, he might have unwittingly absorbed foreign idioms or otherwise departed from the traditional Puritan standards of plain speech:

> The writer has endeavoured to prevent his mental images . . . from being distorted by abstract phraseology, or disguised by foreign idioms. In an attempt to make the clearness of his style in a degree the mirror of his mind, he was solicitous to shun turgid diction, brilliant antithesis, unnatural conceits, affected figures, forced epithets, and, in general, all factitious ornament. Nor was he less anxious to avoid mistaking and admitting vulgarity for simplicity (pp. 122–23).

In this blend of Wordsworthian simplicity and standard decorum, and in his echo of Swift's famous dictum of "the most proper words, in their proper places" (p. 123), Humphreys is at one with a host of other poets of the period, British and American. And yet, as if inevitably, the odd Americanisms do creep in. The word *sleigh* and its compounds, a neologism from New Amsterdam Dutch that would soon become a subject of debate, appears unglossed in Humphreys' text (e.g., p. 196), though it can be found neither in Johnson (1773) nor in Webster (1806). The noun phrase *red men,* again absent from both these dictionaries, is glossed—"the aboriginal inhabitants of America denominate the European the *pale,* and themselves the *red* flesh" (p. 236)—as is the word *leanto,* which is to be found in Webster (not in Johnson), though Humphreys gives more information, specifying that such things are "very common in New England" (p. 218).

None of this, however, amounts to a resounding commitment to Americanisms or to an American style. We will encounter Humphreys again in the next chapter; passing on to his contemporary, Timothy Dwight, this verdict needs to be modified only slightly, though Dwight does seem in principle to have been a linguistic patriot. He wrote to Webster in 1807, in a letter cosigned by nine of the Yale faculty, as follows:

> The insertion of local terms in your small dictionary we approve. No good reason can be given why a person who meets with words of this kind should not be able to find their meaning in a dictionary— the only place where they can usually be found at all (Mencken, 1973, p. 83).

Dwight's *The Conquest of Canaan* (1785), along with its declared intention of creating an eternal and universal history out of the events of the American Revolution, had also spoken up for the principle of Americanisms in language. Speaking of himself in the third person, Dwight says:

> It will be observed that he has introduced some new words, and annexed to some old ones a new signification. This liberty, allowed to others, he hopes will not be refused to him: especially as from this source the copiousness and refinement of language have been principally derived (1785, preface).

With the publication of *Greenfield Hill* (1794), this self-conscious-ness about linguistic innovation appears in the explanatory notes appended to the poem itself. These are not by any means exclu-sively devoted to the explanation of Americanisms; the majority in fact are there to identify allusions to parts of the Bible. In glossing *wain* as "waggon" Dwight is presumably assisting the American as much as the British reader. Similarly, the case for using *firm* as a verb is licensed, according to Johnson (1773), by no lesser figures than Dryden and Pope. It would seem that in both cases, as in that of the word *essoins* (in both Johnson and Webster, and presumably in transatlantic use), Dwight is explaining standard poetic diction to a potentially plain-speaking audience; though the case of *to firm* might have seemed especially sensitive in the light of the way in which American writers were frequently taken to task for their habit of making verbs out of nouns and adjectives. Benjamin Franklin himself had complained of *to progress* and *to advocate* in exactly these terms (see Mencken, 1973, p. 7), and many other commentators followed him in so doing.

If the dominant matter of these notes is not devoted to new words, those relating to Part II of the poem are yet noticeably dense in localisms. Dwight explains the use of *streets* for "roads," translates *nutwood* into "hickory," and explains the word *slump'd* in considerably greater detail than does Webster (1806). The New England term *spring bird,* again glossed in some detail, does not ap-pear at all in Webster's first dictionary.[2]

These are indeed small beginnings, but they do suggest that if the "polite" poetry of the period was not extravagant in its com-mitment to an American vocabulary, it did nevertheless make ges-tures in that direction. Dwight's 1807 letter to Webster (cited above) suggests that even after the language issue had become prominent as a factor in the debate between the Federalists and the republicans, he was still able to preserve a respect for localisms and American-isms as something other than what Joseph Dennie had called "wig-wam words." Any higher degree of linguistic innovation might well have been discouraged by the insecurities that the poets felt about challenging those very figures in the British tradition to whom they owed so much in style and subject. (*Greenfield Hill,* for example, is a poem that in its early sections is an intelligent interpretation of the political economy of Goldsmith's *The Deserted Village.*) They might also have been inhibited by the insecurity of the poetic trade itself. Elihu Hubbard Smith's *American Poems* (1793) did not publicize its main purpose as that of disseminating a new language, but rather as that of remedying a situation where "the frail security of an obscure newspaper" might be the only repository of "some of the hansomest [*sic*] specimens of American Poetry" (p. iv). In a pre-copyright economy in which British authors of established reputation might be freely pirated and cheaply reprinted, there was little incentive for publishers to patronize native talent, and hence perhaps little incentive on the poet's part to stimulate any ideological division within an already fragile audience.

But it must be said that not many of these poets were dependent on their writings for a living, and the career of Joel Barlow was exceptional enough to unsettle any totalizing explanations we might seek to draw from historical and cultural circumstances for an apparent lack of linguistic nationalism. Barlow's career, like that of Humphreys, appears as a contemporary image of the classical ideal—poet, patriot, and politician. What made this apparently ideal synthesis less than universally popular was the fact that the politics were liberal to an extreme, and determined as such the nature of the poetry and the patriotism. Barlow had already established a literary reputation when he left for Europe in 1788. Taking up residence in London in 1790, he became a member of the radical circle that also included Tooke, Paine, and Priestley, and was soon obliged to flee the country, moving to Paris in 1792. His diplomatic career began in 1795, when he became consul to Algiers, and eventually (though not until 1811) minister to France. He died in Poland in the fateful year of 1812, on a fruitless mission to conclude a new commercial treaty with the defeated Napoleon.

Barlow had been a classmate of Noah Webster's at Yale, though by 1798 Webster was taking him to task for his pro-French sympathies and his atheistical tendencies (Webster, 1953, pp. 187–94). Even after Barlow's admiring remarks, in *The Columbiad,* about Webster's linguistic reforms and aspirations, Webster declared himself unable to express any public approval, and sadly explains that he cannot review the poem because of its "atheistical principles" (1953, p. 309). Had he done so, he might have found much to recommend, for Barlow had always shared many of his classmate's convictions. He believed in the power of art and letters as a means of unifying America, and in the power of commerce for unifying the whole world—on which point he is indeed more consistently utopian than Webster himself. In the first version of his American epic, *The Vision of Columbus* (1787), he anticipated the orgy of naming that the new republic had before it, one we shall see beginning to occur in the explorations of Lewis and Clark:

> Lands yet unknown, and streams without a name
> Rise into vision and demand their fame (1970, 2:133)

The commingling effects of commerce on the language, which Johnson had feared and which Webster could ignore because of his sense of the innocence of the early American economy, were applauded by Barlow as working to bring about a whole in which all differences will have been subsumed. Greed and good will go hand in hand as commerce brings about a perfect Smithian cycle:

> That every distant land the wealth might share,
> Exchange their fruits and fill their treasures there;
> Their speech assimilate, their empires blend,
> And mutual interest fix the mutual friend (2:344).

The curse of Babel will be undone as "one pure language" (p. 350) spreads across the earth:

> At this blest period, when thy peaceful race
> Shall speak one language and one cause embrace,
> Science and arts a speedier course shall find,
> And open earlier on the infant mind.
> No foreign terms shall croud with barbarous rules,
> The dull, unmeaning pageantry of schools;
> Nor dark authorities, nor names unknown
> Fill the learn'd head with ign'rance not its own;
> But truth's fair eye, with beam unclouded, shine,
> And simplest rules her moral lights confine;
> One living language, one unborrow'd dress
> Her boldest flights with happiest force express;
> Triumphant virtue, in the garb of truth,
> Win a pure passage to the heart of youth,
> Pervade all climes, where suns or oceans roll,
> And bid the gospel cheer the illumined whole (p. 352).

The same Enlightenment philosophy that we have seen to underlie (in more complicated ways) Webster's arguments about the state of the language is here the guiding conviction of Barlow's poem. Identity of speech represents and redetermines identity of interest, simplifies the acquisition of knowledge, and thus speeds up the progress of truth.

The second and major version of Barlow's epic appeared in 1807, now renamed *The Columbiad*. The author casts himself very consciously in opposition to the tradition of the classical epic. For him, the *Aeneid* conspired simply to "increase the veneration of the people for a master, whoever he might be, and to encourage like Homer the great system of military depredation" (1807, p. ix). Barlow is in agreement with his British contemporary William Blake on this matter; but unlike Blake he remains a devoted rationalist in seeking to replace "the deleterious passion for violence and war" with "the love of rational liberty" (p. x), rather than with Blake's idiosyncratic radical Christianity. Perhaps it was in passages such as this that Webster saw the spirit of atheism at work.

But the most striking thing about *The Columbiad* is not its rationalism, so much as the extraordinarily bold linguistic initiatives it embodies. For Barlow alone among the exponents of high poetry seeks to rewrite the polite language according to patriotic principles. Furthermore, they are largely Webster's principles. The appendix on orthography (pp. 435–38) commends Webster explicitly, and his doctrines are in evidence all over the poem. Barlow employs *-or* rather than *-our* spellings, the *u* being "quite useless in pronunciation" and contrary to the sacred spirit of "analogy." The last three letters in *though* and *through* are also left off, "being totally disregarded in pronunciation and awkward in appearance" (p. 436). Many verb forms are converted from *-ed* to *-t* in the past tense (*fixt, capt*), a movement that began in the spirit of poetic license but needs to be further extended because "it brings a numerous class of words to be written as they are spoken." Similarly, the Johnsonian *musick* and *publick* lose the last letter (p. 437). Barlow also follows Webster in his spellings of *activ, decisiv, determin*, and so forth (p. 438).

Spelling reform is not, however, the only element in Barlow's new poetic language. He tends to omit hyphens (a tendency that twentieth-century American English is at the time of writing beginning to emulate), so that we have *Newyork, liveoaks, midsky*, and other such compounds. There are a host of poetic licenses (e.g., *buffle* for "buffalo") and some strangely prophetic coinages, such as *derouted* and *condependent*, words that might seem incipiently plausible to the modern reader used to words of the *deplaning* class. There are words from the French (*croupe* for "ridge," *brume* for "fog"), and the bizarre coinage *colon* for "colonist" or "immigrant" (perhaps a pun on Columbus' Spanish name?). Barlow also uses words that were beginning to be obsolete in 1807, even in poetry (e.g., *welkin, dight, grume* and the verb *to gride*); and he forms new adjectives from nouns, as poets and Americans were supposed to do. The verb *to methodise* is actually not an Americanism, being found in Johnson, supported by a distinguished cast of British writers. In fact, by far the largest class of neologisms in the poem is made up of words formed by the addition of standard prefixes to words not usually connected with them. Poets had traditionally done this—thus Johnson cites Milton, Gay, and Pope for the verb *imbrown*—but Barlow does it more than most. Thus we have *imban, imbead, bivaulted, impalm, imband, instarred,* and so on. None of these words appears in Webster (1806); but every one is absorbed into the 1828 *Dictionary*, with Barlow in each case given as the sole authority. The entry for *imban* does append the verdict "not well authorized," but otherwise we can see that despite his atheistic tendencies, Barlow was after all allowed to appear in the first major American dictionary.

It is then arguable that most of Barlow's neologisms are not of the sort defended in his postscript, those which arise because the vocabulary "must and will keep pace with the advancement of our knowledge" (p. 435). They are, on the contrary, largely poetic coinages, albeit adhering to the principle of analogy, with prefixes and nouns and verbs being wedded into metrically efficient compounds. The real passion for naming or renaming places seems to have begun, as we shall see, with the expedition of Lewis and Clark and the westward course of empire. But the scope and ambition of Barlow's attempts should not be underestimated or ridiculed. He was after all working within perhaps the most traditionally preconditioned of all the available genres, that of high poetry. Even as this tradition allowed for license, it did not encourage radical deviations from the norms, nor perhaps the sorts of subject matter in which such deviations would most naturally arise. The *Edinburgh Review* took up the poem as "the first specimen which has come to our hands of any considerable work composed in the American tongue."[3] The reviewer finds "a great multitude of words which are radically and entirely new . . . a variety of new compounds and combinations of words, or roots of words, which are still known in the parent tongue," and, thirdly, "the perversion of a still greater number of original English words from their proper use or signification, by employing nouns substantive for verbs, for instance, and adjectives for substantives, &c." Examples of each kind of novelty are given, but the major point of the poem, for this reviewer, is once again political. Barlow's new American tongue

> may also be known from all other tongues by an utter disregard of all distinction between what we should call lofty and elegant, and low and vulgar expressions. The republican literati seem to make it a point of conscience to have no aristocratical distinctions—even in their vocabulary (p. 29).

The irony is, of course, that despite such intentions, Barlow is unable to subvert at one stroke the whole traditionally elitist apparatus of high poetry, so that *The Columbiad* remains in the final analysis the sort of literature that could not have appealed to the average reader, even if it might have gratified the freer-thinking spirits among Webster's yeomen, who were as we have seen a rather sophisticated class. As a form of political statement, its appeal (though not necessarily its message) would have been circumscribed from the start by its appearance in a luxury edition; Paine's *Rights of Man,* it will be remembered, came out in pamphlet form. The reviewer in the *Edinburgh* makes, somewhat coyly, a similar point in deciding that, despite all the fuss, Barlow's poem *is* intelligible to the careful English reader; its "versification is generally both soft and sonorous," and it has passages of real "magnificence." The political point of the poem is almost damned by Jeffrey's faint praise. We now turn to the traditions of prose and prose fiction to see how the American language fared in other contexts.

Prose Fiction and the Dialect Tradition

Students and readers familiar only with the established canon of American literature sometimes tend to assume that Mark Twain invents a language, or at least represents it in literature for the first time. In fact, there is a striking sensitivity to dialect in the writings of the early national period.

We have seen that Webster was very well aware of the differences in American speech that resulted from locality. Although his 1806 dictionary did include New England localisms and was perceived as so doing, and although his 1789 account of the subject relates regional speech differences to different political and environmental factors (suggesting thereby a certain permanence to them), nonetheless Webster foresees neither the genesis nor the survival of fully fledged dialect traditions in America. Nor does he wish to encourage such developments, given the relation between a linguistically differentiated and a politically unfederated nation. In Webster's terms, the presence of local vocabularies may be admitted as long as they do not pass into the standard national language, so that even when he hides behind the democratic rhetoric of a common language his goal is in fact to produce a standard polite usage shared by the educated and influential classes in all parts of the republic. Thus:

> The principal business of a compiler of a grammar is, to separate *local* or *partial* practice from the *general custom* of speaking; and reject what is *local,* whether it exists among the great or the small, the learned or ignorant, and recommend that which is universal, or general, or which conforms to the analogies of structure in a language (1789a, p. ix).

The point is pursued later in the same volume:

> provincial accents are disagreeable to strangers and sometimes have an unhappy effect upon the social affections. All men have local attachments, which lead them to believe their own practice to be the least exceptionable. Pride and prejudice incline men to treat the practice of their neighbors with some degree of contempt. Thus small differences in pronunciation at first excite ridicule—a habit of laughing at the singularities of strangers is followed by disrespect—and without respect friendship is a name, and social intercourse a mere ceremony (pp. 19–20).

Or, Webster might have added, a naked assertion of proprietal rights over the language and everything else, which may be what underlies the continuing incidence of such laughter among some members of the upper and middle classes in the United Kingdom today.

Despite the criticism that his own recommendations in the spelling books and elsewhere transcribe a specifically New England pronunciation (see Neumann, 1924), Webster saw the state of affairs in America as coming very close to an ideal purity:

> The people of distant counties in England can hardly understand one another, so various are their dialects; but in the extent of twelve hundred miles in America, there are very few, I question whether a hundred words, except such as are used in employments wholly local, which are not universally intelligible (1789 p. 289).

We should not expect the tobacco planter of the Carolinas to understand the technical vocabulary of a Massachusetts cranberry farmer; but otherwise there is a very high degree of standardization in the national language.

Not surprisingly, the argument about how much dialect existed in the various parts of America depended very much on the definitions adopted by particular writers, and their purposes in writing on the subject in the first place. It was a commonplace—and it became even more of one after the War of 1812—that the general standard of speech in America was much superior to that in Britain, and even some British writers can be found remarking on this fact (see Read, 1933a, pp. 322–26). Of course, such a position was not incompatible with the British outcry over the incidence of new words or new applications of old ones. In this respect, A. W. Read (1933a, pp. 329–34) goes on to note that almost all the British reactions in this respect were negative. On the question of the norm within the United States, however, the same author argues elsewhere that, from the evidence of the advertisements for runaway slaves in mid-eighteenth century American newspapers, the language was already standardized to a high degree. Because such runaways were often identified as having particular speech patterns—Scots, Irish etc.— Read argues that

> the speaking of English dialects and "broad" English was a noticeable deviation from the body of American speech. Except for the East Anglians, and the southeasterners, those who used the dialects could be identified by them. Thus in the colonial period American

English had a consistency of its own, most closely approximating the type of the region around London (Read, 1938, p. 79).

Because southeastern and East Anglian speech is *not* singled out for attention, Read concludes with some credibility that it coincided closely with the American norm. But we would need far more evidence than this to be sure of exactly what kind of English was being spoken, and where, and by whom. In fact, it was New England that was dominantly populated by immigrants from Norfolk, Suffolk, Essex, and the home counties, but it was precisely New England speech that was most commonly singled out for distinctive representation in the early literature. Of course, much of that literature was written or published *in* New England, and it is likely that we are thus witnessing some kind of humorous exploration of the social differences between learned and common speakers. Patrick Campbell (1793) records meeting a New Englander and asking him where he had come from:

> he swore, vowed, and guessed alternately, and was never like to come to the point, even though he had but that instant come from it (p. 181).

East Anglian speakers in modern England still have a reputation for circumlocution and for slow, well-meditated delivery, and indeed for wit; but it is not clear that this can be identified with the pronunciation and vocabulary of the eighteenth-century New England speaker (as represented). American speakers were themselves even more emphatic than Campbell about the distinctiveness of this speech. *The American Museum* (2, 1788, p. 485) includes a spoof "On Pronouncing Dictionaries" in which it ridicules the "polite" innovations of contemporary British speakers by way of (and perhaps as well as) the homely native alternative:

> Now, where do these grammarians and dictionaries go for authority? Shakespeare is so antique, Addison so solemn, Pope so holy, and Dean so *swift,* that they will not copy after them—No: they can't *endjure* it; they don't think it their *djuty;* so they *keindly* took *hum* to the English theatre, as a brighter *skei,* in hopes of making their *fortshin*—Heard, they say, should be pronounced *hurd,* guide *geide,* creature *creetchur,* &c.
>
> *Neaw,* I advise these *keind* polishers of *awer* language, to go to brother Jonathan, for a *geide:* he'll *larn'um,* to say *keow* for cow,

veaw for vow, *geal* for girl, *heause* for house, and a grate many
other nashun clever things, and he won't *ax'um* a *farding* for't
nother.

This is not the earliest reference to the New England speech. Walter
Blair (1960, p. 8) cites an early eighteenth-century transcription by
Sarah Kemble Knight;[4] and an anonymous wit whom we now reasonably suspect to have been, once again, John Adams (see Adams,
1961, 1:250, 330–32), had written various letters to the Boston
newspapers under the pseudonym of 'Humphrey Ploughjogger', in
which the speech and persona of the plain New England farmer was
used to highlight the problems of the rural class in an expanding
commercial economy. On the front page of *The Boston Evening
Post,* June 20, 1763, Ploughjogger apologizes with "I arnt book
larnt enuff, to rite so polytly, as the great gentlefolks," and goes on
to ask for advice about raising hemp, "for they do say, it fetches a
nation price." He complains about the obsessively political content
of the newspapers, and asks the editors to set themselves the task
of "teeching mankind things they want to know, and helping um
pay their dets and live comfortable." By 1767, however, it seems
that Humphrey has become a bit more literate, even in his campaign against "high-flown words" (*The Boston Gazette,* January 5,
1767), although dialect words (e.g., *botty*) and phonetic spellings
(*Rashosination*) do creep in.

We might quarrel over the degree to which such evidence as this
points to the presence of a fully fledged dialect, and how far it signals some sort of special diction. For dialect was, then as now,
something of a loaded word. In Brockden Brown's *The Monthly
Magazine* (3, 1800, p. 3) 'Candidus' notes that "Every state, every
town, every village, has a *speech* of its own," but this is part of an
obvious polemic against the movement for an American language.
On the very same page, American speech as a whole is defined as
no more than a "dialect." James Carrol is less vitriolic, but he
makes a comparable point in establishing the timeliness of his own
attempt to tidy up the language:

> The pronunciation of the southern states of English America is al-
> most as different from that of the New-England states, even among
> the learned, as any two dialects of the language of any illiterate
> nation can be supposed to be: and yet both these parts of America

abound with men of bright genius, large mental capacities and profound learning. In Great Britain the pronunciation is much more
various than in America; their being scarcely two Shires in which
the English is pronounced according to the same dialect (1795,
p. iii).

Carrol here seems to define dialect as a matter of pronunciation
rather than vocabulary, and indeed both the etymology and the
usage of the word are generally uncertain on the question of
whether pronunciation or vocabulary, or some measure of both, is
the most important characteristic of dialect. This familiar equivocation seems worth noting, because to accuse someone of speaking a
dialect is clearly to imply that there is a standard language from
which they are deviating; a recognition of the complete relativity
of habits of pronunciation is a much less politically assertive gesture. Cobbett recognized exactly this in his *Grammar,* first published in 1817:

> *pronunciation* is learned as birds learn to chirp and sing. In some
> counties of England words are pronounced in a manner different
> from that in which they are pronounced in other counties. . . . But,
> while all inquiries into the causes of these differences are useless,
> and all attempts to remove them are vain, the differences are of
> very little real consequence. . . . Children will pronounce as their
> fathers and mothers pronounce; and if, in common conversation, or
> in speeches, the matter be good and judiciously arranged, the facts
> clearly stated, the arguments conclusive, the words well chosen and
> properly placed, hearers whose approbation is worth having will
> pay very little attention to the accent (Cobbett, 1906, p. 16).

Cobbett's message is emphatic: prejudices about who is or is not
speaking with an "accent" have nothing to do with the real com-
municative efficiency of language.

But if dialect were to be thought of as including a heavy incidence of local words, as well as pronunciation, then we can see that
a stronger case could be made for its interfering with the efficiency
of basic communication. Those who agreed with Webster in seeking to eliminate all principles of distinction, in the interests of political solidarity, tended to be conscious of this implication. Thus
Thornton (1793) argues that, if his initiatives were to be adopted,
"dialects . . . would be utterly destroyed, both among foreigners
and peasants" (p. 38). Priestley (1762, p. 138) had contrasted the

Greek and Latin languages in terms of the presence and absence of dialects. The Greek states were politically discrete and independent, and dialects abounded; the Roman state was a political unity, and dialects were absent. The Roman state proved the more durable; and this was the spirit in which Webster and Thornton saw the question.

Webster's discrimination between the speech of the yeoman and that of the unlettered rustic was in fact the standard way of having the argument both ways: dialect does not exist in the average speaker. Jedidiah Morse essentially repeats the same case:

> It is true, that from laziness, inattention and want of acquaintance with mankind, many of the people in the country have accustomed themselves to use some peculiar phrases, and to pronounce certain words in a flat, drawling manner. Hence foreigners pretend that they know a New Englandman from his manner of speaking. But the same may be said with regard to a Pennsylvanian, or a Virginian, or a Carolinian; for all have some phrases and modes of pronunciation peculiar to themselves, which distinguish them from their neighbours. Men of eminence in the several learned professions, and colleges, ought to be considered as forming the standard of pronunciation for their respective states; and not that class of people who have imbibed the habit of using a number of singular and ridiculous phrases, and who pronounce badly (Morse, 1789, p. 145).

This, of course, presumes the stability and desirability of such a learned class in the first place. Witherspoon, in an account of the subject first published in 1781, had shown himself much more concerned that the habits of the vulgar might in fact come to characterize the language as a whole, the common language:

> But if there is a much greater number of local vulgarisms in Britain than America, there is also for this very reason, much less danger of their being used by gentlemen or scholars. It is indeed implied in the very nature of the thing, that a local phrase will not be used by any but the inhabitants or natives of that part of the country where it prevails. However, I am of opinion, that even local vulgarisms find admission into the discourse of people of better ranks more easily here than in Europe (1802, 4:469).

Already, in 1781, we can see the generation of Toquevillian paradoxes in the elucidation of the implications of democracy.

Despite the degree to which any accurate sense of the state of the language is clearly rendered difficult if not impossible by the way in which the polemical investments of the various writers determine the kinds of analysis offered, it yet seems clear enough that there was a strong distinction between the speech habits of the learned and the less learned orders. Whether we would choose to call this a difference of dialect is very much a matter of opinion. When American writers commented, as they so often did, on the absence of dialect in the new republic, they were making one of two points, or two points at once: first, that the standard of speech was remarkably uniform among the learned classes; and second, that wherever there were differences (at whatever level of the social hierarchy), they were yet much slighter than one might expect given the sheer distances involved and the difficulties of communication, and given the example of Britain itself, where a journey of fifty miles or so could produce three or four transitions in speech patterns. We should not assume that all New Englanders spoke like Humphrey Ploughjogger, even as some surely did; and we must further suspect the likelihood of a considerable degree of confusion and indeterminacy. Thus Miller (1963, pp. 223–24) makes the point that during the impressment controversies of the 1790s, naval officers on both sides found it very difficult to be sure whether potential victims were indeed British or American citizens, to the extent that the United States government thought of handing out certificates of citizenship. Those who have heard recordings of the political speeches of Americans before the middle of the present century will have noticed how much closer their pronunciation was to what is a recognizably British standard. Perhaps the analogy with modern Canada is also helpful: the American speaker who crosses the border is at once aware of the greater linguistic diversity and the relative lack of a national standard (among those born to speak English) in a culture that has experienced a high proportion of recent immigration from the British Isles.

Perhaps we need not labor the point that the evidence of literature and of the language debate itself must be very cautiously handled if we are looking for an insight into the real state of affairs in the early period, or indeed any period before the rise of professional linguistics. In fact, as so often, it is actually the *representation* of the question that is of the greatest interest to the critic or historian. Eighteenth-century British literature was, of course, quite specific in its identification of language, class, and politics, and as such would have been familiar to American writers and readers. Tom Jones' superiority to Squire Western is signalled by his not speaking an ungainly dialect; and when Smollett, in *Humphry Clinker* (1771), has Brambleton Hall occupied by a Methodist natural son and his dialect-speaking bride from the servant class, he seems to be making benevolent nonsense of the whole patriarchal ideal. In the same novel, Bramble advises the Scots to learn the "English idiom and pronunciation," lest they be ridiculed out of hand for their "dialect" (1983, p. 215). Jane Austen, in *Sense and Sensibility,* marks Anne and Lucy Steele as vulgar social climbers by having them speak an affected and archaic language in which tenses are awry and adjectives do the work of adverbs (Austen, 1980, pp. 146, 276, 355). Wordsworth avoided dialect in casting himself as a man speaking to men, yet he was still accused of a breach of decorum; and Clare got into trouble with his publisher largely because he did use dialect. Even Burns, whose Scots diction was to some degree romantically acceptable, and was itself apparently a poetic modification rather than a transcription of common speech (see Bentman, 1965), was widely preferred for his English poems. Henry Mackenzie, the author of the most influential contemporary review (in 1786), noted that even in Scotland Burns' language is "now read with a difficulty which greatly damps the pleasure of the reader," while the English reader requires such constant reference to a glossary as to destroy pleasure itself (Low, 1974, p. 69).

These are some of the prototypes of which American writers might have been conscious as they meditated the question of dialect. At first, it seems that the representation of dialect is not overtly fraught with political implications and decisions, at least for the most part. Potential confrontations or polemical positions are often avoided by good humor, or by an exploitation of the comic opportunities afforded by the material at hand. John Adams' Ploughjogger was quite pointed in his chastisement of the abstracting propensities of the learned and political class, but it would be too emphatic to suggest that he is the conscious voice of an oppressed or misunderstood class of Americans. Similarly, *The American Museum*'s post-independence transcription of the differences be-

tween the polite English and the rustic American speech, already
cited, is humorously deflating rather than sociologically inflammatory. This is the case also for the anonymous author (thought to
have been a British naval officer) of *The Adventures of Jonathan
Corncob* (1787), a comic tale of the encounter between the British
and American cultures, and one in which language plays a significant part. It is linguistic evidence, indeed, that allows the modern
editor (Noel Perrin) to speculate with some conviction about the
author's generic identity (pp. xiii–xiv). Among the dictions present
in the text we find West Indian English (p. 81), polite British in its
particular propensity for French terms (p. 47), and, of course,
most frequently of all, American English. The heroine, Miss Desire
Slawbunk, is named after a Dutch-American word for "something
you lie down on" (p. xi), and the text makes frequent use of italics
to specify words or phrases of American provenance. The words
store and *tarry* are so distinguished (p. 11), and the *skunk* is defined in a footnote for British readers (p. 62). Phraseology—"I
guess you *be* very welcome" (p. 11)—and pronunciation—"get
aloong, let me *alo-one*" (p. 30)—are also highlighted. But, for all
the sharp political antagonisms that underlie these differences, the
author's position is largely disinterested, and the tone is that of
humor rather than of satire.

But this commitment to good humor is not always to be divorced
from the social tensions between the various identities that bring
dialect into play in the first place. Royall Tyler's *The Contrast*
(1790), which claims to be the "first Essay of *American* Genius in
the Dramatic Art," is a highly amusing comedy of manners, and
manners of speaking; but behind them there are serious debates
and differences. Much of the play is taken up with the conversations
between two servants, one Jessamy, the Anglophile servant of the
equally Anglophile Billy van Dumpling, "who has read Chesterfield
and received the polish of Europe" (p. 77), and the other Jonathan
(of course), squire to the upright and loyal Captain Manly. Jessamy says "Egad," breaks into French whenever he can, quotes
Chesterfield, and calls a New Englander a "Yankee" (p. 26). He
does slip once in a while, as when he uses the word *stoop* (p. 31),
for "porch." Jonathan conversely retails all the standard features of
New England speech. He uses Biblical locutions, says "tarnation"
(p. 28), *buss* for "kiss," and *show* for "play" (pp. 34, 38). He

mixes up "I" and "me," finds things *dang'd cute* (p. 46), and knows only the Psalms and "Yankee Doodle," of which he can recite "but a hundred and ninety verses" (p. 46).

This is all very funny. But in the contrast between Manly and van Dumpling (or "Dimple," as he is called), more serious themes are present. Dimple is a coward, a gambler, and a seducer, while Manly makes clear his anti-Mandevillian politics and his suspicion of luxury (pp. 48–49). The conflict between the Chesterfieldian fop, with his polite English, and the stern Yankee, is also a conflict of values, and one absolutely central to contemporary American society.

The question of language is also prominent in Tyler's later work, *The Yankey in London* (1809)—where Tyler himself had never been! British diction is criticized for its "grotesque air of pert vivacity" (p. 103), and Johnson's case against Macpherson's *Ossian* is ridiculed from the perspective of the oral tradition and the "memories of the common people" (p. 128). Nominally a Federalist, and certainly a highly learned writer, Tyler was never an outspoken man of the people; but at the same time he has no respect for the ornaments and titles of the British language. The prologue to *The Contrast* had begun:

> Exult each patriot heart!—this night is shewn
> A piece, which we may fairly call our own;
> Where the proud titles of "My Lord! Your Grace!"
> To humble *Mr.* and plain *Sir* give place.
> (Tyler, 1968, p. 7)

The appeal is to an American audience, if not quite to an American language, for Tyler's is really the plain, unornamented style championed by Wordsworth and others. It ridicules the affectations of the high-flown British speech—see the parodic "Love Varses to the Bucheous Daffodel" (1968, p. 143) and the glossary appended—but does not mean to create a space for an American dialect or a language rife with new words.

It might be expected, not least from the evidence of the later tradition, that the novel would provide a more natural and complex medium for the representation of dialect than either the poem or the drama. This is true, I shall argue, of one writer of the early period: Hugh Henry Brackenridge. Charles Brockden Brown, who is often described as the first American novelist, does indeed deal in American scenes and transcribe American place names; but he is not much concerned with the representation of the linguistic identity of the new nation, perhaps because his motives for fictionalizing are not consciously political or sociological. This is also the case with Washington Irving, who was more concerned with such themes, but not from anything resembling a nationalist perspective. The *Letters of Jonathan Oldstyle, Gent.,* which Irving published in 1802 and 1803, are very free in ridiculing the language of the fops and theatergoers of urban society, and the "common *slang* of the day, collected from the conversation of hostlers, footmen, porters &c." (1977, p. 4); but they do not suggest that American English deviates at all from the traditional "old style," or that it ever should do so. One must speculate that a good deal of Irving's popularity with British readers stems from his reluctance to disturb their sense of national self-esteem and ruling-class self-confidence. *Salmagundi,* which Irving published in 1807–8 (coauthored with William Irving and J. K. Paulding), is quite explicit about its intended alliance with the British ruling class and its values. The United States is parodied as a society ruled by a "pure unadulterated LOGOCRACY or *government of words*" (1977, pp. 142–43), in which anyone with a "plentiful stock of verbosity" may succeed, and the series both begins and ends with a determination to avoid "that carping spirit with which narrow-minded book-worm cynics squint at the little extravagancies of the ton" (p. 70), and to eschew "all spirit of faction, discontent, irreligion and criticism" (p. 316). The author's spirit of "liberal toleration" (p. 70) is actually an espousal of traditional genteel values. John Bull's "jolly countenance" (p. 89) is applauded, along with the "true born, and true bred English gentleman" (p. 206). The parody of the journal of an English traveler is restrained and politic enough ot avoid the thorny and very common question of the American language (p. 103f.), and at one point Burke's notorious reference to the "swinish multitude," such a frequent talking point in the literature of the 1790s, appears in *Salmagundi* with no apparent ironic intention (p. 254).[5]

In 1845, William Gilmore Simms looked back over Irving's career as that of one who "was not accounted in England an American writer, and he himself—no doubt with a sufficient policy—his own fortunes alone being the subject of consideration—took no pains to assert his paternity" (Simms, 1962, p. 265). This is an unkind attribution of motives, but it does describe a definite trait in Irving's literary career, his avoidance of conflict. I have not the space to discuss the complex blend of the idiosyncratic and the historical in Irving's myths of pre-adolescent harmony, themselves darkened by intuitions of violence; but much of his work may be read as an invitation to forget the demands of mature political choices, most conspicuously that represented by the events of 1776. As Rip Van Winkle will sleep through the Revolutionary War, so *Diedrich Knickerbocker's History of New York* (1809) stops short well before the strife of modern times. The pacificist Dutch do not want to fight, and when they do the outcome is purely comic. No one is killed, and the only limb lost is Peter Stuyvesant's wooden leg, easily replaced. Irving's history is only partly satirical in its depiction of an idyllic era before the rule of violence and disputation; it satisfies both a deep cultural fantasy for its American readers, in restoring them to an experience of innocence, and at the same time a scoffing aspiration in its English readers, who can laugh at these grotesque Dutchman as well as deploring the incursions of artful Yankees.[6]

If many of the early representations of dialect exploited the subject for a disinterested good humor, with Irving largely avoiding it in his claim to good taste (so successful that he was often admired for his abilities in despite of his nationality!), we can sense another alternative in Hugh Henry Brackenridge's *Modern Chivalry* (1792–97). Brackenridge was a Scotsman who moved to America at the age of five. Like many men of his time, he tried his hand at various vocations, among them poet, playwright, schoolmaster, minister, lawyer, journalist and member of the Pennsylvania state assembly. A moderate Federalist, he is not easily pigeonholed in political terms. Perhaps his essential profile in this respect was that of a "westerner"; or, in terms of our present study, that of a transcriber of American manners.[7]

Modern Chivalry was published in four volumes between 1792 and 1797, and it opens with an explicit reference to the debate over the viability of an academy of language:

> It has always appeared to me, that if some great master of stile should arise and without regarding sentiment, or subject, give an example of good language in his composition, which might serve

as a model to future speakers and writers, it would do more to fix
the orthography, choice of words, idiom of phrase, and structure of
sentence, than all the Dictionaries and Institutes that have been
ever made (1:5–6).

This is not, however, a Johnsonian case for the precedence of example over prescription, with all its attendant complications and ambiguities. Brackenridge's tongue is firmly in his cheek, when he says
that the kind of example he has in mind can only be set by his pay-
ing "no regard to the idea; for it is not in the power of human ingenuity to attain two things perfectly at once" (1:6). Thus he
offers his readers "something to read without the trouble of thinking" (p. 9). The postscript to this first book takes up the subject
again. Claiming to have based his style on that of Swift and Xeno-
phon, the author has

> carefully avoided the word *unfounded* instead of groundless, a word
> in vogue, among members of Congress especially. The word
> *commit,* is good, but being lately introduced, and too much hack-
> neyed, I have not used it (1:153).

American English is superior to British, especially "since the time
of that literary dunce, Samuel Johnson, who was totally destitute
of taste for the *vrai naturalle,* or simplicity of nature" (p. 155). It
is hard to be sure whether Brackenridge or his typesetter is responsible for the pidgin French, for his irony on this question of the
American language is, to say the least, evasive. The patriotism is
not wholly spurious nor yet wholly serious; he seems to be both
ridiculing and upholding the self-consciousness of the American
writer on the subject. In the body of the novel itself, the irony is
more clearly open to codification: there is a very close correlation
between the political and the linguistic identity of the new republic.
In the very first chapter, Captain John Farrago, the modern
Quixote, comes upon a surgeon whose professional circumlocutions
and learned mystifications are used to delude his audience and "to
increase the perquisities" (1:20)—as they will be in a more subtle
way by Dr. Elnathan Todd in Cooper's *The Pioneers.* The world
through which Farrago travels is one dominated by deceit and exploitation, and much of this is mediated through the manipulation
of language. Farrago's Irish servant, Teague O'Regan, is in great
demand as a potential Indian chief, to be disguised and employed

in the conclusion of fraudulent and profiteering treaties. As the confidence man explains:

> Now you are not to suppose that it is always an easy matter to catch a real chief . . . it is much more profitable to hire substitutes and make chiefs of our own. And as some unknown gibberish is necessary, to pass for an Indian language, we generally make use of Welch, or Low Dutch, or Irish (1:107).

Teague could be made "a Kickapoo in about nine days" (p. 108), and could soon be taught to speak "the language":

> That is an easy matter. . . . Indian speeches are nearly all alike. You have only to talk of burying hatchets under large trees, kindling fires, brightening chains; with a demand, at the latter end, of blankets for the backside, and rum to get drunk with (1:111).

Similarly, a figure later encountered by Farrago "had the advantage of some education with a Welsh schoolmaster, who passed his native language upon the young man for Latin" (4:88).

Brackenridge's novel represents an early analysis of what was to become the "confidence man" tradition, in which nothing is as it seems, and in which the plurality of languages in the new nation is exploited by the unscrupulous to further their own interests. The targets of his satire include both the manipulators of the rhetoric of democracy and equality, and also the naive exponents of a well-intentioned but inept spirit of egalitarianism—for example, the recruiters for the American Philosophical Society, who seek Teague's membership because there are "hundreds, whose names you may see on our list, who are not more instructed" (1:51). As the United States is not yet politically or socially solidified, so it is also linguistically chaotic, and the clash of languages produces misunderstandings and deceptions. A. W. Read has made further use of the information provided by advertisements for runaway slaves in deducing that "the American colonies of the middle quarters of the eighteenth-century abounded with speakers of languages other than English" (1937a, p. 99; cf. Heath, 1977), with Dutch and German especially prominent. Farrago's two servants, Teague O'Regan and Duncan Ferguson, are, respectively, Irish and Scots, and they provide all kinds of comic relief in their dialect speeches. But an earnest realization exists at the heart of the novel that there is more

at stake than this; the clash of languages embodies a wider struggle
for recognition, in which mutual intelligibility is but the first, essential step. Black English and Quaker English also figure in the text
(2:74, 107), but it is the Irish and the Scots dictions that are most
carefully transcribed and explored. Teague and Duncan are both, in
a sense, innocents abroad, caught up in processes of social and political change they cannot understand or control. This makes them
consistent targets for the conscious manipulations and sheer misconceptions of others. Farrago's contempt for Teague's constant
willingness to be tempted beyond his natural rank in life is explicit—
"this servant of mine is but a bog-trotter; who can scarcely speak
the dialect in which your laws ought to be written" (1:31)—but in
his inflexible belief in the fixity of all social hierarchies, Farrago too
is not beyond the reach of the author's irony, and he too commits
the odd grammatical blunder, as when he sounds forth in the voice
of cultural patriotism:

> Our politicians have wrote, and our patriots have spoke as well as
> your Burkes, or your Sheridans, or any other . . . (2:17).

As Teague narrowly escapes being made into a Kickapoo, so Duncan is charged by a constable with being the father of an illegitimate
child, simply because all Scotsmen sound the same to him: "his
Scottish dialect sounded the presumption or identity so strongly,
that it was difficult, if not impossible, to get over it" (4:82).

We should not become too heavyhanded in arguing for this sociological intensity in Brackenridge's representation of language
and dialect, but it would also be a serious misunderstanding to
assume that he is writing simply at the dictates of a comic interest.
In his transcription of the struggles and tensions between the languages of liberty, he departs from the polite assumption that these
tensions are minimal or ephemeral, or that they do not reflect on
the instability of liberty itself. He also produces some startlingly
earthy dialogue; startling, that is, in comparison with the more
decorous writings of Irving and Cooper, and with the Websterian
commitment to euphemism and the exclusion of vulgar language.
Farrago persuades Teague away from the vocation of preaching by
threatening that the devil's "very scullions will piss upon you"
(1:78; cf. 3:xiv). He describes Britain as an island "which, taking
in its whole extent, would be little more than a urinal to one of our

Patagonians in South America" (2:18), and is not too prudish to voice his observation of the universal inclination for "kissing a great man's backside" (2:112). Brackenridge's village moll calls Duncan a "son of a bitch" (4:85), and his obligatory Frenchman dispenses "foutres" at regular intervals in the scenes in which he is involved (3:7, 22f.); this word, as we have seen, found its way (by accident) into only one American dictionary, that of Samuel Johnson Jr. Farrago is willing to discuss the process of castration in decidedly indelicate detail, and his creator does not hide the fact of the existence of brothels in the land of liberty. Unlike Barlow, Brackenridge does not seem to aim at any conscious innovations in the way of vocabulary: words like *homely* and *barbecue* can actually be found, in their American senses and without comment, in Johnson. I have found two apparently original words: *quashaw* (3:1), for the species of pumpkin that came to be known as "squash" (Webster 1806 gives *quash;* neither *DAE* nor *DA* gives *quashaw*); and *haubucks* (3:11), which I have been unable to trace but which looks very like a Scotticism for "loungers" or "common fellows." In thus being relatively free of self-conscious neologisms, and in not in this sense publicizing an American national language, Brackenridge's analysis of dialect may be thought to be exposing to scrutiny the incoherent raw materials of any *possible* national language. There is no Enlightenment assumption of a body of common speakers inventing together according to common principles and needs. His version of the state of the nation is thus very different from the pre-revolutionary vision of linguistic and social tolerance imaged in Thomas Campbell's popular *Gertrude of Wyoming* (1809):

> And scarce had Wyoming of war or crime
> Heard, but in transatlantic story rung,
> For here the exile met from every clime,
> And spoke in friendship every distant tongue.
> (Campbell, n.d., p. 165)

Cooper was to use the last two lines of this passage as the epigraph to Chapter 8 of *The Pioneers,* not without an (at least) implicit irony. The different tongues in Brackenridge's world are the vehicles of deceit rather than the images of toleration. S. Brice Heath (1977) has argued that the early republic was marked by the conscious tolerance of a multilingual society, taking as evidence the fact that some of the early congressional documents were also printed in French and German where the local readership required them. This is an appealing argument, not least for its relevance to an urgent twentieth-century debate; but it does not seem to me to suit the evidence. Willingness to compromise with local differences, in the short term, does not imply a maintained policy of linguistic pluralism. Men like Webster and Jefferson believed that America would of necessity come to speak a standard language, and that language would be an American version of English. Theories aside, Brackenridge begins to chronicle some of the tensions (as well as the comedies) in that process of inevitable standardization, and to suggest also some of the exclusions it must involve.

The Exposition of Lewis and Clark

Differing from both the high poetic tradition that reaches its neo-logistic peak in Barlow's *Columbiad,* and the more skeptical analysis of language and ethnicity that I have argued to be at the heart of Brackenridge's *Modern Chivalry,* the journals of the expedition of Lewis and Clark to the far west offer a further representation of the state of the language, and one in some ways more prophetic of what was to come than the other texts considered in this chapter.

Meriweather Lewis and William Clark were army officers rather than university men. Although Lewis had been Jefferson's private secretary before taking on the command of the expedition, neither of them were in any formal sense learned, though they were both highly intelligent and even scientifically minded. The orthography of their journals is chaotic and inconsistent, and offers fascinating evidence of the pronunciation of Virginia English in the early nineteenth century. Vowels are highly unstable, dipthongs added or simplified, and certain consonants tend to intrude or disappear. But there is little enough consistency within patricular words to give the lie to the Websterian thesis about the naturally analogizing habits of the untutored speaker.[8] Lewis' entries include such spellings as *thim* for "them," *whin* for "when," *clift* for "cliff," *geathered, intestens,* and *bofore* (May 26, June 13, June 11, June 14, 1805). Clark uses the forms *brackfast, furin* (for "foreign"), and *git* (June

14, November 1, 1805). The troublesome insect that they encountered throughout their journey is almost as protean in its linguistic as in its physical form. I have counted at least four spellings, without doing an exhaustive search, three by Clark and one by Lewis: *musquiters, muskeetors, musquetors,* and *musquetoes* (June 17, September 13, 1804; May 23, June 26, 1805). Metathesis is a common feature of both their styles: thus *perpotion, prosued, pervale,* and *preswaded* (May 25, June 18, 20, 30, 1805).

Perhaps surprisingly, in the deluge of orthographic variations of which the above list is only a tiny sample, both men tend to preserve the Johnsonian *-our* forms in words such as *colour* and *favourable*. Whether this is because they actually sounded the word that way, so that it is in fact a phonetic spelling, or whether it was an especially persistent primary school lesson they both preserve, is hard to say with complete confidence. Websterian *-er* is more common than *-re* in words like *center* (e.g., September 26, 1804); but Clark, who is generally the more linguistically innovative of the two (see Criswell, 1940, p. xxiv), manages to hang on to the *k* in *traffick* (November 1, 4, 1805).

It may be assumed that neither Lewis nor Clark wrote with any degree of linguistic self-consicousness, which makes the journals all the more valuable for what they tell us of the actual state of the language. They include words that had been and would continue to be the subject of learned commentary and debate as Americanisms, for example, *creek, bottom, bluff* (all very common in the journals), and *slay,* their version of *sleigh*. In the naming of new species, of which they did a great deal, Criswell argues that they tended to be conservative, preferring to denominate by way of "a fancied resemblance of a new species to an old" (p. cxxxi). In this respect they are indeed demonstrating the principle that Webster and others had argued as central to the practice of neologism in America; extending the senses of old words to new objects, rather than inventing new words out of nowhere.

The list of innovations recorded by Criswell, consisting of new words and old words used in new ways, is truly staggering, and much longer than anything that could be claimed for any contemporary literary writer. We cannot assume that Lewis and Clark's text had any direct influence on any of the writers who followed them, since the actual publication of the journals was spasmodic and slow (see Jackson, 1961). Some of their spellings give us clues about the pronunciation of at least one form of regional English, though their sense of the relation of letters and syllables to spoken sounds is too unstable for any complete correlation. Their vocabulary, at least, may be taken as typical of that of the intelligent layman in 1805, and it does include many of the Americanisms already defined by the grammarians and dictionary-mongers.

Lewis and Clark are also conceptually significant, for they represent one of the earliest examples of the expansionist vocation, which was soon to become the westward migration. Part men of the Enlightenment, like their patron Jefferson, and thus concerned to describe, measure, and catalogue with scrupulous taxonomic intelligence, they were also (again like their patron) apostles of commerce and forerunners of empire. Both ambitions are transparent in Jefferson's instructions to the expedition (Lewis and Clark, 1953, pp. 481–87). Their transcription of the native American languages they encountered (which was extraordinarily scrupulous) will be discussed in a later chapter. Generally, their behavior was not characterized by any Wordsworthian "wise passiveness" of watching and receiving, and as namers of places they do not give any evidence of the hesitations and ambivalences that mark the English poet's meditations on the relation of nomination and appropriation. Criswell comments noncommittally that in the orgy of naming involved in the expedition, they

> were especially interested in preserving a bond with the known, for were they not naming and describing all these things for a world eagerly awaiting the issue of their voyage and desirous of learning the essential facts about this new country, a world which would understand only in terms of what it already knew? (p. cxix)

Indeed they were, of course. But it is, I think, insufficient to suggest that conscious efficiency of communication is the only habit of mind behind the act of naming. The pilgrims who named the towns and villages of New England after the ones they had left behind in East Anglia and the home counties did not do so to make things clearer for the folks at home; and we must further note the historical and cultural mutability in this process, as evidenced, for example, in the fashion for the *remote* and mysterious that typified some later periods in the nineteenth century.

In fact, many of the names bestowed on the landscape by Lewis and Clark were so rooted in the moment, and in their immediate mnemonic needs, that they have not survived. But, while we must preserve a respect for and a recognition of the disinterested intelligence of these men when it occurs (as it often does), it would be blindness to ignore the degree to which they were also apostles of a particular culture. As such they display some of the connections between power and language that have so preoccupied modern critics and historians. The names that have not often survived are those resulting from timely events or coincidences peculiar to the expedition itself; thus *Elk rappids, birth Creek* (for Clark's birthday), *Panther Creek,* and *rattle snake clifts* (May 26, August 2, 3, 10, 1805). Some of these names have the platitudinous familiarity of modern holiday homes; for example, *Travellers rest* and *camp disappointment* (September 9, 1805; July 26, 1806). But the more significant features of the landscape reveal a more aggrandized and aggressive nomenclature: *Smith's River* is named after the Secretary of the Navy, *Dearborn's River* after the Secretary of War, and *Jefferson's River* has as its two grandiloquent tributaries *Wisdom* and *Philanthropy,* "in commemoration of two of those cardinal virtues, which have so eminently marked that deservedly selibrated character through life" (July 15, 18, August 6, 1805). It is very rare that they show any sense, implicit or otherwise, that such places or features might have been already named; to have done so would indeed have involved challenging their assumption of originality and discovery with the complicated ethics of native rights and prior possession. Such considerations were neither in their mandates nor in their inherited cultural outlook. One of the ironies of the westward migration is that, as we shall see, the fashion for native American words usually appeared well after the natives themselves had been displaced or destroyed. Lewis and Clark's journals, with their western ambiance and their prefiguring of a new phase in the clash of cultures in America, look forward to the Jacksonian period and to a later chapter in this study.

4

1812 Overtures
and Jacksonian Operas

Patriotic Irony: James Kirke Paulding

Historians have argued over who, if anyone, won the War of 1812, but they generally concur in the judgment that the United States certainly did not lose it. The war itself was never a unanimously popular enterprise. Those states committed to a producer economy were more in favor of belligerence than those dependent on the carrying trade. The northeast was still strongly Federalist, and was perceived to differ from the other parts of the republic to the extent that Britain apparently authorized a plan for a separate peace with New England after hostilities had begun.[1]

Leaving aside the military and political ambiguities of the war, commentators on American culture have often concluded that for the spirit of national self-confidence emerging in literature and elsewhere it was a resounding victory.[2] James Fenimore Cooper, for whom nationalism was not an uncomplicated sentiment, felt that 1812 was the important date in the process of achieving *mental* independence. He has John Cadwallader, the main character in *Notions of the Americans* (first published in 1828), explain that

> So far as Europe was concerned, for many years after the peace of 1783, the great mass of the American people saw with English eyes, and judged with English prejudices. This was a fearful position to

122

be occupied by a nation whose policy is so greatly controlled by the influence of public opinion (1832a, 1:312).

This "mental bondage" continued "during the first ten years of the present century" (p. 313), until the War of 1812 relieved America from

> the thraldom of mental bondage. So generally and so forcibly is this truth felt, that while the war of '76 is called the war of the revolution, that of '12 is emphatically termed the war of independence (p. 315).

Cooper here has the authority and perhaps the luxury of hindsight. For we might expect that if the bonds of "mental bondage" were indeed broken once and for all by this particular corporeal war, then the new spirit of the age might have become manifest in the writings on the state and prospects of the national language. In fact, it seems that neither the declaration nor the cessation of hostilities produced anything so unambiguous. Most of the energy in the campaign for literary hegemony seems to have come from the British reviewers, and many of the most extreme American statements came in response to them. James Kirke Paulding's *John Bull and Brother Jonathan* (1812) remains dominantly humorous rather than rancorous in its analysis of the political and cultural tensions between the two countries, which are presented as a larger species of family quarrel. It is the French relative, Beau Napperty, born near "Frogmore" and nurtured under the patronage of "Lewis Baboon," who is held largely responsible for the dispute between father and son (1812, p. 21f.). At the level of language, the United States does not pass unscathed. Jonathan's wife speaks the "confusion of Babel" in the uncertainty of her dictions:

> at one time she talked like a Frogmorean, at another like Bull's wife herself; sometimes she talked crooked like a negro-driver, and very rarely she talked as became Brother Jonathan's wife (p. 62).

The same vacillations can be seen in her dress (pp. 62–63). Paulding's satire is evenhanded, unimpassioned, and deliberately lacking in analytical weight. Squire Bull exiled the New Englanders, we are told, because they liked to "sing psalms through their noses" (p. 90). In their *"cuteness* in making bargains, and *swapping* horses," these same New Englanders exceed in craftiness even the inhabitants of "Oatlands"—that is, the Scots (p. 92). The point is made, but made with a lightness and insouciance all the more notable given Burke's famously intense appeals to the language of fathers and sons some twenty years earlier. Paulding comments

> It is a thousand pities to see father and son fighting and squabbling, when they ought to be a stay and a staff to each other in the troubles of this distracted world. Still, when the father deals out to the son nothing but unkindness, and makes use of his superior power to depress rather than to exalt his offspring, it is not to be wondered at if the ties of relationship are broken forever (p. 134).

Paulding is in agreement with Cooper in that he does not consider these ties to have been definitively broken in 1776. And much of the energy for the breakage seems to have come, as I have implied, from the British reviewers. Charles Jared Ingersoll's anonymously published *Inchiquin's Letters* (1810) is a good example of the spirit of the age in America. Inchiquin is a fictional monk traveling in the United States, and responding to requests from his friends in France to provide confirmation of their derogatory prejudices. These imaginary correspondents want America to adopt French as its language, French being "the most general language of the civilized nations of the world" (1810, p. 18). Inchiquin's reports are far from extravagant in their praise of the state of the nation. He does see in Marshall's *Life of Washington* and Barlow's *Columbiad* two works that are "at least comparable, if not superior" to anything written in Europe since 1776 (p. 80). But the account of Barlow's poem is in fact quite censorious on the subject of neologism; the poem "teems with words that are unusual, technical, and unmusical, without any perceptible reason or apology for their introduction" (p. 89). Ingersoll does support the contention that there are no dialects in the United States, but this was a standard belief; and he further claims that German is the only non-English tongue spoken, and that even this is dying out (p. 105).

Modest as these propositions might now seem, they were enough to bring about a heated exchange in the reviews. The *Quarterly Review* (January 1814) printed a long and hostile account of the book, and takes up among others the topic of the American language, which is "neither native nor foreign, neither English, Scotch, nor Irish, but a mixture of all, made up from bad samples of each (pp. 514–15). It is a language (and a culture) marked by *bundling, tarrying,* and *gouging,* and among those responsible for bringing it into being and publicizing its vocabulary the reviewer attacks Jefferson, Dwight, and Thornton (pp. 517, 522, 528–29).

Timothy Dwight himself replied to this review (see Mencken, 1973, p. 24) and, perhaps because the very same issue of the *Quarterly* contained a brief but damning notice of his parody of Scott, so too did Paulding, again anonymously. Although his rhetoric is highly vitriolic at the expense of the *Quarterly* in general and of Southey in particular, much of Paulding's argument in fact accepts the secondary status of American literature as a matter of historical necessity. Burdened with a language and a tradition held in common with a highly developed nation, American authors are struggling against fate in trying to be original: "They may invent new combinations of events, and new associations of ideas, but they must always think, and talk, and write English," and because of this they can never achieve "the charm of originality" (1815, p. 94). Paulding contends somewhat lamely that "the want of a school of national literature is no argument of a want of original genius" (p. 95), touching on a sensitive pairing that we have encountered before, whereby each was thought necessary for the creation of the other! In his reluctance to embrace a specifically linguistic nationalism, and to employ (as Barlow had employed), consciously American words and Websterian spellings, it often seems that Paulding's regret at being rejected by the parent culture is stronger than any spirit of rebellion in inaugurating a new American alternative. In *The Backwoodsman* (1818) he declared

> Thrice happy he who first shall strike the lyre,
> With homebred feeling, and with homebred fire.

But even as "Europe's ancient honours fade away" (1818, p. 8), there is no sense that homebred feeling should come out in homebred words or inflections. Those words in the poem's vocabulary that are descriptive of distinctly American phenomena—for example, *whip-poor-will, nighthawk, prairies, screech-owl, calumet* (pp. 16, 19, 91, 97)—are of the sort that could also be found in Campbell's *Gertrude of Wyoming* and a host of other British and American precursors; they were part of the decorative literary evocation of the American scene, and not obviously implicated in any strident commitment to Americanisms.[3]

There is no doubt that in the early part of his career Paulding is a nationalist rather than an anglophile, but his nationalism rarely emerges into an extreme or easily identifiable position on doctrinal matters. As a colleague of Washington Irving's in the publication of *Salmagundi,* he might have learned from his more successful peer the usefulness of writing a language relatively devoid of American markers. We have seen that Irving was a great success in the English market. Alternatively, we might choose to explain Paulding's position as that of a natural humorist, able to see the absurdity in all extreme positions, or that of a New Yorker, who was as uncomfortable as Cooper was later to be with the prominence of New England culture and New England speakers within the new nation. None of these explanations for Paulding's comparative reluctance to write an aggressively American English needs to be seen as excluding the others, and we may add to them one more. We have seen that Americanism in speech and populism in politics were closely identified by the more conservative spirits in the Jeffersonian period; and, despite his later career as a Jacksonian democrat, Paulding was just as evasive as we have seen Webster being on the subject of the common man. In *The Backwoodsman* we can see strong traces of a developing nativism, whereby the more recent immigrants are typed as not the sort of people the nation really needs:

> But beggary's now the fashion of the times,
> And paupers hither flock from distant climes;
> Thousands of brawny rogues unblushing stand
> Whining, and lying, cap and crutch in hand,
> Cover'd with dirt, as though e'en water here
> They cannot buy, forsooth—it is so dear!
>   (1818, pp. 71–72)

This image of the poor as idle and deceitful, and essentially poor by their own choice, was a common one in the inherited British rheoric against public relief; and in his strong support of the interests of the employed and the industrious against the apparent challenge of the newly arriving dispossessed, Paulding was not out of step with many other men of his time. The point may then be made, that his defense of an "establishment" in this sense might have made it difficult for him to support a policy of continual development and inclusiveness at the level of the language; perpetual innovation in a sphere as important as that of the language might have seemed all too close to a similar tolerance regarding the social contract of which language was a central constituent.

As I have said, Paulding does not usually commit himself to such unambiguous declarations as the above; more often, the political allusions are framed within a variously complex irony, a play of dramatic voices and perspectives from which the author seems almost to have disappeared. The ironic mode is not however completely incompatible with a polemical direction. If Paulding was indeed the 'Lemuel Lengthy' who wrote to the editors of *The Analectic Magazine* (Irving, Verplanck, and Paulding himself) with an article on Americanisms, then he did make at least one contribution to the language debate in which his affiliations are decidedly anti-British, even if they are at the same time ironic in their linguistic patriotism. The word *lengthy* was, of course, a notorious Americanism. Jefferson had used it (and, according to some, abused the language), and Brockden Brown's *Monthly Anthology* (1800) had included, in both jest and earnest, a piece on 'The Trial and Condemnation of LENGTHY' (3:172–74), claiming the word as a New England coinage and therefore a localism. This being so, any author who uses it "may not offend *one* class of readers," but "he will, by omitting it, please every class" (p. 173). Webster (1806) provocatively gives the word without commenting on the controversy at all.

Such, then, is a sample of the many references that provide the context for the appearance of "Lemuel Lengthy" in 1814. His criticism of the British attitude is pointed:

> Nothing can be more provoking than to see, when one of these critics encounters a "lengthy" or a "progressive," how the wretch begins to grin. He immediately puts it in italics, or posts a tall note of admiration at the end, to allure his readers to come and gaze at this curious transatlantic monster (?Paulding, 1814, p. 404).

"Such is the ingratitude of these people," he goes on, "that I have actually heard an unfeeling assassinator of the king's English rail at the 'ideous habsurdity of the Hamerican abit of speaking' " (p. 405). Lengthy himself maintains that since the Americans have conquered the states, they have also conquered the language, and may if they wish "make a French revolution among the alphabet" (p. 405). He echoes Webster in his sense of the British conviction that "to furnish a nation with books is to hold it in complete subjection," and in his belief that America "ought to have a dialect at least somewhat distinct from all others, as a proof of its independence" (p. 406).

As we might expect from his very name, Lengthy verges on hyperbole in his zeal for a new language. It is unlikely that Paulding himself would have supported a French Revolution in any walk of life, language included. At the same time, we cannot dismiss as comically excessive such declarations as the following:

> We shall never be truly independent, I am afraid, till we make our own books, and coin our own words—two things as necessary to national sovereignty, as making laws and coining money (p. 408).

This view comes with too famous a history and too obvious a logic to be receivable as mere parody. Moreover, such convictions are not in themselves incompatible with the defense of the establishment that appears elsewhere in Paulding's writings. Webster himself had supported Americanisms without endorsing the rights of *every* section of the population to contribute to the language and be thus "represented" within it, and the element of irony in Lengthy's persona certainly contributes to his creator's avoidance of any radically democratic position.

A similar balance is visible in Paulding's later (and again anonymous) *A Sketch of Old England* (1822). Here the persona is that of a New England man traveling in Britain. This figure loudly objects to the spread of prison reforms, "this habit of devoting ourselves to deploring and pampering, instead of stigmatizing and punishing the guilty" (1:85). Even the extreme reactionaries among Paulding's British contemporaries might have blushed at describing the poor house as a palace (1:91). For the *working* poor, Paulding's New Englander has nothing but sympathy. They are the true sufferers, and they are driven to radicalism only by want and hunger: "Give them plenty to eat, and they will lie down as contentedly as a pig in a sty" (1:145). Once again, the irony is hard to decipher with any conviction. It is unthinkable that Paulding would not have known of Burke's famous reference to the "swinish multitude," made back in the early 1790s but taken up and disputed by a whole generation of radicals. It is possible that some satirical presentation of Yankee thrift might be intended here, as well as an invocation of Burke's notorious condescension; but the remark is very much in the spirit of these made in Paulding's own voice in *The Backwoodsman,* so that it is difficult not to conclude that the criticism of Britain, and of the hierarchy and oppression it embodies, is mounted on behalf of industry and self-determination. Britain is here viewed as the prototypical welfare state that is too kind to its dispossessed poor.

This middle-class standard of social behavior in the traveler's implicitly ideal America is also a standard of literature and language. The "expiring phantom of despotism" in Britain is "beginning to be afraid even of American literature, and every effort is made to exclude all republican books, but such as are in a greater or less degree anti-republican" (2:178). But the republicanism that America threatens to export is not to be of the Jacobinical sort, nor is it imaged as a divisive or contested entity. It is represented in the mythologized universality of the common man and his speech habits:

> To one, who in America has been accustomed to hear the commonest people speak with the fluency and almost the correctness of a gentleman, it is intolerable to listen to the *haw-hawing* and *yaw-yawing* of these terribly thick-headed fellows, who, with all their really good qualities, and these are many, are most stupidly deficient in ideas, and possess no language to express the few they have. I long to get among the sprightly, saucy Americans, whose tongues run like mill-tails, and whose brains are the inexhaustible reservoirs that keep the mill-clappers going (1:98).

The true American commoner speaks like a gentleman and embodies in his articulation and inventiveness both the regularity and the ingenuity of a machine. As such, he speaks for a system founded in uninhibited industry and free enterprise. There is no intimation of a linguistic and social differentiation within the body of the people, of the sort we find implied by Brackenridge and analyzed further (I shall argue) by Cooper. The image of the language embodies once again the image of national unity.

Paulding's satirical coherence is much more complete in his *John Bull in America* (1825), which is a very funny parody of a journal kept by an Englishman—specifically, the "writer of American criticisms in the Quarterly" (p. xii)—on a visit to America. Among the outrageous misconceptions that John Bull retails to his British readers, there is, of course, that concerning the state of the language:

> I may as well remark here once for all, that if I make these republicans talk good English in my journal, it is only because it is utterly impossible to reduce their jargon to writing, and if it were, no civilized reader could possibly understand it. There is not a being living, who is a native of the states, that can talk or write English (1825, p. 137).

This is much more obviously absurd than the reverse experience transcribed by the New Englander in England:

> In the various counties, particularly Somerset, Yorkshire, Cumberland, and elsewhere, I give you my honour, not one in a hundred can speak the English language. Were not my servant a sort of booby, who speaks all the languages of this island, except the English, I should be quite at a loss to understand or be understood (1822, 1:63).

It was a truism even among the Anglophiles that British English was much more marked by dialects than American; whereas the degree to which John Bull is obliged to misrepresent the state of things in America is once again an intimation of the increasing sensitivity that the British are feeling about all things American. Earlier in his career, Paulding had cast his own nation as the suffering child of a cruel and unloving parent. By the 1820s, that child is beginning to stand on its own feet and to care less about the grumblings of the declining relative.

Paulding remained alert to the question of the American language, and he was one of the earliest authors to turn to literary account the emerging genre of western "tall talk." *The Raw Kentuckian, or the Lion of the West* (1831), featuring one Nimrod Wildfire, was one of the most popular plays of its day.[4] But he is too much the satirist and humorist ever to emerge as a committed linguistic patriot, as Webster and Barlow were, or to entertain any very searching analysis of the different languages and interest within the United States.

Democracy and Eloquence

The second decade of the nineteenth century also marks the beginning of what has proved to be a continuing tradition of glossaries of American English. There had been word lists before, but nothing consciously systematic. David Humphreys' glossary, which appeared as an appendix to his play *The Yankey in London* (?1815, pp. 103–10; reprinted in Mathews, 1931, pp. 56–61), is itself rather slight. Despite the familiar claim that English "is not generally spoken any where with greater purity than in many parts of America" (p. 12), Humphreys' list exists mostly as a guide to the localisms of his standard New Englander, one Dolittle. So little does the author defend this diction that he points out that the actor playing the role was "merely acting an assumed part," and was in his own person "free from every YANKEE PECULIARITY" (p. 111).

The transcriptions are significant in that they reproduce the famous vowel instabilities in New England speech—*agin, bile, bin, heerd, darter, hull, hum, keow*—as well as its contractions—*cuss, critturs, hoss,* and so on. Dolittle says *ax* for "ask," a usage Webster had authenticated, and uses *lengthy* and *tarnation.* The whole vocabulary, in fact, is close enough to that of Cooper's rustics in *The Pioneers* for us to suspect that Humphreys might have been one of the later writer's sources.

John Pickering's more extensive *Vocabulary* was published in 1816. A largely conservative document, it laments the possibility of an essentially distinct American English, and defends the British reviewers' hostilities on the grounds that they are just as disapproving of the "Scotticisms of their *northern brethren*" (1816, p. 15). Pickering tends to be happy with those reputed Americanisms that he can trace to the best British writers, but others are dismissed as vulgar provincialisms. Webster, never slow to rise to the challenge, responded in a letter (1953, pp. 341–94), also published as a pamphlet (Webster, 1817),[5] in which he takes particular exception to Pickering's alliance with the very British polite speakers who have introduced more corruptions in fifty years "than were ever before introduced in five centuries" (1953, pp. 392–93). Moreover, many common words do not occur in the speech of the upper orders of society. Dryden and Addison, says Webster, might have written ten times as much as they did, without ever needing the words *hub* or *tire,* but this does not make them "illegitimate words" (p. 354). He himself strongly objects to a policy that would have "the young Hercules of genius in America chained to his cradle" by passive obedience to a "foreign press" (pp. 382–83).

Much of Webster's response is a word-by-word refutation of Pickering's entries, but his letter is also a restatement and updating of the convictions about the language that we have already examined. He asserts once again that most neologisms are only reputed such, being derived from British sources, and doubts whether there are "ten words" in the United States that are authentically new (p. 346). But he is a sadder and a wiser man on the subject of spelling reform, lamenting that "error and prejudice" must continue to inhibit the standardization and thus the spread of the English language (p. 373). Webster is not alone in concluding that the project for spelling reform has failed. Writing to John Wilson in 1813, the aging Thomas Jefferson comments wistfully on the power of habit to prevent even positive change, and concludes that we must be "content to follow those who will not follow us" (1903, 13:348). The idealism of the 1790s about rational and radical reform has passed into a quieter hope for what Jefferson calls "small changes at long intervals."

Much the same arguments about American English and its place in an American literature are voiced after 1812 as had been before. On the one hand, John Bristed regrets the spread of the "mouthing, monotonous rant" and *"nasal* twang" of the New Englanders (1818, p. 331); on the other, Timothy Dwight's *Travels in New England and New York,* first published in 1821–22, asserts that there is no such thing as a *dialect* in America (1969, 4:196). Gorham Worth's bombastic (though anonymous) *American Bards* (1819) drew a stinging reply from Robert Waln (1820), in which he once again upbraids the unfortunate Barlow:

> Now BARLOW's muse the sword of Epic girds;
> Domestic manufacturer of words!
> Unnumber'd thoughts in one new word condense,
> And murder English while they murder sense;
> Vapid and harsh the coin'd expressions flow,
> Incorrigibly quick,—obtusely slow (p. 19).

And expansionist idealism continued to sound in Solyman Brown's prospectus for an age free from "the loathsome filth of Scotch reviewers" (1818, p. 24), and marked by a linguistic federation wherein a single language would be heard "from torrid Darien to th' Arctic Pole" (p. 68). Bland as such sentiments might now seem, they were enunciated before the annexations of Texas and California (and Darien, at the present time, still speaks Spanish!).

As the American periodical press expanded and diversified in various and mostly familiar directions (see Cairns, 1898), the utopian strain was not completely absent. Under the chairmanship of John Mason, and with William S. Cardell as the (actively) corresponding secretary, the American Academy of Languages and Belles Lettres was formed in 1821 with the aim of conforming and adjudicating the development of American English.[6] There were no parades through the streets, as there had been for the members of the earlier Philosophical Society of New York. Mason's task was to collect words and phrases charged upon America as "bad English," and to take some "practical course" in response to them (Cardell, 1821, p. 13). The general policy seems to have settled somewhere between the Anglophilia of Pickering and the more aggressive nationalism of Webster. *Circular no. III* (1822) transcribes the enthusiasm of such luminaries as Madison, John Adams, and John Trumbull, with some modest support from Jefferson and some high flown language from Thomas B. Robertson, Governor of Louisiana, extolling the need for new words for which the English, "in their state of stability or stagnation, have no occasion whatsoever" (p. 27). Samuel Latham Mitchill also welcomed the scheme (1821, p. 29), seeing in it a chance to revive his old Fredonian ambitions of 1804. He predicted also a veritable orgy of naming, in which the vitalized world would conspire joyfully in the baptisms of the American Adam:

> Every vegetable will respond to its name, and tell its excellent or noxious qualities. Ores and rocks shall rise from the bottom of the mine and descend from the top of the mountain, and arrange themselves in museums. The species of the animal race shall approach and ask the lord of the soil to notice and know them (p. 34).

Needless to say, this was not to be! The three circulars were all that the academy ever published, and it failed as so many projected academies had failed before it. Edward Everett reviewed the circulars in his *North American Review* (14, 1822, 350–59), finding therein a "colossal organization of officers" and a plethora of grand intentions, "without a single practical hint, that we can fix on, or so much as the project of the plan, by which these objects are to be obtained" (p. 357). At the same time, Everett himself was on the way to becoming an impassioned advocate of the rights of the national language. By 1824, in his Phi-Beta-Kappa *Oration,* he was looking forward to America expanding "with a pace more like romance than reality," and with the national language in the vanguard of the process (Blau, 1946, p. 87).[7]

Cardell stayed in the field rather longer than the academy of which he was the secretary. He published his *Essay on Language* in 1825, and a *Grammar* in 1826. This last, although it never challenged the hegemony of Murray, was in its fourth edition by 1828. The argument of the *Essay* is a conventional nominalistic one, according to which language is the chief means of mental cultivation for both individual and society. And it takes a conventionally patriotic turn. Since "we have no account of any nation, a prime object of whose government was to diffuse instruction among the entire body of their people," America represents a unique forum for the development of a "national language" (1825, p. 30). The argument is Tookean in its preference for seeing all verbs as implicitly transitive and active, and for relating as many words as possible to sensible objects. While a conformity of the spoken to the written would indeed be desirable, it is not to be expected given "the imperfection of human skill" (p. 42).

After Cardell's rather moderate arguments, John Sherman's *Philosophy of Language* (1826), promising in its very title to be "wholly divested of scholastic rubbish," comes as something of a shock! In his democratical gestures, Sherman goes well beyond even the infamous Horne Tooke. His patriotism verges on sheer rant: "I thank God, that I live in a country whose forefathers were driven to a wilderness, because they were *innovators.* I thank God, that I am a citizen of a Republick . . . which had its birth in *innovation*" (p. 7). In a voice that almost makes Walt Whitman appear modest, Sherman speaks of an "atmosphere of unadulterated liberty" that "feeds with electric fire the energies of genius" and "bursts asunder the shackles of barbarous domination" (p. 16).

The true legislators of the language are not the grammarians but the "multitude": "as well may the starcht philologist attempt to arrest them, as for kings or nobles to stem the tide of popular revolution" (pp. 147–48). Spurning not only Murray and Cardell, but also Tooke and Webster—"let me be anything rather than an Anglo-Saxon etymologist" (p. 146)—Sherman takes on the "filth and rubbish of long accumulated absurdity," his only weapons the "spade, the pickaxe, and the crowbar" of the "full blooded labourer" (p. 293). There is much that is disingenuously hyperbolic about this posture of the grammarian as humble laborer, and the whole argument has the flavor of the extravagant democratism that would come to typify the political rhetoric of the Jacksonian era. Sherman's populism is romantic and impulsive, quite different from the cool, idealist rationalism of the men of the Enlightenment. It has its limits, moreover. The use of the subjunctive is dismissed because the "great multitude" does not use it, but the egalitarian motive here is somewhat compromised by the author's comparing it scornfully to *the lingo of Negroes* (pp. 198, 200). The great multitude seems once again to exclude some language users, as it had so often done before.

Sherman's book prefigures a style and posture that would become, in various forms, much more popular from the late 1820s onward, and that would prove to be a cause of grave concern to many of the more sober intellects, Fenimore Cooper among them. The degree to which the rhetoric of populism was ever genuinely expressive of the needs of all the people is arguable, to say the least. At the same time, it is one symptom of the confident patriotism that allowed Cooper, in 1828, to look back at the War of 1812 as the true war of independence. Perhaps a similar hindsight assisted the publication, in 1827, of Richard Emmons' *The Fredoniad,* the "Epick Poem" of the War of 1812, and a late flowering of Mitchill's ambition for a new name for the nation—this despite Pickering's assertion that such "extraordinary words" as "Fredonian" are "never now used in the United States, except by way of ridicule" (1816, p. 94), and the word's complete absence from Webster's 1828 *Dictionary* (which does however give the Saxon word *fred*). Emmons' poem is largely a Miltonic-Homeric account of the various battles of the war, with little beyond the obvious ulterior moralizing, least of all on the subject of language. A Kentuckian publishing in Boston, Emmons apologizes for having been unable to read over the proof sheets. Perhaps the Johnsonian spellings that abound in his text are to be read as the revenge of a Bostonian typesetter!

Leaving aside such texts as Sherman's *Philosophy of Language,* the terms of the debate about the national language are familiar enough. *The North American Review,* founded in Boston in 1815, printed Walter Channing's plea for a national literature (Channing, 1815), but its general policy was judiciously middle of the road, combining what C. J. Ingersoll (1823, p. 19) called a "pure, old English style" with its "American spirit." Barlow's *Columbiad* is still being censured in 1821 (*NAR,* 13:20–47),[8] and Cogswell's review, in *NAR* (15, 1822, 224–50) of Schoolcraft's *Narrative Journal* is passionately critical of all "sin against the King's English," declaring that it would be better to vote out the language completely rather than to carry on corrupting it (p. 248). Even among the more overtly Democratic journals, linguistic patriotism was relatively restrained.[9]

The British periodical press was itself divided along political lines, with the *Westminister Review* generally sympathetic to America, and the *Quarterly* and the *Edinburgh* less so. The former even took Irving to task for being insufficiently American in his affection for old-world institutions.[10] Thus, Irving was a favorite with the Tories (Cairns, 1922, pp. 58–111). But in whatever political guise, Americans had to put up with seeing the names of their writers misspelled: thus, for example, "Erving" and "Paulsen."

Among the major writers, most seem to have followed Isaac Candler's advice (1824, p. 332) not to reject "the authority of those standard authors whose works are common property." Timothy Flint's writings produce a modest list of Americanisms (see Krumpelmann, 1969), but not until his frontier novels of the 1830s did Irving begin to transcribe them (see Kime, 1967). Moreover, a text such as that of *Astoria* is so derivative that it is hard to be sure about which elements of its vocabulary to attribute to Irving himself. John Neal's articles for *Blackwood's Magazine* (1824–25) are not at all concerned to publicize an American language, although his own novel, *Brother Jonathan* (1825), is full of American locutions, signalled by italics or speech marks for the benefit of the British reader. This narrative of 1776 is notable chiefly for its parading of various American speech habits and colorful "ethnic" personalities. Neal could hardly have failed to be aware that he was providing his British readers with a good deal of material for ridiculing the New England and Virginia dialects. Despite the case made recently by Benjamin Lease (1981, pp. 51–68) for Neal's patriotic credentials, his representation of American speech is carried to the point of parody. Thus Edith Cummins is "a 'smart', whimsical Virginia girl; the prettiest one, though, 'by all accounts', there 'was a goin', as everybody 'allowed' " (1:10). In a similar spirit, Neal purports to scan the Yankee speech, famous for its irregular stress patterns: "$h\bar{e}$ nĕver, $s\bar{o}$ mŭch, $\bar{a}s$ tŭrns, $h\bar{\imath}s$ nŏse— $n\bar{o}t$ hĕ, $t\bar{o}$ bĕ sŭre" (1:159). The pages of the novel abound with such typographical calls to attention, but they are not accompanied by any apparent valuation of the claims of an American English.

In poetry, the most important newcomer on the American scene in the decade or so after 1812 was William Cullen Bryant. In the context of the American language, Bryant began and ended a conservative, however original he might or might not have been for the tradition of American lyric poetry. It is one of the ironies of the history of the language that the reputed coiner of the memorable expression "to bite the dust" would probably have defended it (with complete credibility) as the proper translation of the passage in *The Iliad* that occasions its first appearance, in 1870.[11] Thus, we see the Homeric origins of the countless long, tall strangers who would walk the landscape of the American West.

Bryant began his literary career as a precocious thirteen-year-old with *The Embargo* (1808), a satire on Jefferson's policy of restraining American commerce as a sympathetic gesture to the French in their war against England. It is an overtly Federalist tract, seeking to expose "a weak ruler's philosophic dreams" (p. 4). A year later it went into a second edition, prefaced by the familiar cry that "*faction* and *falsehood* exert themselves with increasing efforts to accelerate the downfall of our country" (1809, p. 5). We would not expect any great enthusiasm for a national language in a context such as this!

Around 1818, Bryant seems to have drawn up a "dictionary" of the New York dialect (since discovered among his papers), but there is no evidence confirming its mood or intention. The list contains only about thirty words, and most of these are transcribed to indicate pronunciation, rather than standing forth as new words of American origin; thus Bryant lists *pome* for "poem" and *potry* for "poetry" (see Bryant, 1941). His own volume of *Poems,* often cited as the origin of significant American verse, was a small paper-bound volume of forty-four pages, published in Cambridge, Massachusetts, in 1821. It was the antithesis of Barlow's splendid *Columbiad* in more ways than one. Of the eight poems in the book, only "The Ages" has epic rather than lyric pretensions, and in none of them is there so much as a word that would have registered to a contemporary reader as a recent Americanism. We find *mocasin* [*sic*] and *snow-shoe* (p. 35), but these had seventeenth-century origins and had become familiar even in the language of British poets. It is perhaps a mark of Bryant's excessive caution in this respect that *battle-axe* replaces the expected *tomahawk* (p. 22).

As he wrote, so was he reviewed, even by the British magazines. No one complained of any impurities in his diction, though some wondered why he bothered to call himself an American at all (see Cairns, 1922, pp. 158–64). Bryant found favor with the same audience that was rewarding Irving, though his poetry does not take as clear a side in the political debate as does some of Irving's prose. There seems little evidence of the need to challenge Mencken's view (1973, p. 78) that Bryant was "essentially a conformist" in the realm of language, and this despite the fact that he was perceived as a radical later in his career, in terms of the sentiments he espoused. Once again, we may observe that, with the notable exception of Barlow, poetry seems to have proved even less receptive than prose to the proliferation of Americanisms and to the analysis of American English. Thus, it is somewhat ironic that Bryant has so often been canonized as the first American poet. His lyricism and romanticism certainly fit in with the received idea of what American literature was to become, but he is still writing an impeccably correct version of the language of the parent culture. A separate self is being sung, indeed, but sung in a received language.

There would, of course, be much more to say of Bryant, and especially of the later Bryant, in any complete account of his career as a writer or as a patriot. But we may see in the 1821 *Poems* an example of a reticence that is not merely personal to a young and unestablished poet. It belongs also to a culture, one that is at once conscious of the weight of an inherited tradition and also somewhat suspicious of aesthetic writing itself. Madame de Staël, in *The Influence of Literature Upon Society,* first published in America in 1813, had queried the role of "literary" writing in a republican society that should properly commit itself to a "manly eloquence" and an "independent philosophy" (1847, p. 13). American writers should follow the lead of American magistrates in declaring "simple truth and pure sentiments" (p. 68). Aesthetic complexity is suspicious, because it cannot be understood by all, and because it has traditionally been employed in the flattery of tyrants.

De Staël here enunciates what had already become a telling truism for many American authors, aware that the written word ought to be useful before it is attractive, and comprehensible rather than complex. Robert Ferguson, in his important study of the role of law in letters during this period, has shown how this suspicion of the literary might go so far as to discredit writing itself as a less immediate and thus socially cohesive medium than speech (1984, pp. 77–84). Daniel Webster, Ferguson shows (pp. 207–40), built a career around such tensions. But if speech proclaims itself more immediate than writing, it also threatens to free itself (especially when the norms are forensic ones) from the test of private adjudication and rational judgment in the reader's own time. By exploiting the heat of the moment, the speaker can often get away with more than the writer. As the century progresses, we can see a developing concern with the demogogic potential of this privileging of the spoken word.

Versions of the "Common" Language

Very little of the political imagination of the United States in the 1820s and 1830s seems to have been focussed on critical questions of foreign policy. It was a period of westward expansion and internal tension. Expansion, as we have seen in the example of the Lewis and Clark expedition, might be seen as the natural historical and demographic corollary of a favorable view of neologism. New places and new things need new names, or new applications of old ones. Our old friend *Fredonia* was invoked once again in the quarrels over land grants in East Texas in the late 1820s (see Billington, 1962, p. 117), but by 1845 Texas was part of the Union, and much of the rest of the west soon followed.[12] The notion that the language should not expand must have seemed especially untenable at a time when the nation itself was doing so at such a spectacular rate.

With such exceptions as Poe, whose vocabulary may be credibly studied without any mention of Americanisms (see Fletcher, 1973, pp. 63–84), many writers of the period do display a moderate linguistic nationalism in their approval of a number of new words, and new objects of attention. They were not generally defenders of anything resembling a "common" style, but they were definitely prepared to introduce patriotic gestures into their fastidiously correct prose. The so-called "skylark" campaign provides a good instance of this. Reviewing a reprint of Sidney's *Defense of Poetry* in *NAR* (34, 1832, 56–78), Longfellow demands that American poetry become "more national" and bear on it "the stamp of national character" (pp. 69, 70). Poets should write "from the influence of what they see around them," so

> let us have no more sky-larks and nightingales. For us they only warble in books. A painter might as well introduce an elephant or a rhinoceros into a New England landscape (p. 75).

In the same year of 1832, William Cullen Bryant sent the same message to his brother John, who had himself written lines on the skylark, pointing out that the "skylark is an English bird, and an American who has never visited Europe has no right to be in raptures about it" (cited in Spencer, 1957, p. 86). Thoreau and others said their pieces, and the poetic propriety of catbirds and whip-poor-wills became a minor talking point.[13] In revising *The Last of the Mohicans* for the 1831 London edition, Cooper added a footnote remarking that the "powers of the American mocking-bird are generally known," and claiming that the songs of both catbird and ground-thresher are "superior to the nightingale or the lark, though, in general, the American birds are less musical than those of Europe" (1983, p. 187). The mocking bird is applauded again in *The Oak Openings* (p. 305), and in *The Water-Witch* Cooper makes fun of the gullible Dutchman who builds platforms for storks' nests on his chimneys, and who could never understand that there was "no such bird in America" (p. 81).[14]

The skylark campaign was, of course, no very radical challenge to the good humor of any of the parties involved. Few even among the staunchest Anglophiles had ever doubted that American poems could properly record American objects, as long as general purity of diction and conventional standards were preserved. Even the fastidious Washington Irving was, in the 1830s, sufficiently carried away by the westward migration to write three "prairie" novels in which, according to Kime (1967), no less than fifty-one words are recorded in *DAE* as first used therein. Even Wordsworth had made reference to the "merry Mockingbird" and "melancholy Muccawiss" (*The Excursion,* 3:946–47).

Americanisms had then become a relatively stable part of the literary as well as the common language by the outset of the Jacksonian period. Arguments continued to occur, of course, and even when they were the same old arguments, they meant different things in a new context. To approve an American vernacular in 1840 meant something very different from the same approval in 1800. The most famous linguistic controversy of the period 1828–50 was surely the dictionary war between Webster and Worcester and their publishers. I have space here only for a very brief account.

Webster's great two-volume *American Dictionary* appeared in 1828.[15] Not least because of its size and sheer professionalism—Webster claimed a vocabulary of seventy thousand words, an increase of twelve thousand over the latest edition of Todd-Johnson—this is a much less aggressively nationalistic work than its 1806 predecessor. Even where arguments are repeated verbatim, they are diluted by the extra quantity of material. Webster likes to cite American writers, but dilutes his earlier Saxonism and considerably diminishes his debt to Horne Tooke (1831, p. xlii). Americanisms and republican principles continue to be defended, but this case sits together with an acceptance of the biblical account of the origin and dissemination of languages.[16]

In general, the reception of the *Dictionary* was much less divided than that of Webster's earlier thoughts on language. The old Federalist party, with its often passionate Anglophilia, was dead, and America had perhaps survived enough crises of its own to feel confident of its identity as a nation. Fastidious British travelers continued to complain about the state of the language. Basil Hall (1830), Captain Marryat (1839), and the notorious Fanny Trollope, whose remarks were quite frankly designed to disprove the wisdom of "placing all the power of the state in the hands of the populace" (1832, p. iii), all spoke their minds, and were answered in kind. Paul Paterson's anonymous *Playfair Papers* (1841) presents American diction as an outlandish lingo, and Dickens' *American Notes* (1842) and *Martin Chuzzlewit* (1843–44) were famously negative.[17] But the British were already starting to fight the rearguard action against the importation of Americanisms that has continued to this day. Coleridge used *reliable* in 1800 and *influential* in 1833; Bentham committed the word *lengthy* in 1816 (Mencken, 1973, p. 267); and Tennyson uses *bluff* in the notorious American sense in section 103 of "In Memoriam," a poem that was to console Queen Victoria herself.

Even where Webster's views had not been modified through the passing of time, as they mostly had, they thus fell on more receptive ears in 1828 than they had done in 1800. The *Encyclopaedia Americana* (1829–33) spoke up for the linguistic rights of a "free, industrious and thinking people" (1:211), and Robley Dunglison (1829–30) made much the same case in his supplement to Pickering's 1816 *Vocabulary*. Theodoric Romeyn Beck was still speaking the old Federalist language in 1830, arguing that the "standard writers of a language are, like the guardians of a well-ordered state, its preservers from anarchy and revolution" (p. 25). But his attempt to remind Americans that their language was a *"derived* one" and their literature a *"foreign* one" (pp. 26–27) must have fallen on many deaf ears. Samuel Lorenzo Knapp argued that America had kept the language "unpolluted and unchanged" (1829, p. 9), and Peter du Ponceau echoes Webster's prospectus for American English free of the "barbarisms" introduced in England by the "second Norman invasion" of the language (1834, pp. 33, 36). Against the extremists on all sides, "Borealis" (1836) offers a judicious middle ground in which neither the "entirely Britannic" nor the exponents of a "pye-bald dialect" (p. 110) should be encouraged.

Why then was there a dictionary war at all? Joseph Emerson Worcester, the challenger, had published a composite dictionary (Todd-Johnson-Walker) in 1828, in which he generally defended the norms of metropolitan London, albeit with the demurral that the retaining of *-ick* endings seemed now to savour of "affectation or singularity" (1828, pp. xi, xv). He does include an appendix of Americanisms (pp. 1035–53), but tends to follow Pickering rather than Webster here. Worcester's next work was an 1829 edition (more words, less etymology) of Webster 1828, though the additions were supposedly of the sort licensed by Webster himself (see 1830b, p. iii). There followed a forty-three thousand word dictionary based on Webster (who is generously acknowledged) and others, and in which the credibility of the London standard is very much lessened (1830a, pp. xiii–xiv). The *-or/-our* crux is now resolved in favor of the modern American norm, and Worcester goes even further than Webster in giving *frolic, mimic,* and *traffic* without the final *k* (oddly preserved in Webster).

Webster promptly accused Worcester of plagiarism, so that the appearance, in 1846, of Worcester's *Universal and Critical Dictionary* was bound to be controversial. Despite continued agreement on many issues, Worcester here prefers *centre* over *center* and *traveller* over *traveler,* as well as some other elements of the London standard (pp. xxii, xxvii). He also prefers to cite British authors, even at the expense of Americans of "higher respectability," in order to assure his readers that "respectable English authority" can be found for doubtful words (p. v), and aggressively disavows having taken anything at all from Webster.

Thus the war was on, carried on by Webster's publishers (Webster himself died in 1843) through the 1850s and 1860s.[18] Commercial rivalry was clearly the dominant motive in this war over words, but once again we should not ignore the substantial implications. Webster's dictionary *was* more American than Worcester's, and the struggle for literary-economic hegemony between Britain and America was still very much alive. It was not until 1891 that Congress finally authorized reciprocal copyright arrangements with foreign nations; until then native authors continued to be at a disadvantage against pirated and cheaper editions of British writers.[19] Worcester's concessions to Websterian policies really speak for a consensus about American English, but some shots still remained to be fired; and it was far from true that there had been established in America an economically secure class of writers who could use that language.

The above must suffice as a brief account of the quarrels between the dictionary makers. Their version of a common language was, of course, always as much prescriptive as descriptive. The literature of the Jacksonian period is dominated by James Fenimore Cooper and his followers. (A reading of Cooper will be the subject of the next chapter.) Among the followers, who are too numerous to be dealt with here in any satisfying detail, we may notice an almost obligatory interest in dialect speech, and in the identity of the American Indian, as the Native American was called. In such instances as Paulding's *Konigsmarke* (1823) the fashion for historical novels is treated with more than a measure of irony. But Paulding's deliberate disruption of the historical illusion is untypical of the period. At the same time as the vernacular speech is widely represented in the fiction of the period, it is not, however, in any simple sense endorsed. The tall talk of "Roaring Ralph" Stackpole and the habits of the various Quakers, New Englanders, Kentuckians, among a host of others who populate the pages of Robert Montgomery Bird's *Nick of the Woods* (1837), are never allowed to escape from the control of the fastidious narrator and his hero, who preserve a decorum that is at once linguistic and social. A. B. Longstreet, who was doing for Georgia very much what Bird was doing for Kentucky, prefaces the first edition of *Georgia Scenes* with a reminder to those taking exception at

> the coarse, inelegant, and sometimes ungrammatical language, which the writer represents himself as occasionally using; *that it is language accommodated to the capacity of the person to whom he represents himself as speaking* (1835, p. iv).

The transcriptions of dialect are very convincing, not least for the degree to which they overlap with the conventional representations of New England speech (Georgia having been settled largely by New Englanders); but there is no sense in which they are endorsed as a desirable standard. The same may be said of William Gilmore Simms, Cooper's follower in South Carolina. We may be instructed about regional speech, but we are for the most part also invited to register some amusement at its features.[20] In poetry also, the American vernacular usually appears as part of an ironic purpose, as in the writings of N. P. Willis (*pace* Shulman, 1948), or in Lowell's famous *Biglow Papers* (1848). Serious poetry by the likes of Longfellow and Whittier does not seem committed to an American English, dialect or not. Even Bryant, who was by 1830 regarded by Edward Everett as "poisoned with the gall of Jacksonism" (Schlesinger, 1946, p. 186), chose not to depart from the purity of style that we have remarked in the 1821 *Poems*.

In the writings of Brackenridge, above all, I have argued for a represented relation between different "languages" or dialects and the sociological tension in the early American community. It does not seem that the sense of crisis was any slighter in the 1830s than it had been in 1800. It was perhaps even greater. The nation was geographically larger, the electorate even more volatile, universal suffrage was being proclaimed, and for many of the conservatives and supporters of the national bank, who formed the mainstream of the opposition to Jackson and Van Buren, the specter of a bloody social revolution was just as evident as it had been to the men of 1800. If anything, the discourse of class confrontation was more developed than it had been before. The working men's movement was afoot, and was supported by a coherent rhetoric, and Loco-focoism was established both inside and outside the Democratic party. We might then wonder why the representation of dialect or common usage seems to have been less of an issue than it had once been, and why the panic about "wigwam words" seems to have been relatively absent. Why are the same questions that prompted passionate debates in 1800 now tending to call forth responses that take the form of humorous distractions wherein confrontations are either displaced or only very gently intimated?

It is hard to offer a conclusive answer to such a question, but some suggestions may be made. Obviously, the spirit of the age had moved further away from the typical Enlightenment equation of language with mind and culture; the revolutions of 1848 did not have the same implications for theorists of the language as had that of 1789. Perhaps more important, in the years preceding the election of William Henry Harrison in 1840, the new conservatives (now called whigs) began to take over the rhetoric of populism that had hitherto worked so well for the Jacksonians and the radicals. According to Schlesinger (1946, pp. 269–305), the whigs began to realize that Jackson's campaigns had profited considerably by a popular interest, or at least a populist rhetoric, that could no longer be ignored. The way to fight Jackson was not to stand forth on the explicitly argued doctrines of a necessary elitism, as the old Federalists had done, but rather to begin to claim that the whigs themselves were the genuine party of the people. Thus, an explicit recognition of class distinctions and differences of interest, in Federalist discourse, is replaced by a disingenuous rhetoric of equality in which there are no workers and no employers, and in which all have the same interests and the same opportunity for profit and progress. Thus was born that enduringly vague entity and smoke-screen for a multitude of political priorities, the American people.

If Schlesinger is right, then the election of 1840 might well have signaled the end of a European-style political discourse in America, one based on clearly confessed and argued differences of interest and opportunity. Such a discourse has certainly never been success-fully re-established, and its absence is very obvious in the political language of America today. The effects of this development on the language and literature must have been significant. The defender of patrician values can no longer afford to look down on the political and linguistic initiatives of the people, whatever he may really be-lieve in his heart; he is now obliged to pretend to be one of them, as every candidate for office has since done. Outbursts against im-propriety must have tended to become increasingly counterproduc-tive in a world committed to the image of absolute equality. The task of the conservative was then clear: to increase the appearance of popular affiliation while maintaining the fact of continued social control. The politician is obliged to become, in a very simple sense, dishonest.

The vernacular speech of the common man had never been of-fered as any kind of ideal model for a national speech. In the con-text of the above situation in the Jacksonian era, we might specu-late that the maintenance of the linguistic hierarchy becomes even more important because the *image* of the acceptability of the ver-nacular has to be more thoroughly developed. Not only must all factions now support Americanisms in the official language; they can no longer afford to present the speech of the lower orders (usu-ally dialect) as improper, ridiculous, or sociologically charged. Hence the appeal of *humor,* which may be always on the edge of a belittling satire without quite settling into it. And, if both ends of the political spectrum are now speaking the same language, that of the "people," we can no longer make any easy assumptions about the political affiliations of the writers who represent it. On the one hand, no writer or speaker can be assumed to be of the people just because he sends out populist signals in the form of racy idioms and dialect words, as Emerson and Whitman were to do. On the other hand, no one who chooses not to invoke such a style should be defined without closer inspection as a conservative or an aristocrat. The rhetoric of the Jacksonian period, both political and fictional, has thus to be studied very carefully indeed. As an example of the political, we may take the first volume of the *United States Magazine and Democratic Review,* which attracted the efforts of many of the progressive writers of the period, and made all the right noises about freeing America from the shackles of "such an utterly anti-democratic social system" as the British (1:14).[21] But in its faith in "our industrious, honest, manly, intelligent millions of freemen" (p. 2) it made "legislation . . . the fruitful parent of nine-tenths of all the evil, moral and physical, by which mankind has been afflicted since the creation of the world" (p. 6). Here, it must be seriously questioned whether the ideology of minimal government, of "getting government off the backs of the people," to use a modern rubric, is conceivably an adequate *popular* proposal at a time when a rapidly developing manufacturing economy is introducing stronger than ever differences of interest and opportunity between some people and others. Lack of restraint is all very well as long as all have the same limits and the same opportunities; if they do not, then it becomes part of the rhetoric of oppression.

In the sphere of fiction, the increased popularity of colloquialism after 1830 has been studied by Edwin Ray Hunter (1925) and by Kenneth Lynn (1959), who has argued that the vernacular style began in the fiction of the southwestern frontier as something carefully subordinated to the control of the polite narrator, but then came to claim more attention for itself as the people who spoke it became more politically important. In accepting this useful argument, we must, however, always remember that literature presents an image of life, never the thing itself. These images call for very careful explanation, especially if opposing political interests really did decide, sometime in the 1830s, to use the same language. Tocqueville, whose remarks on language may in some sense be derived from his visit to America in 1831, noted that a democracy will tend to display a literary style that is loose, vigorous, "vehement and bold" (1945, 2:62–63).[22] In his account of the language of democracy (2:68–74), he cautioned against the tendency toward the proliferation of abstractions, which are "like a box with a false bottom; you may put into it what ideas you please, and take them out again without being observed" (p. 74). The vaguer the term, the more unlikely it is that any member of an audience or readership might take exception to it: each will simply interpret it in ways most convenient to himself. At a time when American English was well enough established for *Webster's Pronouncing Dictionary* to appear in the British market, albeit with the omission of some "localisms and obsolete vulgarities" (1856, p. v),[23] the English spoken by Americans to each other was conforming more and more to the image of a common language. The plight of anyone outside that image, or anyone suspicious of its coherence, would now become all the more difficult for anyone inside the consensus to understand. Of all the writers of the period, none is more sensitive to the implications of this development than James Fenimore Cooper.

5

The Languages
of Cooper's Novels

Cooper on the State of the Language

It is almost truistic to declare that the publication of *Precaution* in 1820 marked the inauspicious beginning of the most distinguished literary career in America so far. Over the next thirty years Cooper published more than thirty novels as well as other occasional works on historical and political subjects. A professional author in the fullest sense of the word, Cooper was also a patriot—no easy achievement at a time when the copyright laws were making life very difficult for American authors in general, and especially for those whose writings did not conform as comfortably to the needs of the British readership as did those of Washington Irving. Cooper's patriotism was complex and never hyperbolic, so that it was misunderstood on both sides of the Atlantic. His faith in the glorious political future of America took a severe shock in the 1830s, from experiences both personal and national. But the accusations of "aristocracy" that were lodged against him by his political enemies in the last fifteen years of his life, while not completely unjust, yet partake far too glibly of the political shorthand that was coming to characterize the rhetoric of the times, as it had characterized the turbulent years around 1800. After a close reading, Cooper's apparent ideological transition can be made to seem just that: apparent. As with so many writers of his times, he is often best understood as a mixture of ideological impulses, not always coherent one with another.[1]

Cooper wrote travel books and treatises in which American English is discussed explicitly, and we can also arrive at a sense of his linguistic personality from a perusal of the scrupulously edited modern text of his letters and journals (Cooper, 1960–68). These writings are a useful introduction to the image of language in the novels, even as they do not exhaustively predict the complexities of that image. *Notions of the Americans* (1828), *The American Democrat* (1838), and *Gleanings in Europe: England* (1837) all comment in some detail on the relation of American to British English. In *Notions,* most of these comments come in the dramatic voice of the patriotic Cadwallader, who expounds the rather Websterian case that America has an "equal right" to the language, that its speakers have neither the localisms nor the "slang of society" that infects Britain, and that it will eventually produce a literature that will be "felt with a force, a directness, and a common sense in its application, that has never yet been known" (1832a, 1:323, 327; 2:122). Cadwallader upholds the notion of the rationalizing tendency of common usage (2:122–36), and explains the New England dialect as a result of "the intelligence of its inhabitants" (p. 132), who tend to conform the spoken to the written even where the conventions are otherwise.

Cooper's task as an apologist or at least a publicist of American English does not stop with Cadwallader's remarks. The narrator himself uses conscious Americanisms, and not all of them are explained. Words like *canvas-back, live-oak,* and *bottoms* in the distinctly American sense defined by Webster 1828 occur without gloss (1:137, 2:75, 1:248). Otherwise, words are italicized to make clear their novelty, for example, *blazed* and *cradle* (2:4, 116), or (more often) glossed in some detail for the benefit of the British reader. Among the latter class are *stage* (i.e., "stage coach"), *fall, slips, stoop, lumber-men, store, "new countries," logging, worm fence* and *long fence, polls, creek, mess, caucus* (as a place of meeting), and *patroon* (1:68, 87, 115, 149–50, 243, 246, 254, 255, 256, 257; 2:10, 23, 18, 50).

The tone of *England,* where Cooper speaks in his own voice, is more measured (see Spiller, 1928–29), but maintains the case for the "purest English" as that spoken in New Jersey, Maryland, and

Delaware (1982, p. 11). However, this time the standard is that of the very best *British* speech, which more Americans than Britons happen to be able to achieve. The best British speakers cannot be rivaled, and their women have more pleasing voices! (pp. 96, 270). But he does not care for the British "coldness" (p. 142), nor for the rhetoric of parliament, which he calls the "cheering and coughing system; or, perhaps it were better now to term it the *bah-ing* system" (p. 111). Aimed at an American reader, this volume now seeks to explain British speech, as *Notions* had explained the American. Vocabulary and pronunciation are transcribed (pp. 16, 69–70, 134), and on two occasions Cooper uses the telling word *Anglicism* (pp. 170, 267), as if to make the point that there is no one standard from which all *isms* are to be derived!

Cooper does not here uphold any faith in "reason" as the arbiter of language reform (p. 96), as Cadwallader had done; and he scoffs at

> a puerile and a half-bred school of orthoepists in America who, failing in a practical knowledge of the world, affect to pronounce words as they are spelt, and who are ever on the rack to give some sentimental or fanciful evasion to any thing shocking. These are the gentry that call Hell Gate, Hurl Gate, and who are at the head of the *rooster* school (p. 70).

Cooper here approves neither of spelling reform nor of the Websterian commitment to euphemism, preferring the aristocratic vulgarity of Hell Gate to the middle-class piety of the substitution.

The American Democrat, first published in 1838, has a whole chapter on language (1969, pp. 171–77). While Cooper's faith in the high quality of the average speaker is preserved, the great concern of this volume in general, and of its analysis of language in particular, is with the abuse of eloquence in a democracy. In the spirit of Toqueville, Cooper notes "an ambition to effect, a want of simplicity, and a turgid abuse of terms" (p. 171). The case for innovation and neologism is now more precisely circumscribed: "In all cases in which the people of America have retained the *things* of their ancestors, they should not be ashamed to keep the *names*" (p. 175). The orthography of this volume, published in Cooperstown, is almost as chaotic and inconsistent as were the texts of 1776 examined at the beginning of this study. The coexistence of *-ick* and -*or* endings (with some deviations) suggests that Cooper's typesetter was not much concerned with the Webster-Johnson controversy, and the evidence of the *Letters and Journals* confirms that Cooper himself was a poor speller, as he well knew in writing to Goodrich, the publisher of *Precaution,* confessing that "My writing is so bad and I am so very careless with it that unless great care is taken with the printing and orthography—the Book will be badly gotten up" (1968, 1:44), as indeed it was. He later declares that "In future I shall not notice the spelling at all—leaving it solely for you—unless a proper name occurs spelt wrong" (1:60).

Orthographically speaking, Cooper's was a somewhat bewildered imagination. In those letters (in the modern edition) reprinted from holograph rather than from newspaper or other printed sources, the first ten years or so of Cooper's career show him as opting generally for -*ick* endings, though there is no evidence that he was consciously following Johnson. There is more indeterminacy over the choice between -*or* and -*our*. He usually prefers the first, but in the travel journals of 1828 *our* tends to become more common, perhaps under the European influence. The Websterian *theater* goes along with the rather outmoded *controul,* though they are nine years apart (1:399, 58), and Cooper consistently spells -*cei* as -*cie* (e.g., *recieve, concieve*), a habit he never quite conquered and one that demonstrates, incidentally, a rationalizing instinct at work in his own practice, even as he denies its incidence elsewhere! In the very year of publication of *The Pioneers,* its author was indulging in such spellings as *Secratary* and *responsabillity* (1:105–6).

It seems that Cooper was not deliberately disregarding such orthographic decisions, which had by the 1820s of course become political talking points in both Britain and America, but that he was too generally unsure of his spelling to be making any fine discriminations. This is, as we shall see, conformable to the linguistic policy implicit in the range of his writings, wherein spelling is presented as considerably less important than neologism in the definition of American English. His own confusion was to continue. Writing to President Andrew Jackson in 1832, he juxtaposes *labor* and *labour* in the same letter (2:234–35). He uses the forms *defense* and *staid* (for "stayed"), both sanctioned in Webster 1806, but at the same time declares himself disinterested on the matter of whether British or American spellings are to be printed in his novels. Sending the corrected proofs of *The Bravo* to Colburn and Bentley in 1831, Cooper still professes to "pay no attention to any of the spelling, except in words of particular signification and proper names" (2: 93). He notes the differences in British and American conventions, including an American habit of transcribing *visitor* as *visiter,* of which Webster himself did not approve (1831, p. xxx) but which was to remain a hallmark of Cooper's own style. At the same time, he does not seem to want to make an issue of it. This is not just a result of Cooper's concern for his British readership, for he continues to claim both in private and in public that the "prodigious influence that England has and still exercises over American thought is both amazing and mortifying" (2:294). But at the level of spelling, Cooper is no Joel Barlow, being happy to preserve the "usages of polite life" (1969, p. 173) when he can determine them. As we shall see, his attitude to vocabulary is more complex.

The printed texts of Cooper's novels offer a more complicated archive than that to be discovered in his letters, journals, and political writings. We have to consider not only their passage from script to print, but also their double life as American and British imprints. British house styles often obeyed different conventions, and Cooper's own revisions of his early books for republication in Bentley's *Standard Novels* series reveal not only general stylistic and grammatical changes but also explanatory footnotes specifically intended for the British reader, who could not be expected to understand aspects of the American language. For the novels are full of the material of that language. They employ Americanisms, they discuss them at length, and, most important of all, they often incorporate sophisticated dramatizations of the relation between linguistic and social tension, in the manner we have seen anticipated by Hugh Henry Brackenridge. The dramatic status of the characters of Cooper's fictions seems to make it possible for the author to present and explore a greater range of problems in the language than he might be able to manage in his own voice, made didactically consistent. Since D. H. Lawrence's account, it has become part of the standard wisdom that Cooper is something of a schizophrenic, or that his novels present irreconcilable perspectives and convictions. This is one corollary of the dramatic mode, whereby different views can be pushed (through different characters) to the point of complete contradiction. Instead of judging him as an in-

consistent thinker or a flawed artist, it is more helpful to find ways
of making these contradictions meaningful. In the largest sense, I
think that they speak for a consciousness divided by precisely the
tension that informed so much of the theory and experience of the
Jacksonian period, that between innocence and expansion. Destiny
perhaps, and politics definitely demanded a bigger and more popu-
lous America, but one that placed greater and greater strains on the
maintenance of civic virtue and of a positive relation to the natural
environment. It is not so much that one part of this dichotomy was
myth and the other reality; both seem to have been essential elements in what historians like to call the Jacksonian experience.

All the variants on this and related contradictions appear in the
treatment of the theme of language in Cooper's novels. One of
the most obvious cases involves the representation of the speech of
the Native American. This will be discussed in the next chapter.
Here I shall account for the other substantive and thematic aspects
of Cooper's image of the national language, or rather languages.

By the time Andrew Jackson came to the presidency in 1828,
Cooper had published no less than eight novels, as well as *Notions
of the Americans*. The first of these, *Precaution* (1820), was his attempt to imitate Jane Austen. In its ironic distance from the *mores*
of the English ruling class, it does not, however, duplicate Austen's
more sophisticated (though also ironic) conservatism. The language
of the polite classes is not a target of Cooper's satire, though Lady
Jarvis does refer to shooting "the *h*arrows of Cupid" (p. 318).
Generally, there is not much evidence here for a developing curi-
osity about the language, but the subject is, after all, not an American one. In the following year Cooper published *The Spy,* the first
of his tales to have an American setting. It is also, in many ways,
the closest to the example of Sir Walter Scott, with whom Cooper
was to be continually compared throughout his career. Set during
the Revolutionary War, the novel focuses less on the well-known
deeds of the great than on the comings and goings of the under-
cover characters and the unofficial antagonists, the Cow-Boys and
the Skinners. Like Scott, Cooper is interested in the degree to which
the official moralities that beget or accompany armed violence are
subverted or exploited in the course of that struggle itself; all pieties
are threatened when the "law of the neutral ground is the law of the
strongest" (p. 204). Like Scott, again, Cooper explores the gap

that opens between profession and practice in such situations. The Skinners become "men who, under the guise of patriotism, prowl through the community, with a thirst for plunder that is unsatiable. . . . Fellows whose mouths are filled with liberty and equality, and whose hearts are overflowing with cupidity and gall" (p. 329). Already, in this early tale, there is present the basis of Cooper's later obsession with the dangers of a populist rhetoric, and with the resultant contradiction between appearance and reality. The greatest of these contradictions afflicts the reputation of the spy, Harvey Birch, who is of further interest for the way in which he prefigures Natty Bumppo as an image of ecological innocence. He knows every tree in the forest, comes and goes with unerring regularity and accuracy, and, leaving no footprints, passes inscrutably across the landscape without defacing it in the slightest.[2]

The changes made between the first edition of *The Spy,* published in 1821, and the revised edition prepared for Bentley's *Standard Novels* series in 1831 have been studied by McDowell (1930). Additionally, the editors of the recent and authoritative text of *The Pioneers* (1980) have been able to make good comparative use of the annotated printer's copy of the second edition of *The Spy* in the preparation of their own text. Many of the changes noted by McDowell are grammatical and stylistic rather than inspired by any consciousness of the needs of an American English, and the editors of *The Pioneers* have confirmed this judgment (1980, pp. 467–68, 491–94). Such revisions do not then relate to Cooper's identity as an *American* writer so much as to his increasing competence as a writer of standard English prose. But some of the changes are significant in other ways. Although Harvey Birch himself does not speak an identifiable dialect—McDowell says that Cooper was "determined to elevate his spy in the social scale" (1930, p. 514)— the treatment of Black American diction is made more consistent. McDowell notes two techniques used here for the first time: "the apostrophe to indicate omission of a letter, and inversion of word order, today familiar to all dialect writers" (p. 513). The editors of *The Pioneers* have similarly decided that Cooper took considerable trouble to refine his representation of dialect between the first and second editions of that novel (1980, pp. 479, 483). This suggests that by 1831, the year in which both novels were revised for Bentley, Cooper had learned something about how to write dialect.

Even more significantly, it suggests that he became more highly motivated in developing dialect as a central theme in his novels. I shall develop this point in the discussion of *The Pioneers*.

The 1831 edition of *The Spy* also contains some explanatory notes designed specifically for the convenience of the British reader. Geographical and political details are explained (1831, p. 1), as is the term *improvement,* which is "used by the Americans to express every degree of change in converting land from its state of wilderness to that of cultivation" (p. 4). This sense of the word appears in Webster 1806 and 1828 without specification as an Americanism, but both Pickering (1816, pp. 108–12) and Worcester (1828, p. 1043) describe it as a New England localism. Cooper also explains the term *Cow-Boys* (1931, p. 204), recorded by *DA* from 1779, but otherwise the text is not marked by an exceptional number of Americanisms. It is also relatively unemphatic about its representation of American dialects. The New England "twang" is noted but not reproduced (p. 327), and Betty Flanagan's Irish-American diction is transcribed with rather less sophistication than Brackenridge had shown a generation earlier, being indeed strangely blended with obviously Scottish locutions (pp. 394–95). To appreciate the full range of Cooper's sensitivities to these and related questions, we must turn to *The Pioneers*.

The Language of the Leatherstocking

First published in 1823, *The Pioneers* is one of the half dozen or so seminal American novels, one of those books without which any model of the development or continuity of American literature simply makes no sense. Its linguistic themes and practices are much more complicated than those of *The Spy,* or those of any other previous work of American literature. Like its immediate predecessor, *The Pioneers* is really two novels, one published in 1823 and the other in 1832, in the *Standard Novels* series. Cooper's revision in fact began immediately after the publication of the first of the 1823 texts, thanks to the large number of errors disfiguring the first printing. Thus, the last three 1823 texts differ from the first (see 1980, pp. 468–69). The modern edition of the novel is a model of editorial tact and sophistication, and it is possible to reconstruct from it all the variations between the chosen copy-text and all other texts. From the analogous evidence available for *The Spy*, the editors suggest that the normalization of dialect forms found in the 1832 Colburn-Bentley edition is likely to be non-authorial. They contend that Cooper "never willingly curbed his experimentation with dialect" (1980, p. 483), and suggest that the tidying-up process apparent in 1832 may be a result of the compositor's misinterpretation of the author's instructions. Cooper declared his willingness to allow the printers to decide on spelling, but he made an exception for "words of local use, the names, or those which are evidently intended to be corrupt." Thus, the 1980 text rejects two hundred and one normalizations of dialect introduced in 1832, and accepts twelve substitutions *of* dialect *for* standard forms.

We may infer, then, that Cooper was not responsible for the conversion of dialect profiles into more standard forms in the 1832 text (previously the version most often chosen for widespread reprinting), anxious as he was in other respects to make the novel available to British readers. This seems appropriate, given the degree to which the thematic and argumentative weight of the book is embodied in and nuanced by its representation of the disparate speech patterns of the frontier society it depicts. The guiding image of the novel is perhaps that of the "composite order," the hodgepodge of architectural styles and improvisations that characterizes the doings of Richard Jones. Templeton itself is similarly made up of elements from various parts of America and Europe. Cooper notes that

> half the nations in the north of Europe had their representatives in this assembly, though all had closely assimilated themselves to the Americans, in dress and appearance, except the Englishman. He, indeed, not only adhered to his native customs, in attire and living, but usually drove his plough, among the stumps, in the same manner as he had before done, on the plains of Norfolk, until dearbought experience taught him the useful lesson, that a sagacious people knew what was suited to their circumstances, better than a casual observer; or a sojourner, who was, perhaps, too much prejudiced to compare, and, peradventure, too conceited to learn (1980, p. 124).

This notion of a general assimilation to the American standard (the Englishman aside) is not, however, simply borne out in the lin-

guistic profiles of the characters in the novel, who in this respect
seem to demonstrate a hum of misunderstandings and idiosyncratic
languages rather than anything resembling the famous model of the
"melting pot." The epigraph to chapter eight, quoted from Campbell's *Gertrude of Wyoming,* tells us that they "spoke, in friendship,
every distant tongue" (p. 96), but the friendships are often strained
and mutual understandings compromised. Some of this has, of
course, sheer comic potential, as when the nautical Cornishman
Ben Pump quarrels with the transplanted New Englander Remarkable Pettibone over the pronunciation of the language. Pump concludes that "Miss Lizzy has been exercising the King's English
under a great Lon'on lady, and, for that matter, can talk the language almost as well as myself"; Pettibone rejoins that the true
standard is to be found in her own speech, having "always heer'n
say, that the Bay State was provarbal for pronounsation" (p. 176).
Most of the inhabitants of the Temple Patent are in fact "from the
moral states of Connecticut and Massachusetts" (p. 98), so that
the novel can be said to chronicle an early stage in that process
which Webster and Franklin, among others, had identified as crucial to the preservation of the civic virtue of the republic—the westward migration of surplus population. Most of the characters who
speak the New England dialect in this novel are anything but para-
gons of such virtue. Pettibone is one of the most opinionated and
the most heavily marked by regional speech. She says *tuck* for
"took" and *wownd* for "wound" (p. 80). The following is a fair
sample of both her diction and her personality:

> I heer'n say that the Judge was gone a great 'broad, and that he
> meant to bring his darter hum, but I didn't calcoolate on sich
> carrins on. To my notion, Benjamin, she's likely to turn out a
> disp'ut ugly gall (p. 175).[3]

There are other New Englanders in the novel. Elnathan Todd, the
quack doctor, is from "western Massachusetts" (p. 71) and has
been educated from "Webster's Spelling-Book." As a child he had
lounged about the "homestead" hunting for "yarbs" until he was
discovered to have "a naateral love for doctor-stuff" (p. 72).
Jotham Riddle (p. 158) and, possibly, Sergeant Hollister, who says
fout for "fought" and *larning* for "learning" (p. 147), are from the
same area of the map. Hiram Dolittle, the most negatively por-

trayed of all the secondary characters, is even more heavily marked by Yankee speech habits than Pettibone. He is the most noncommittal and the most circumlocutive of all (pp. 119, 377), in the style defined and explained by Noah Webster as early as 1789, though in rather more flattering terms than those admitted by Cooper.

The linguistic identities of these incidental characters thus faithfully represent the demographic profile of western New York state in 1793, the year in which the novel is set. The New Englanders are just the bedrock of the population, and there are a host of other speech patterns evident in the village. Hollister's wife Betty has a "strong Irish accent," though Cooper is once again not very precise in its transcription. The Scotticisms (e.g., *Och*) seem out of place, unless she is an Orangewoman, but in her use of some New England locutions, such as *sich, calkilating,* and *ind,* Cooper may be meaning to make a subtle record of the habits she has acquired from her peers and from her husband. Ben Pump's Cornish English is not very convincing, often sounding more like East Anglian— "this here painter . . . that there dog" (p. 352)—or Cockney— "ship them 'ome" (p. 394)—than Cornish. With Monsieur Le Quoi's French-English Cooper had even more trouble, so much so that large tracts of his speech in the first edition were omitted or heavily amended in the second (1980, pp. 510, 517, 546). Similarly, Major Hartmann, who is meant to have a "strong German accent" (p. 48), speaks something much more like a Dutchman's English, with which Cooper would presumably have been much more familiar.[4] Thus, where the first edition reads *der teufel,* 1832 and the modern editors have *ter deyvel* (pp. 51, 93, 517), in line with Hartmann's consistently Dutch sounds: "put you will preak ter sleigh and kilt ter horses" (p. 50). To complete the picture, there is, besides John Mohegan's Indian talk (which will be discussed in the next chapter), the Black English of Agamemnon, wherein *he* does the job of all the pronouns in a language of considerable grammatical contraction (pp. 53–56, 195).

The misunderstandings that arise from this babel of voices are, as has been said, often just comical; but they are always poised upon a point of seriousness which at times emerges into full articulation. Cooper does not seem very adept at dialect transcription in such cases as those of Pump and Hartmann, but it is clear that he is trying to indicate thereby the diversity of the community, and this registers as a theme of the novel in despite of the author's apparent inconsistencies. Misunderstandings between national or ethnic groups, though they occur (e.g., Pump and Le Quoi, p. 120), are in fact less important in this respect than those between members of different professions or vocations, for the novel also abounds in the languages of special interest groups, people who are either trapped by their language or committed to it as a way of exploiting and deceiving others. I give two examples of characters who are trapped or betrayed by their languages, one major and one minor. The minor case is that of Judge Temple, who was raised a Quaker, and who can be observed "uniformly, when much interested or agitated, to speak in the language of his youth," with its famous "thees" and "thous" (pp. 35, 48, 201). Even the "politely" spoken Elizabeth can be found "unconsciously adopting the dialect of her parent, in the warmth of her sympathy" (p. 234). Although he makes it lightly, Cooper makes a serious point here, and one that bears directly on the question of consensus within the developing community. Not only do children tend to mimic parents, thus preserving (albeit in a diluted form) original diversities of speech through the generations; but the most traditional speech habits tend to be most strongly evident at the moments of greatest tension or excitement. Since the important decisions in life tend to be made at such moments, we may infer that linguistic differences are strongest at precisely the points where they ought to be weakest, that is when mutual comprehension is most necessary and might make the greatest positive contribution. This point is never made incremental to the action of this novel, at least in the case of Judge Temple, but it is there nonetheless, and Cooper returns to it in other novels.

A more significant example of a character who is in the fullest sense trapped by his inherited or acquired language is, of course, Ben Pump. Along with his natural self-satisfaction as an Englishman, already tending (as Cooper has told us) to insulate him from any new experience and any creative social intercourse, there is his vocational diction, whereby everything is described in terms of the parts and operations of a ship-of-the-line. This means that he is often not understood by others around him. Again, Cooper continues in his later novels to transcribe the languages of such obsessives, and they are often sailors (like Master Cap in *The Pathfinder*).

The recourse to a familiar vocabulary in which total competence has been achieved (especially true of sea language, which is so limited and specialized) does provide the mind with an anchor in a sea of new experience. At the same time, it also holds the users at a distance from properly engaging with such experience on its own terms. Much of *The Pioneers* is about the various kinds of and reactions to new experiences, so that Pump's effective language means that he is always going to remain an outsider from whatever consensus might be established. Subjectively, it is the mind's need for familiarity and security (or perhaps sheer obstinacy) that compels it to repetition; objectively, the result of this is to distance us further and further from the common language. Thus, at the moment of the closest human solidarity, when Ben opts to enter the stocks along with Natty in order to share his punishment, Natty can understand the intention but not the expression:

> The hunter appeared to appreciate the kind intentions of the other, though he could not understand his eloquence; and raising his humbled countenance, he attempted a smile, as he said—
> "Anan!" (p. 375)

In this case Cooper does not choose to develop the "tragical" potential in such misunderstandings, as he does in those of Natty himself, and of John Mohegan; but we must still take the point that Pump's language prevents him from becoming a fully functional member of the community.

Pump's nautical diction does remain largely a comic principle. This is less clearly the case with some other special dictions in the novel, notably those of medicine and the law (which have continued to perplex many Americans since!). These special dictions are even more effective than the ethnic languages in causing divisions within the community, as they had been (incipiently) for Brackenridge and (more ambiguously) for Samuel Johnson (see 1957, pp. 123–24, 860). In one sense we may say that struggles of interest and vocation take the place, in this novel, of the struggles between the classes that we might expect to find in a European novel of the same period. Edward Tyrell Channing, writing on Brockden Brown for the *North American Review* (9, 1819), had opined that one of the great difficulties facing the American writer was the lack of a properly developed class system, offering recognizably

constant and distinct identities to the creator of fiction. He interpreted this as a problem, since the American writer thus had no
means of signaling the generic qualities of his characters, who must
thus remain mere individuals. It is true that we do not find a
European-style class system in the representation of Templeton,
but Cooper shows that the facts of struggle and conflict can be just
as strongly evident between individuals as between classes. These
individuals do, moreover, become generic in their functions within
a system of competitive individualism, and they all subsist by some
kind of manipulation of language.

Again, I offer a minor and a major example. Elnathan Todd, the
New England doctor, can talk "with much judgment concerning
intermittents, remittents, tertians, quotidians, &c.," but he is all
the time building "on this foundation of sand, a superstructure,
cemented by practice, though composed of somewhat brittle materials" (p. 74). He learns as he goes along, in other words, and with
his "shrewd mind" he is not a complete hypocrite. But there is at
the same time a definite disjunction between what he says and what
he knows and does, exemplified in the extraction of the ball from
Oliver's shoulder, where a very simple *deed* is made much of in
words. This is further heightened by the argument between the
native medicine of Mohegan, who *says* very little, and the kind of
physic that Todd has to offer, accompanied by a barrage of technical terms. But at least no serious harm comes to anyone as a
result of his efforts.

Cooper's representation of the language of the law is more complex and troubling. McWilliams (1972) and others have rightly
emphasized the importance of the legal theme in the novel, and
Cooper's opening remarks speak of a present (1823) that "hourly"
displays "how much can be done . . . under the dominion of mild
laws" and where "every man feels a direct interest in the prosperity
of a commonwealth, of which he knows himself to form a part"
(pp. 15–16). Some commentators have used this and other such
statements to conclude that Cooper means to show the evolution
of such a commonwealth in the novel, wherein some residual and
primitive elements (Natty and Mohegan) must necessarily, albeit
regrettably, be displaced. Following the model offered by D. H.
Lawrence, however, we may choose to see Cooper's consciousness
as more ambiguous than this, at least in his fiction. I shall return

to this question. At the level of the language, we can see a problem with the law at the very beginning of the tale, where Natty questions Temple's humorous but nevertheless condescending invocation of the "act of supererogation" (p. 23) by asserting the simple facts and being proven, as it happens, dead right. Here is a specimen of lawyer Van der School's diction, his morning greeting:

> "Good morning, Mr. Edwards, (if that is your name, (for, being a stranger, we have no other evidence for the fact than your own testimony,) as I understand you have given it to Judge Temple,) good morning, sir" (p. 281).

Later, in the courtroom scene, where Natty is on trial for shooting a deer in violation of the Judge's new game laws, Van der School's summary is "recounted in such a manner as utterly to confuse the faculties of his worthy listeners" (p. 368). Natty himself is more confused than any. The simple resolution of the quarrel that the direct discourse between him and Billy Kirby threatens to achieve is judged totally out of context and unsatisfactory. The law has been put into motion and must have its way: personal settlements are no longer possible. And, while the law is in principle necessary for the popular good, it is crucial to this scene that there is *no* popular support for the law. The only characters who want the case to be pursued are those who stand to profit from it, Dolittle chief among them. The very first occasion of the application of this theoretically "necessary" common law is also the first occasion of its misuse by vested interests. It is the game law that Natty has transgressed, one passed with the aim of inhibiting wasteful slaughter but ironically invoked here against a subsistence hunter who generally kills only what he needs to eat. Elsewhere in the book, he himself comments on the evils of wasting nature's resources, when he is confronted with the slaughter of the passenger pigeons (a species indeed now extinct) and the frenzied destruction of the fish in the lake (pp. 247, 260). Judge Temple also is disgusted at these excesses, as he is by the wanton felling of trees (pp. 105–6, 228–29). But he passes no *laws* against these spoliations, although they are imaged in the novel as far more serious than the taking of a deer out of season. Why then does he pass a law at all? The answer lies, I think, in his own habits and interests. The game law is of the Judge's own making, it is not imposed from elsewhere, and the opening scenes make it clear that he is a keen if not a fanatical hunter. The game law may then be a direct product of his own personal obsession, a way of making sure that there will always be something for him to hunt. Critics have often missed this point in arguing for the necessity of this particular law. It is surely the case that communities in general require laws as they become larger and more complex. But there is nothing in the novel that subsumes Temple's game law under such a dignified philosophical category. It is only the letter of the law that Natty has offended, imaged in his exclusion from its language. Its spirit is highly questionable.

As Natty is at odds with the language of the courtroom, so he is also set apart (and again ambiguously) from the dominantly polite language of the narrator and the (other) most admired characters. The very name of the village, Templeton, might be taken to indicate that its future would lie in the hands of the genteel class of whom the Judge is an exemplary representative. It is a convention in the novels of this period that the dialect speakers be held at a distance by the refined and even fastidious narrator in alliance with his favorite protagonists, and there are any number of examples in Cooper of the habit noted by Richard Bridgman as typical of the genre:

> Overt definition also frequently occurs in the narrative itself when opposed points of view come into conflict. With at least an upper and a lower linguistic world recognized in the United States, a good deal of inter-translation was necessary. Sometimes the genteel narrator served as the interpreter, either furnishing a paraphrase of the vernacular, or actually defining the troublesome word (1966, p. 26).

This tendency was reinforced, as we shall see, by Cooper's sense of the need to "translate" the book for a British readership in 1832. But it was there from the start, and is even repeated within the narrator's own voice as he paraphrases his own terms as if to make sure that he gets them right, for example, when he refers in the very first paragraph of *The Pioneers* to "hills and dales, or, to speak with greater deference to geographical definitions, of mountains and valleys" (p. 15). The polite standard is quite definitely the one that Cooper generally endorses and tries to practice, often with the comically euphemistic or hyperbolic results that made him such a tempting target for parody. When Bret Harte has *his* version of Judge Temple complain that the noise from the fire is spoiling his concentration, he is devilishly close to some of Cooper's own prose in declaring that "The sibilation produced by the sap, which exudes copiously therefrom, is not conducive to composition" (1867, p. 12). In *The Pioneers,* it is crucial that both Oliver Edwards (Effingham) and Elizabeth Temple, the ideal couple heralding the future, should speak an impeccably correct English. We have already seen Ben Pump commenting on Elizabeth's speech. In the case of Oliver, the point is made from the start that he speaks "with a pronunciation and language vastly superior to his appearance" (p. 24). The Judge comments again on his "chosen language; such as is seldom heard in these hills" (p. 110), and Mr. Grant also notes his complete lack of "dialect" (p. 137). In a manner symmetrical with this emphasis on polite diction, the character of Richard Jones is appropriately expressed in a language just one step away from propriety. His pronunciation falls to pieces when he is excited (p. 50), and he says *don't* for "does not," just like Jane Austen's Lucy Steele. He is a man trying to pretend to be more than he is, an early version of the hyperbolic democrat on whom Tocqueville was to comment, one who calls a plain entrance way a "portico" (p. 60). The controlling presence of the polite is further established by Cooper's habit of putting speech marks around unusual or local words (e.g., p. 123), and of defining them by parentheses. At times he refers to "the language of the country" (p. 96), at times to "the vulgar language of the country" (p. 28), though on at least one occasion he tactfully amended "called in vulgar parlance" to "commonly called" (see p. 544).

There is, then, a generally intact alliance between Cooper the narrator and his exemplary characters in preserving the standards of a rather fussy transatlantic English. If this were all there is to say, however, Cooper would have no claim to distinction as a linguistic patriot and the founder of a national fiction. There are at least two further dimensions of Cooper's art that serve to complicate this situation: the portrayal of Natty Bumppo and the narrator's own commitment to a regular use of Americanisms.

In the representation of Bumppo—himself an awkwardly named hero if ever there was one—Cooper clearly departs from the otherwise intact alliance of narrator and polite language. Whereas the dialect speakers in most novels of the period are held at a distance and not allowed to voice the important themes and arguments of the tale, Natty clearly enunciates some of Cooper's own strongest convictions. Louise Pound (1927) has analyzed his language, and has concluded that Cooper is not therein differing significantly from contemporary representations of lower characters.[5] But, as a dialect speaker, Natty does differ significantly from the other such speakers in *The Pioneers*. He speaks a kind of generic common language, one definitely based on the norms for the transcription of New England speech, but yet devoid of all the hostile or comic markers by which Cooper usually represents that speech. He does not *guess* and *reckon* at the same rate as the other New Englanders, who tend to use more of the words defined by Pickering (1816) as typical of their regional language: *clever, calculate, guess, curious,* and so on. This is appropriate in at least two ways. First, Natty is a figure whose exact origins are vague, and whose whole identity is premised on a predicament of perpetual displacement and dispossession. His language must then also be suitably unmarked by a strong regional personality. Second, his function as an image of righteous innocence would not be enhanced by any tendency to speak like a "calculating clever" Yankee. Much of his past is left unexplained, most obviously his role in the Revolutionary War. He is the protector of the old Tory, Effingham, and he was on the side of the British in the Seven Years' War (1756–63), but beyond his admission that he has "seen the inimy in the 'seventy-six business" (p. 374) we learn nothing of his exact career at that time. Cooper clearly wishes to preserve him from an extreme connection with either faction, and as one thus not responsible for the division within the colonies which it is the function of this novel to present as, in Cooper's particular way, healed with the restitution of the Effingham line. He is an abstract and generic character, almost a principle. But he does have some of the features of Humphreys' (1815) Yankee, Dolittle. He says *druve* (Humphreys has *druv*), *n'ither, sartin, kivered,* and *heerd* (Humphreys has *nuther, sartinly, kiver,* and *heerd*). He says *used to could* and *mought,* which Pickering (1816) had proposed as a Londonism, and he has the long New England vowels in such words as *ha'arths.* He also has a distinct vocabulary, including such words as *gaunty, hatchel, squinch,* and the omnipresent *anan.* Pound (1927, p. 486) notes this last as

one of his "most annoying and hard worked mannerisms," and
Bridgman (1966, p. 67) finds it "as evocatively mysterious as
David's 'Selah!' and Turoldus' 'Aoi!' " But, whether Cooper knew
it or not, *anan* is a word with a significant history. Natty uses it
when he does not understand what is happening or being said, as
in the courtroom scene (pp. 361, 364) and immediately thereafter
(p. 375). Smollett's Roderick Random also heard it when he came
to London from his native Scotland (see Barrell, 1983, p. 179).
For Horne Tooke, it was the Anglo-Saxon verb meaning *give* or
grant, of which *an* is a contraction (1829, 1:107). Noah Webster
had made something of this:

> It is used for *what,* or *what do you say;* as when a person speaks to
> another, the second person not hearing distinctly, replies, *nan,* or
> *anan;* that is, *give* or *repeat* what you said. This is ridiculed as a
> gross vulgarism; and it is indeed obsolete except among common
> people; but it is strictly correct, and if persons deride the use of the
> word, it proves at least that they do not understand its meaning
> (1789a, p. 188).[6]

Natty's archaism has thus both a context and an integrity, though
Cooper would probably not have cared for the support of Noah
Webster in this respect! It signals that he is part of a disappearing
class—the other dialect speakers do not use it because they understand all too well what is going on around them—and that he is in
touch with a primitive linguistic integrity (as with several other sorts
of integrity). He also says *sin'* for "since" (p. 454), another word
Webster (1789a, pp. 190–91) finds in the "ancient authors" and
among the "common people in New England." Webster repeats the
Tookean explanation that *since* comes from *seen that,* hence from
an allusion to "sensible objects" (another aspect of Natty's affiliation is to the *seen* rather than to the *imagined*). Hence the form
sin or *sen* is closest to the original *seen.* Natty's dialect is a purified,
essential version of the Anglo-Saxon substratum of the common
language, as befits one whose own given name signifies, as House
(1965, p. 283) has pointed out, "the 'given of God,' or the prophet
in whom, Jesus said, there 'is no deceit.' " The further development
of his dialect in the 1832 text (see 1980, pp. 521–24) only adds to
the distance between Natty and the other characters, whether they
speak the vernacular or the polite language. His ability to mediate

the two, and to speak a common language that is not vulgar, is precisely what is most needed in the increasingly polarizing society of Templeton. It is also what is most inexorably being excluded.

We have, then, in the case of Natty Bumppo, a (modified) dialect speaker who is not simply subordinated to the polite usages and values of the socially superior characters, and who seems to bear about him a definite degree of authorial approval and conviction. It is as if Cooper appears twice in the tale, once as the fastidious narrator in alliance with the Temples and the Effinghams, and once as the voice of Natty Bumppo. As a man of letters and a patriot, Cooper clearly has an investment in an American literary style that measures up to the standards imposed by the British tradition. At the same time, in the figure and voice of the hunter, he explores an alternative dignity in the image of an unlettered hero. For, at a crucial point late in the novel, we learn what we should have assumed from the start but have not yet been told: that Natty cannot *read* (pp. 451–52). It is a corollary of his innocence, perhaps, that he is outside the contract of the written language and outside all the arguments that had gone on about it, including the argument about whether civilization could be possible without such a language—an option Dr. Johnson had denied. With a painful sense of irony, we make this discovery about Natty as he stands in puzzled contemplation of the grave of Chingachgook, which stands on the very site "where the cabin of the Leather-stocking had so long stood" (p. 449). The graves are thus the symbols of his own imminent disappearance from the landscape, and they commemorate Mohegan in an even more disjunctive way by virtue of being not only *written* but also in English. Natty is mentioned honorably on Effingham's grave, and thus himself entombed by association, and in the very mode of the written language that has always been outside his control. His joy at this discovery—" 'tis a gin'rous gift to a man who leaves none of his name and family behind him in a country, where he has tarried so long" (p. 452)—is a perfect image of his identity as a man caught between two worlds, those of primitive innocence and socialized (linguistic) complexity. Much of the subtlety of Cooper's image of Natty and of Chingachgook consists in the way in which the emergence of a fully revolutionary confrontation between the two worlds is prevented by the complex demands of their personal and political loyalties and divided identities.

Natty does embody some virtues that would be worth preserving in any emerging culture, in spite of (and perhaps because of) his being illiterate. He also contributes to the developing vocabulary of the American language. Some of his words, like *squinch* for "quench" (p. 164) and *gaunty* for "lean" (p. 454) do appear to be genuine dialect terms that were not to become any part of an emerging standard. (*DAE* gives *squinch* from 1835, but in a different sense.) His use of *hatchel* as a verb meaning to "vex" or "hector" (p. 296) is supported by Webster 1806 but never seems to have become a common one. The beast that threatens the life of Elizabeth and Louisa is variously called by him a *painter* (*DA* from 1764) and a *cat-a-mount* (pp. 292, 455), in contrast to the narrator's *panther* and Mohegan's *cat of the mountain* (pp. 307, 400). Pump remarks with some justice that "some calls it one, and some calls it t'other" (p. 341).[7] Natty is the single user of the term *red-skin* (p. 403), not in either of Webster's dictionaries but recorded in *DA* from 1699. He uses *sundown* twice (pp. 207, 453), as does Billy Kirby (p. 430), a word that is not technically an Americanism but had been preserved in America longer than in Britain (*DAE,* 1620–   ). Among the authentic Americanisms he does voice are *betterment* (*DA,* 1785, also discussed by Pickering, 1816, as a New England word), *shanty* (*DA,* 1822), and *windrow,* the last of which he shares with the Judge himself (pp. 202, 236), therein anticipating *DA*'s first recorded citation (from a later Cooper novel) by six years.

We may still choose to agree with Bridgman (1966, pp. 68–69) that Cooper "possessed no fixed linguistic conception of a character like Natty by which he could monitor his speech," but we may at the same time come to suspect that the very lack of such fixity might have a point to it. Both thematically and linguistically, Natty is to be distinguished from those who pronounce a strong regional identity (most commonly that of western Massachusetts). He speaks a generic dialect form that is open to a measure of authorial endorsement, one further enhanced by his use of words that were becoming part of the national language, and increasingly endorsed as such by the various lexicographers and commentators whose views we have already discussed. Cooper has created a very special place for the figure whom he will later call "the Straight-tongue."

This brings us to the second way in which Cooper departs from his apparent endorsement of a fastidiously correct transatlantic style. He too, as narrator, is a publicizer of Americanisms. Bret Harte, again, catches the point very aptly in describing how "the log cabin of Judge Tompkins, embowered in buckeyes, completed the enchanting picture" (1867, p. 11). Along with the platitudinous and vapid "enchanting picture" and the elevated "embowered" there is the friction of the common and precise "buckeye," an American tree in an American place. In an analysis of the vocabulary of *The Pioneers* (not to be taken as absolutely exhaustive), I have found four items for which *DA* cites this novel as the first recorded source: *down countries,* "High Dutchers," *dicker* (as noun), and *sugar-bush* (pp. 58, 97, 158, 219, 227). *DAE* similarly cites Cooper's use of the word *roily* (p. 225), though the word can be found in Pickering (1816, p. 164).[8] Among other words that *DA* records as first appearing in the period just prior to Cooper's novel are the title word itself (*DA* gives *pioneer* from 1817; but see *OED,* 1605), *flood-wood* (p. 7, *DA* 1822), *Otsego bass* (p. 259, *DA* 1822), and *chicker-berry* (p. 108, *DA* 1821, in *The Spy*). The following Americanisms, recorded in *DA* as eighteenth-century innovations, also appear: *portage, jobber, store, blocks,* "rides post" (*DA* gives *post rider*), *half-breed, sugar camp, batteau, squatter,* and *door-yard* (pp. 7, 74, 96, 99, 112, 242, 256, 266, 327). Those traced to seventeenth-century sources include *settler, sleigh, clearing, patent, resolutions, beaver-dam, scow, posse,* and "pull up stakes." Possible Americanisms not recorded in *DA* or *DAE* include *stubbs, eating-parlour, wood-path,* and "break-gaol"; also *lathy,* which Webster 1828 lists as a New England term, but which appears in Scott's *Heart of Midlothian* (ch. 50) and in Todd-Johnson, without comment. Cooper's *craneberry* is presumably a form of *cranberry* (p. 108); and Ben Pump's *younker* (reported from Natty, p. 111) does not imply the Dutch-American sense defined by *DAE* (as man of property), but is a synonym of young man (as in Webster 1806) with a specifically nautical flavor. Mohegan uses the word *spry* (p. 400), which Pickering (1816) gives as a "vulgar" Americanism with a possible origin in British dialect. Other Americanisms in the novel do, of course, include a whole range of names of birds, fishes, and trees, among them *whip-poor-will, fish-hawk, bull-pout, salmon-trout, suckers, curled maple, black walnut, sumach, dog-wood, bass-wood,* and so forth.

Such elements of Cooper's vocabulary, taken together with his book's implicit endorsement of the character and thus perhaps the speech of Natty Bumppo, must qualify the familiar assumption that Cooper's stylistic inspiration comes from other writers and traditions. Much has been made of his debts and borrowings: critics have noted echoes of the King James Bible, a number of debts to Shakespeare (see Gates, 1952) and to Ossian (see Fridén, 1949). All of these echoes—and others—are indeed there to be found. Most famously of all, Cooper is certainly indebted to Scott, though he was never a mere follower. He perhaps took from Scott the terms *"firstly"* and *"lastly,"* though where Scott speaks simply of the development of the sermon (*Old Mortality,* ch. 26), Cooper extends the sense to the features of a building (1980, pp. 9, 42–43; cf. 1960–68, 4:77). Some items in Cooper's military vocabulary, such as *fusee* and *vidette,* are also common in Scott, and Shakespeare is for Scott, as he is for Cooper, the most common source of epigraphs (see Tulloch, 1980, p. 23). Further, Scott also demonstrates a sophisticated sense of the relation of dialect to common speech, though he is much more interested in archaisms than Cooper is (see Tulloch, 1980).

Cooper's borrowings from Shakespeare are also significant and obvious, though they are equally extensive in other nineteenth-century writers.[9] The point is, of course, that Cooper's inability or unwillingness to appear as a complete original has taken on greater importance because of his being an American. It has also, I would argue, inhibited a fair recognition of the degree to which he *is* original. The words and phrases listed above as Americanisms are an important part of the vocabulary of the novel, and they are made the more obvious when they are paraphrased in the narrative as being local or national usages (e.g., *patent, clearing,* "High-Dutchers," *stubbs, down countries, store*), or set off for the reader's attention by being placed in italics or parentheses (e.g., *portage, flood-wood, betterments, blocks, resolutions, ride post, sugar bush*). Other words are the subjects of lengthy etymologies, for example, that of *Otsego* (p. 7), or of explanatory footnotes (e.g., *jobber,* p. 74).

Two particular words, *sleigh* and *Yankee,* are dealt with in great detail in the 1832 footnotes. The first is defined as follows:

> Sleigh is the word used in every part of the United States to denote a traineau. It is of local use in the west of England, whence it is most probably derived by the Americans. The latter draw a distinction between a sled, or sledge, and a sleigh; the sleigh being shod with metal. Sleighs are also subdivided into two-horse and one-horse sleighs. Of the latter, there are the cutter, with thills so arranged as to permit the horse to travel in the side-track; the "pung," or "tow-pung," which is driven with a pole, and the "jumper," a rude construction used for temporary purposes, in the new countries.
>
> Many of the American sleighs are elegant, though the use of this mode of conveyance is much lessened with the melioration of the climate, consequent on the clearing of the forests (1980, p. 17).

Sleigh had appeared in Pickering's list of Americanisms (1816, p. 174), where it was attributed to New England speakers. Webster 1806 gives a brief definition, under the spelling *sley,* and in 1828 a longer one under *sleigh.* Cooper's note is considerably fuller than any of these, and goes into unique detail about the various kinds of sleigh and their attributes. Webster made much of the *sled-sleigh* distinction in his reply to Pickering (1817, p. 23), along with some complicated etymological speculations; and later (1823, pp. 46–47) he asserted that the "distinction *sleigh* and *sled* is a very important one in this country, where two forms of carriage are used." Cooper goes further. He seems to have been wrong about the derivation of the *word,* if he implies that it comes from British English; it is almost certainly a borrowing from the Dutch. But he may mean to say that the *thing* is derived from England, in the spirit of his general interest in things before words. His relative ignoring of etymology serves to remove the word from potential dismissal as a coinage, and there is a way in which the very detail of Cooper's description, with its focus on different kinds of sleigh and on aesthetic appeal, further contributes to removing the term from any merely linguistic context or contention.

On the subject of the etymology of *Yankee,* Cooper's modern editors have noted (1980, p. 459) that he follows the explanation in Heckewelder (1818, p. 60). Cooper's contribution to what was already a notorious debate is as follows:

In America the term Yankee is of local meaning. It is thought to be derived from the manner in which the Indians of New England pronounced the word "English" or "Yengeese." New York being originally a Dutch province, the term of course was not known there, and further south different dialects among the natives, themselves, probably produced a different pronunciation. Marmaduke and his cousin being Pennsylvanians by birth were not Yankees in the American sense of the word (p. 56).

Thus Todd is a Yankee to Richard Jones.

Once again, Cooper's note can be set against a context of speculation about this infamous word (still not conclusively explained). Royall Tyler surely had his tongue in his cheek in claiming that

The term Yankey is but a corruption of Yorkshire, being simply the Indian pronunciation. The natives of the country hearing the white men, during their early habitancy, frequently speaking of Yorkshire, styled them Yankeys. To be satisfied of this, I once requested a Cognawagha Indian to pronounce Yorkshire: he immediately replied—"oh, Ya-ankah, you—you be Ya-ankah" (1809, pp. 75–76).

But this spoof is not significantly more far-fetched than Webster's explanation, in a letter to the *Connecticut Herald* scornfully reprinted in *The Monthly Anthology* (8, 1810, pp. 244–45). Here he argues that *"Yankee . . . was an epiphet descriptive of excellent qualities,"* deriving from nothing less than the Persian!:

Now in the Persian language, *Janghe* or *Jenghe* [that is Yankee] signifies "a *warlike man*—a *swift horse*—also one who is prompt and ready in action—one who is magnanimous". . . . The word Yankee claims a very honourable parentage; for it is the precise title assumed by the celebrated Mongolian Khan, Jenghis; and in our dialect, his titles literally translated, would be, *Yankee King,* that is, *Warlike Chief.*

By 1828, Webster is (more credibly) citing Heckewelder's hypothesis, as Cooper had done in 1823, though his 1830 abridgment for schools adds a possible derivation from the French *anglais,* the explanation also preferred by the editors of *Household Words* (see Lohrli, 1962, p. 93). Paulding (1814, p. 165) noted the word as a "term of contempt applied to the people of the United States, by the English naval officers." Once again, we can see Cooper picking his way through this range of opinions, some of them absurd, some of them comic, some of them uncomfortably serious, and coming up with an explanation depending on a "native" origin and application. The word originates with the American Indian, is not a term of contempt, and should be properly applied within the United States, rather than by foreigners to all Americans.[10]

So much, then, for the languages of *The Pioneers*. I have not commented in any detail on the orthography of the text, since it duplicates the habits of Cooper's journals and letters, already described in the previous section. Thus p. 40 of the modern text (1980) reproduces both *vapors* and *vapours, color* and *colour;* p. 243 reads *equipt,* and p. 425 has *skipt; sithes* occurs for *scythes* (pp. 189, 358); and *visiter* prevails throughout.

It is not possible to go into the same lengthy analysis of the rest of Cooper's novels as has been lavished on *The Pioneers*. I take this to be a particularly important novel for the subject of the American language, because it was written early, because it was extensively revised for a later (British) edition, and because it contains a great deal of information about Cooper's vocabulary (as narrator), about his treatment of dialect, and about his thematic exploration of linguistic tensions in the frontier society. It thus provides perhaps the best possible basis for a general account of the rest of his fiction.

When we move on to *The Pathfinder,* for example, first published in 1840 and also available in a carefully edited modern edition (1981), we find that many of the features of Cooper's earlier text are repeated. The manuscript has, moreover, survived, and thus is available as a copy-text (1981, p. 474), which has been modified by the kinds of authorial variants typical of the earlier tale. Cooper's perusal of the proof sheets of the first edition seems to have caused him once again to *develop* Natty's dialect (pp. 474–75, 479), as he had done before.[11]

Because the novel was published simultaneously in America and in Britain and never went into a revised edition, there are no footnotes of the sort that appear in the 1832 text of *The Pioneers*. Perhaps Cooper was also less aggressive than before about expounding the American vocabulary (and he was not getting paid for any extra notes). Some words are identified as belonging to the "language of the country," for example, *wind-row, bass-wood, rifts, garrison* (1981, pp. 7, 9, 34, 48), but at the same time the notorious

Americanism *bluff* is allowed to stand without any comment at all (p. 259). Cooper seems generally less anxious about catering to the possible perplexities of the British reader. Perhaps he is less solicitous than before about preserving his good will; or, alternatively, less assertive about the rights of the American language. Italics and parentheses are similarly less common than in *The Pioneers*, although many of the Americanisms of the earlier novel appear again, for example, *wind-row, bass-wood, flood-wood, portage, red skin, betterments, batteau,* and *Yengeese,* the prototype of *Yankee* (pp. 7, 9, 30, 33, 77, 98, 113, 346). Among other words listed in *DA* as Americanisms, a high proportion are once again spoken by Natty Bumppo: *woodchuck, trail, back-woodsman, wampum, buffaloe, cat-bird, lick* and *salt lick, improvements, hedge-hog, sugar-maple,* and the verb *to jerk* (pp. 27, 32, 39, 53, 79, 79, 89 and 445, 98, 126, 275, 436). Natty's *rattler* (p. 429) is cited by *DA* as first recorded in *The Prairie* (published in 1827), though in fact it appeared one year earlier in *The Last of the Mohicans* (1983, p. 114). Thus, he is once again of great importance as the expounder of the language, and his status as a speaker of modified dialect, without the strong (and comic) New England markers, is correspondingly preserved. He continues to use *anan,* speaks of *sarcumventions* (p. 50) and of *ambushment* (p. 50, *DAE,* 1638), and uses the colloquial *trampoose* (p. 113, *DAE* 1725). He says *used to could* (p. 275) and *squinched* (p. 395), as he did before, as well as the word *hist,* glossed by Webster 1806 as "an exclamation commanding silence."

The thematic continuity with *The Pioneers* is also strong. This is a "nautico-lake-savage romance" (p. xv), one putting together all the elements on which Cooper's success as a writer had been founded; once again, he is conscious of the relation between the struggle of dictions and the struggle for social recognition and control, so that the desire for attention or supremacy tends to appear as an attempt to take over the "standard" language. Jasper and Mabel, the emerging happy couple and the founders of the new generation, once again speak the language that is closest to that of the narrator himself. But Natty's dialect speech is also, again, affirmed as authentic, despite not being integrated into the polite norm. There is even more emphasis on *translation* than in the earlier tale, though since this chiefly takes the form of Delaware to

English it will be discussed in the next chapter. Among the English speakers, it is (besides Natty) the Scots and the sailors whose languages are most frequently called to our notice. Cap's intellectually limited and stubborn view of the world takes, like Ben Pump's (though with rather less sympathy), the form of a completely closed vocabulary. All things are defined in terms of the sailor's life, and the salt-water version of it at that, so that Natty is obliged to declare that he is "none the wiser for your words, and in ticklish times the plainer a man makes his English, the better he is understood" (p. 49). Jasper's honorific pseudonym, 'Eau douce', is variously misinterpreted by Cap as "Oh! the deuce" and "Eau-de-vie" (pp. 38, 94), a fact of merely comic potential until Jasper's possible disloyalty is proposed and related to his knowledge of the French language (p. 194). Like Temple with his Quaker phrases, Lundie and his fellow Scotsmen fall into the "pronunciation and dialect" of their youth when remembering past times or when excited, just as they retain a preference for the foods and drinks of their homeland (pp. 146, 149, 125). Once again, this corresponds to an unwillingness to adapt to new situations, so that Natty remarks that "Exper'ence makes them but little wiser" (p. 51).

As with *The Pioneers,* the title of this novel is again worth noting. Coined as another of Natty's honorific names, those given to him as a result of his talents, *DA* notes Cooper as the inventor of word, later taken into more general use. In fact, in three of the five Leatherstocking novels, Cooper is taking as his title a word having a definite identity as Americanism. *Pathfinder* is a coinage, and the two others had recent recorded origins (*prairie, DA* 1770; *pioneer, DA* 1817), although *OED* disputes the second. The identity of the series as a chronicle not only of the American experience (the five tales span the period from the 1740s to 1805) but also of the American language is thereby signaled. If this seems a slight point, we may note the British review of *Notions of the Americans* cited by Cairns (1922, p. 143), which remarks that "the very title is objectionable, as containing a *slang* term, which (in the sense in which he uses it), good taste has long ago banished both from polished composition and discourse."

Both *The Last of the Mohicans* and *The Prairie,* published respectively in 1826 and 1827, were revised by Cooper for publication by Bentley. Of the twenty-eight footnotes added to the 1831 text of *The Last of the Mohicans* for the benefit of the British reader, and which mostly interpret American Indian customs and laws, six are devoted to the definitions of words, and another six or seven are about names or naming. Almost half, in other words, are concerned with language. There are a number of Americanisms in the text, some of recent recorded origin. *DA* gives this novel as the perpetrator of the (probably mistaken) use of *wish-ton-wish* (1983, p. 227), a word that would soon appear in the title of another tale. The words *blazed, licks, relish,* and *suc-ca-tush* are all glossed in footnotes (pp. 318, 122, 54, 287); although *DA* does not give *relish* as an Americanism, it was widely thought to be one, and discussed as such (*OED* gives a British use in the 1790s). *Rifts* is explained (p. 12), as it was to be again in *The Pathfinder*. The word *pale-face* is common (DA 1823), and terms for which *DA* records eighteenth-century origins include *kill-deer, war-path, warwhoop, blazed, pepperage,* and *succotash*. This novel also has the first recorded use of the phrase *war-paint,* as well as the unrecorded (in *DAE*) incidence of *rattler* (pp. 56, 114).

The next novel in the series, *The Prairie,* has been the subject of a detailed study that contains much useful information on its vocabulary and its textual evolution. Orm Överland (1973) has identified and described the close use made by Cooper of the narratives of the Lewis and Clark and the Stephen Long expeditions, and this is reflected in the vocabulary. Natty has now become a *trapper,* a word for which *OED* gives a British source but which was certainly more common in America, and is therefore glossed by Cooper as an "American word" (1832b, p. 16); similarly, *fall* (p. 90). Once again, many of the footnotes included in the 1832 text concern language; eight out of eighteen propose etymologies or translations (*trapper, partisan, brave, plunder, half-breed, long-knives, hommany, fall*), and two more are about names or naming. The word *prairie* is explained at length in the introduction (pp. vi–vii). *DA* gives *rattler* (mistakenly), *burnt-wood,* and *crowdy* as first occurring in this novel, all spoken by Natty (pp. 10, 42, 425), and other words with citations postdating 1800 include *"acclimated," brave, fixen, metiffs,* and *plunder.* Again, a heightening of the dialect forms has been traced in the revisions (see Överland, 1973, p. 119). There is a positive war of words over the naming of the largest mammal of the prairies. The debate between *bison* and *buffaloe* is

pursued throughout the novel, and perhaps represents the model for
Bird's use of the distinction as an index of social status in *Nick of
the Woods* (1837). *Buffaloe* is "the popular nomenclature of the
country" (1832b, p. 116), and is used by Natty Bumppo. It had
been the preference of Lewis and Clark, exclusively, and even
though Cooper's own note says that the true word is *bison,* which
is only "vulgarly called the buffaloe" (p. 108), the tone of condescension of the writer revising his text is not borne out by the
dramatic representation of the argument within it. For, in the person of Dr. Obed Battius, Cooper clearly satirizes the learned scientist and the mouther of definitions, the exponent of that Enlightenment mentality we have seen latent in the exposition of Lewis and
Clark, though expressed there in much less intimidating language.
Battius, whose real name is presumably just plain Batt, takes Natty
to task for his "vulgar error":

> The animal you describe is in truth a species of the bos ferus, (or
> bos sylvestris, as he has been happily called by the poets,) but,
> though of close affinity, it is altogether distinct from the common
> bubulus. Bison is the better word; and I would suggest the necessity
> of adopting it in the future, when you shall have occasion to allude
> to the species (p. 80).

Cooper here parodies a tendency of which he was himself often
to be accused; that of redundant grandiloquence or overfastidious-
ness. Natty's reply is in the spirit of his familiar appeal for tolerance
and for the precedence of things over names: "the creatur' is the
same, call it by what name you will." He is voicing an alternative
priority to that of learned definition, one wherein social and educational distinctions are not unnecessarily heightened. For him the
demands of survival and cooperation are stronger than those of
science; as in the other Leatherstocking tales, he is proposing a
contract within which language (or culture, or race) does not constitute a divisive principle. There is comedy here, of course, but
it is not unqualified by gravity. Natty's rendering of the Latin
horridi as "horrid eyes" (p. 228), like his hearing of *incisors* as
"inside overs" (1832b, p. 107) and Harry March's reporting of
compos mentis as "compass meant us" (*The Deerslayer,* pp. 24–
25),[12] has no actual harmful consequences, unlike Cap's misreading
of "Eau douce." But it is nevertheless an index of his exclusion

from the more complex linguistic and social contract that is coming into being. This contract will depend on a legal-scientific synthesis in which both the beasts of the field and the laws of civil society will be expressed as impersonal schemata whose interpretation will require a sophisticated inference of particular items from general terms. Webster, in the preface to his 1828 dictionary, had commented on words of foreign spelling as "very embarrassing to readers who know only their vernacular tongue," and tending to introduce "an odious difference between the pronunciation of different classes of people" (1831, p. xlvii). For Natty, Batt's words "hide their meaning in sound" (p. 230), and he recognizes in them the restless symptoms of the imperial imagination, however ineptly embodied in this particular scientist: "I have always found that a conceited man never knows content" (p. 273). Batt's mistaking his own ass for a new species, under the influence of a fearful imagination that is intimidated by the unfamiliar even as it tries to tame it, makes it clearer than ever that Natty's perceptions and expressions are those best suited to this particular environment, despite his vulgar insistence on calling a *bison* a *buffalo.*

In these two novels of the mid 1820s, *The Last of the Mohicans* and *The Prairie,* the materials of the national language are as evident as in any others. The character of Natty especially is developed beyond what it had been in *The Pioneers.* As he becomes even more central to the narrative than he had been before, so the questions and controversies he raises become more important to the argument of the tales. *Mohicans* includes the most complex of any of Cooper's images of Native American languages, and will be discussed in the next chapter; suffice it to say for now that much of Natty's linguistic integrity is marked by his assimilation into the language contract of the Delawares. Not only does he abjure all books except one—"what have such as I, who am a warrior of the wilderness, though a man without a cross, to do with books!" (1983, p. 117)—putting forward the "primitive" case that books can stand between a man and a proper appreciation of what is around him; but the English language itself becomes one "he was apt to use when a little abstracted in mind" (p. 272). When he wishes to be precise, he speaks in Delaware.

Cooper's art is a complicated one, and I do not mean to imply that this is all there is to say about Natty Bumppo.[13] He is, as

Lawrence and others have pointed out, a killer as well as an innocent, and the images of death, infertility (or unfecundity), and the
negation of the female occur throughout the novels in which he
figures. His identity is to be found in his attachment to his rifle, a
positive fetish form at times, the very killdeer that first appears in
Mohicans and whose name marks it out as a many-sided symbol.
The bird's name is an Americanism (*DA,* 1731), and comes from
the sound the bird makes; it thus has the poetry of onomatopoeia,
suggesting the coincidence of man's language with that of nature.
But when Natty calls his weapon by the same name, other senses
accrue. He does indeed *kill* deer, and much besides, with unerring
accuracy. In this nominal synthesis of the poetic and the deathly,
it is as if Cooper has imaged the whole paradox of the hunter's
character.

   Any full analysis of that character must then take account of this
and other related paradoxes and indeterminacies. In the sphere of
language, however, Natty is generally presented as the speaker of
truth, the voice of natural justice and of a sympathetic relation between man and nature The end of *Mohicans* (p. 348) has him "deserted by all of his colour" in more ways than one. In *The Prairie*
he has become "the trapper, whom in future we shall choose to
designate by his pursuit" (1832b, p. 16); the Native American
practice of honorific naming is here applied with a sad irony. In
this novel, as we have seen, Natty's language is on the defensive,
and his locutions are more Indian than ever, although he no longer
lives within a society that he can educate by voicing them. The new
homo americanus, Ishmael Bush, speaks a very different language
from that of the trapper, one full of violence and Old Testament
fire, articulating a moral code that is not completely hypocritical
but yet is definitely at the service of an irresistible self-interest.
Ishmael's turning back is one of the great moments of wish fulfillment in the American novel, given how few of the actual emigrants
did so. A space is thereby cleared for Natty Bumppo to die in peace,
"without kith or kin in the wide world" (p. 440). It is a space between cultures and between languages, as he is "always changing
his language to suit the person he addressed, and not infrequently
according to the ideas he expressed" (p. 438). Like an Indian, he
lies with his rifle and with the stuffed figure of his dead hound, but
like a Christian he must qualify the superstition of his pagan friends

and request a gravestone (p. 439). The grave will, however, be tended only by the Pawnees; and as he dies expressing his hopes of an after-world in which the white and red races might be mutually reconciled, the whole logic of the book makes it clear that they will never be happy together in this one.

By the time of *The Deerslayer* (1841) and its revision (1850), Cooper has returned to the career of the young Natty Bumppo; so young, indeed, that the novel opens with his having lost his way, something that never happens to the older man. This is one of Cooper's most difficult and dark novels, imaging a world in which white men go scalping and wherein violence, while beginning as "Homerically" specific and personal, with man facing his enemy and knowing him by name, ends in a scene of indiscriminate slaughter. Louise Pound (1927, p. 481) has noted that of all the Leatherstocking tales this one is most committed to the representation of Natty as a dialect speaker. This may be partly related to the increasing fashionability of dialect writing, as described in a previous chapter. But Cooper is not simply responding to market factors; or if he is thus responding, then he is doing so skeptically. For as well as the deerslayer himself, now incarnate as "the Straight-tongue" (p. 68) among other names, there is Harry March, who also speaks in the vernacular but is as much committed to noise and hyperbole as Natty is to the minimal language of truth. Cooper observes somewhat fastidiously that "the reader will have remarked that Deerslayer had not very critically studied his dictionary" (p. 227), but at the same time he is clearly one who is in tune with his environment and with his creator "without the aid of forms or language" (p. 299). When Natty comments on language itself, Cooper takes even more trouble than before to emphasize the integrity of his priorities. His somewhat homespun account of the etymology of *furlough* is aimed at the conclusion that "the vartue of a pledge lies in the idee, and not in the word" (p. 424). Again, in a later discussion of the meanings of generally held as against personal associations and feelings, he declares that, although he can hate the word *serpent:*

> Yet, ever since Chingachgook has 'arned the title he bears, why the sound is as pleasant to my ears as the whistle of a whip-poor-will of a calm evening—it is. The feelin's make all the difference in the world, Judith, in the natur' of sounds (p. 459).

Appropriate as these reflections are to the speculations of a young man slightly touched by the rub of love, they also have a place in the novel's examination of the relation between reality and its appearance in words. Judith Hutter is the most politely spoken person in the book, speaking the language closest to that of the narrator himself. Cooper takes pains to point this out:

> her language was superior to that used by her male companions, her own father included. This difference extended as well to pronunciation as to the choice of words and phrases. Perhaps nothing so soon betrays the education and association as the modes of speech; and few accomplishments so much aid the charm of female beauty as a graceful and even utterance, while nothing so soon produces the disenchantment that necessarily follows a discrepancy between appearance and manner, as a mean intonation of voice, or a vulgar use of words (p. 152).

In *The Pioneers,* it will be remembered, Cooper made much of a similar linguistic alliance between the narrator and his favored characters, Oliver Edwards and Elizabeth Temple. Here, however, the pattern is reversed. Judith Hutter is, in the somewhat restrictive morality of the tale, a false woman, one whose appearance is not her reality. Her relation to society has been improper, so that she is forced to admit that she can never

> be justly called the equal of a man like Deerslayer. It is true, I have been better taught . . . but then his truth—his truth—makes a fearful difference between us (pp. 338–39).

Cooper makes a similar point later on in asserting that "truth was the Deerslayer's polar star. He ever kept it in view; and it was nearly impossible for him to avoid uttering it, even when prudence demanded silence" (p. 594). The narrator's conviction is thus now much more behind the dialect speaker (despite his tendency to self-righteousness), at the expense of the character who is closest to him in speech, Judith Hutter. Polite speech is here projected as the bearer of false forms and fallen manners.

This apparent inverse symmetry must itself be disturbed, as I have hinted at before. For it is not *all* dialect that is thus privileged, but only that of Natty Bumppo. Harry March is the other major vernacular speaker, but he is as negative as Natty is positive. He is the prototype (the tale is set in the 1740s) of a type Cooper already (in 1841) saw all around him, both in fiction and in life, the "ring-tail roarer" or tall talker, whether incarnate as a boisterous backwoodsman or an astute Whig politician. In this novel, appearance is not to be taken for reality in any way except in the personality of the deerslayer. As there are good and bad Indians, all speaking the Ossianic language of high poetry, so there are good and bad dialect users (though no good polite speakers). No simple inference of character from speech can be made, despite the narrator's declaration of his own preferences (p. 152, cited above). Natty's minimal speech signifies maximum integrity; it is his preference for silence or near-silence that is more telling than his use of dialect. He remains as different from the frontier "blowhard" as the older Natty was from the other dialect speakers of Templeton in *The Pioneers*. As with the truths of the Christian religion and the fact of the rotation of the earth (pp. 468–69, 495), seeing is not believing, and surfaces do not always speak the truth. Natty's career in the five novels in which he appears is founded on a lifelong attempt to bring together appearance and reality, and his failure to do so is an index of Cooper's despair at the sophisticated deceptions of the society Cooper saw coming into being around him. As communities must become larger and civilization more developed, so the necessarily *specific* exploration of the relation of appearance to reality must become harder to undertake; and this alone, along with the reliable evidence of trial and error, can produce a firm idea of the truth. Moments of origination and conclusion are continually changing places in the Leatherstocking cycle. Thus, it is appropriate that the tale of Natty's early career should be one of Cooper's darkest novels, in which language and truth are at odds in all but one case; and appropriate also that the first novel to be written, *The Pioneers,* should already show a world from which the "Straighttongue" has been once and for all displaced and sent forth into the wilderness, both herald of and alternative to what he leaves behind him.

Cooper's Other Languages

In the many novels Cooper wrote between the first and the last of the Leatherstocking tales, as well as in the novels of the 1840s, he remained sensitive to the rights of the American vocabulary. His patriotism was never belligerent or extreme, however, and the policy expounded in *The American Democrat,* that new words should not be invented when old ones will do, is repeated throughout his career. In the same spirit, he comments at least twice, in *The Chainbearer* (p. 264) and in *Wyandotté* (p. 20), on the improper use of the word *creek,* whose application to small rivers rather than to inlets of the sea was a notorious Americanism.[14] In *The Monikins* Cooper parodies the American inclination for novelty at all costs. When the commodore is challenged in his use of the term "rotatory," he rejoins that *rotary* is "not expresssive enough for our meaning; and therefore we term it 'rotatory' " (p. 256).

Scornful as he was of what he saw as a mindless enthusiasm for neologism, Cooper yet remained sympathetic to the transcription and publication of such new words as were necessitated by the particular circumstances of the new nation, as well as terms that had become too popular to be resisted. *Home as Found* has *DA's* first recorded use of *sockdollager* (p. 228), and words and phrases such as *A no. 1* (*Miles Wallingford,* pp. 79, 160), *grave-yard* (*The Redskins,* p. 238, in the voice of Littlepage), and *real estate* (*Afloat and Ashore,* p. 217) are used either very close to or in advance of their first recorded *DA* entries. In *The Oak Openings,* Cooper goes into a long digression on the usage and etymology of *shanty,* and then into another discussion of the infamous problems of *Yankee* (pp. 27–28). *Satanstoe* (pp. 233–34) includes another account of *sleigh,* for the benefit of "others than Americans," which predicts that it *"will* become English ere long, as it is now American. Twenty millions of people not only can make a word, but they can make a language, if needed." Thus, even as Cooper is engaging in one of his most skeptical inquiries into American political developments, he never reneges on the rights of the American language. In a similar spirit, the word *sun-down,* though noted as a "New England provincialism that has got to be so general in America" (*Homeward Bound,* p. 417), is not censured as such.[15]

The above remarks are not intended as a complete summary of Cooper's vocabulary, but they may at least stand as evidence that his concern with the publication and defense of American English did not cease with the revisions for Bentley's *Standard Novels* in the early 1830s. In particular, it did not cease during the years when his general faith in the positive future of American culture and society was at a very low ebb. Nor does Cooper cease to explore and dramatize the conflicts of language that we have seen to be central to *The Pioneers*. It cannot be claimed that he is ever very sensitive to the rights of Black English, and he prefers to avoid as far as he can the whole argument building through the middle years of the century about the rights and prospects of Black Americans. Otherwise, linguistic tension remains an important part of his analysis of the wider strains emerging within the republic. This is especially true of the Littlepage trilogy and of the Effingham novels, though here it tends no longer to take the form of disputes and misunderstandings between English and foreign speakers, whether they be Frenchmen, Germans, or Native Americans. Although these ethnic minorities continue to appear, both as picturesque or comic relief and as indices of serious tensions within the community, they no longer seem to constitute the major focus of Cooper's interest in language. With the exception of the Native American question, this interest becomes more and more fixed on the profile and "sociology" of New England speech, often presented as a negative challenge to that of New York and the middle states, the repository of Cooper's preferred national standard. This change of direction, or emphasis, may be taken as a sign of an increasing urgency on Cooper's part about the internal quarrels between different factions of English-speakers with different *regional* affiliations and practices.

Cooper had, of course, always been sensitive to the New England dialect, and we have seen the care with which, in *The Pioneers* especially, he had purified Natty Bumppo's speech of many of the more flagrant localisms that mark the speech of the other inhabitants of Templeton. The images of New Englanders are seldom positive in the early novels, even if they are not emphatically negative. Hiram Dolittle and his kind are always hated by Cooper, but Tom Coffin of *The Pilot* is not the object of any disapproval on the grounds of his New England origin, nor is Noah Poke of *The Monikins* treated more cynically than the rest of the cast of characters. Moses Marble, who is "an uneducated Kennebunk man, and by no means particular about his English" (*Afloat and Ashore*, p. 147), is no villain, and while the portrayal of the New Hampshire-born Ithuel Bolt in *The Wing-and-Wing* is considerably more complex, no more is he. Cooper plays on Ithuel's use of the words *clever* and *despise* (pp. 59, 69), on his pronunciation of *Italians* (p. 166), and on his "propensity to pass all the modulations of his voice through his nose" (p. 274). But, despite his generally cynical self-interest and the irony of his ending his career as Deacon Bolt, he is not a completely negative character, and he is allowed one very justified complaint about the British prejudices against his speech:

> What I found hardest to be borne, was their running their rigs on me about my language and ways, which they were all the time laughing at as Yankee conversation and usages, while they pretended that the body out of which all on it came, was an English body, and so they set it up to be shot at, by any of their inimies that might happen to be jogging along our road. Then, squire, it is generally consaited among us in Ameriky, that we speak much the best English a-going; and sure am I, that none on us call a 'hog' an ' 'og', an 'anchor' a 'hanchor', or a 'horse' a ' 'orse' (pp. 68–69).

Ithuel's "consait" may be risible, but not so his observations on unreasonable arrogance of his Cockney peers, least of all appropriate at a time when he is suffering impressment in the British navy!

In fact, the New Englanders against whom Cooper's animus seems to be strongest are those hailing from Massachusetts and Connecticut, rather than from the states to the north. He always disliked Puritanism, which he seems to have associated with these two states, and he must also have inherited a strong antipathy toward a region traditionally regarded as a stronghold of Federalism and thereafter a hotbed of Whiggery. These religious and political predilections often led in Cooper's eyes to a distinct kind of personality. It projects a commitment to plainness and simplicity, avoiding such arts of life as that of cookery, for which no one would ever go to the "land of the Pilgrims" (*The Oak Openings,* p. 219). Admirable as this is up to a point, it can be hypocritically exploited at such times as self-interest is disposed to mask itself as egalitarianism. This was, as we have seen, exactly the strategy of which the new Whigs were being accused in much of the commentary of the times. Thus, Cooper says, under the guise of a profound humility, "our kinsmen of New England pay homage to the golden calf" (*The Sea-Lions,* p. 155). Similarly, while pretending to an egalitarian culture, "the deference to *English* rank . . . is undeniably greater among the mass in New England, than it is anywhere else in this country. . . . Perhaps the exclusively English origin of the people may have an influence" (*Satanstoe,* p. 150). As Webster had fought the prevailing Anglophilia of the Boston press, so Cooper (who did not much respect Webster) satirizes Steadfast Dodge's obsequious behavior before an (apparent) English baronet (*Homeward Bound,* pp. 199–200, 251), Dodge being "an American demogogue precisely in obedience to those feelings and inclinations which would have made him a courtier anywhere else" (p. 199).

Although Cooper was never a Tory in the true sense of the word, he was a believer in traditions (up to a point) and in some measure of social stability. Thus, he was naturally uncomfortable with the mobility and restlessness of the New Englander, who was familiar to him in the figure of the settler. We have seen that Templeton was peopled largely by migrants from western Massachusetts. In *Home as Found* the commodore protests:

> I call him a bad neighbor who never remains long enough in a place to love anything but himself . . . heaven is no place for a Yankee, if he can get further west, by hook or by crook. They are all too uneasy for any steady occupation (p. 329).

The Yankee entrepreneur is thus a persona who represents the principle of instability always unleashed by a commercial economy, though here it takes the form of a movement across the land. Samuel Johnson had expressed concern about the disturbing effects of commerce on the language (and on much else besides), and Webster had explained the New Englander's circumlocution as an egalitarian trait that might all too easily be prone to misuse. All of these elements inform Cooper's portrayals of New Englanders and their diction in the novels of the late 1830s and the 1840s. Dodge comes from a "part of the country in which men were accustomed to think, act, almost to eat and drink and sleep, in common" (*Homeward Bound,* p. 48), and among other things he sees himself as an arbiter of the language, declaring that it is "rather unpopular to differ from the neighborhood, in this or any other respect" (p. 108). In other words, everyone must conform to the New England standard, a proposition Cooper reports with obsessively sarcastic tenacity. Whole pages are given over to the transcription of Dodge's linguistic misdeeds, and the disdain they occasion in the truly polite characters (e.g., pp. 212–19). *Home as Found* is similarly punctuated with Dodge's delusions about "his superiority on the subject of language" (p. 425). For Cooper, Dodge is the image of the new man, one who hides self-interest behind the rhetoric of populism.

In the Littlepage trilogy, the persona of the New Englander offers Cooper an opportunity for parodying Noah Webster, of whom he had as we have seen (1982, pp. 70–71) a very low opinion. Jason Newcome—"or, as he pronounced the latter appellation himself, Noocome" (*Satanstoe,* p. 45)—is a Yale-educated schoolmaster:

> the whole energies of his nature became strangely directed to just such reforms of language as would be apt to strike the imagination of a pedagogue of his calibre. In the first place, he had brought from home with him a great number of sounds that were decidedly vulgar and vicious, and with these in full existence in himself, he had commenced his system of reform on other people. . . . His first step was to improve the language, by adapting sound in spelling, and he insisted on calling angel, *an*-gel, because *a-n s*pelt an (p. 48).

Cooper delights in pointing out that Jason contradicts his own principles, calling "stone" *stun* and "home" *hum;* he also puts "verbs in the places of substantives" (p. 52), Here, as throughout the later novels, Cooper misses no opportunity to make fun of the Websterian ambition to conform sound and spelling. In *The Chainbearer,* "the Yankees in the camp" are said to have "a mania to pronounce every word as it is spelled" (p. 18). In *The Sea Lions* Cooper opines that the "discrepancy between the spelling and the pronunciation of proper names is agreeable to us, for it shows that a people are not put in leading-strings by pedagogues, and that they make use of their own in their own way" (pp. 18–19). Here, it must be pointed out that Cooper himself is using the rhetoric of populism to affirm a convention that is not at all unambiguously in the interests of "the people." No account is taken of Webster's reasons for advocating his reforms: that literacy might be made more generally attainable and that communication between the various orders within society might be less divisive. Thus, in *The Sea Lions* especially, while Cooper's position on dialect seems to have turned around, with the colorful vagaries of common speech in this respect being almost celebrated (e.g., pp. 135, 172, 200, 477), we can see that what is in fact being covertly excluded from the linguistic commonwealth is exactly the troublesome category of the middle-class literates for whom Webster most commonly spoke. In Cooper's world, it is also aristocratic or genteel to use names that are not pronounced in ways we might predict from their spelling. Hence Gardiner as " 'Gar'ner'—as it would be thought almost a breach of decorum, in Suffolk, not to call him" (*The Sea Lions*, p. 30); Woolston as "Wooster," despite the efforts of the "Yankee schoolmaster" to persuade our hero otherwise (*The Crater*, p. 13); and Wilmeter, "which, in the family parlance, was almost always pronounced Wilmington" (*Ways of the Hour*, p. 12). This pleasure in the whimsical unpredictability of names is, of course, dominant in the family designations of the British ruling classes—Cholmondeleys, Cokes, Beauchamps, and so forth—a fact with which every aspiring English social climber and bewildered foreign visitor has had to cope. So, in certifying the disjunctions between the spoken and the written as common to the uppermost and the lowest social orders, Cooper is supporting a familiar conservative compact in which the entire existence of the unstable middle orders (with their pious insistence on linguistic conformity), as well as the arguable needs of the lower order itself, are completely effaced. Although he celebrates the traditional pronunciations of dialect *speakers* as differing from the written forms, he entirely fails to explore the probability that they cannot *spell* the words they speak, if indeed they can read and write at all. The very sounds they enunciate are of the sort to keep them less capably literate than they might otherwise be.

The other area of Jason Newcome's pedagogy that Cooper satirizes is his commitment to euphemism. Webster's dictionaries had been famously sensitive on this subject, going to great lengths to avoid any hint of impropriety. A. W. Read (1933b) has pointed out that the 1833 edition shows revisions directed at the further exclusion of any potentially embarrassing words. Newcome similarly finds the word "Satanstoe" (not by accident the title of the novel) to be "irreligious and profane" (p. 52), and becomes a supporter of the alternative "Dibbleton," "under the pretence . . . that it once belonged to a family of Dibblees" (p. 494). Cooper's most frequent target in this respect is the campaign to renominate "Hell Gate" as "Hurl Gate," which draws the following response from Squire Dunscomb (*The Ways of the Hour*, p. 137):

> Heaven knows what the country is coming to! There is Webster, to begin with, cramming a Yankee dialect down our throats for good English; then comes all the cant of the day, flourishing finical phrases, and new significations to good old homely words, and changing the very nature of mankind by means of terms.[16]

Cooper's scorn for the habit of euphemism is, like his attack on the campaign to conform the spoken and the written, very much an aristocratic posture. Euphemisms have usually been more fashionable among the aspiring, middle order of society, those most anxious about the proprieties they themselves have created, but which they tend to regard as imposed from above. The lower and upper orders are both, then as now, less self-conscious about such matters.

No more does Cooper seem to care for the sound of the New England dialect. It must be said that Littlepage is a man "who feels that he has been grievously injured, and who writes with the ardor of youth increased by the sense of wrong" (*The Redskins*, p. 535). But even if he is not to be simply identified with Cooper himself, it is hard not to conclude that his obsessive criticisms of New England speech, which he finds "strong and unpleasant" (p. 136), are in line with the author's own sentiments. Webster's role in the popularizing of his own regionalisms (a role often noted by the reviewers of the 1806 dictionary), together with his general convictions in favor of the reform of language, make him an obvious target for Cooper, who always intuits and often articulates a connection between language and the social order. As New England was exporting its surplus population, so its language spread beyond its natural boundaries, along with the values and social practices that the language expressed. Nelson's objections to the "infernal jargon" and "false philosophies" of the French (*The Wing-and-Wing*, p. 217) are hardly less extreme than those elsewhere directed at the New Englanders. Steadfast Dodge's newspaper changes its name from *Enquirer* to *Inquirer* when it ceases to support Adams (*Homeward Bound*, p. 192); in it he publishes not only his views but the language appropriate to them, being "an advocate for rotation in language, as well as in office" (p. 215). Somewhat uncomfortably,

Cooper looks back to 1776 as a time when "the English language had not undergone half of its present mutations" (*Wyandotté,* p. 311). We must assume that he means less to approve a pre-revolutionary standard than to lament the subsequent rise of a factional tradition in American politics, and one expressing a commitment to change for its own sake. In *The Crater* (p. 33–34) he sardonically suggests that since "new things require new names," the government should be called "Gossipian" instead of "Republican."

One further linguistic symptom of the middle-class self-interest Cooper identified with the New England Yankee is the fashion for hyperbole, also remarked by Tocqueville. Although Cooper disavows any complete alliance with the dramatic narrator of *Afloat and Ashore* (p. ix), he is clearly not unsympathetic to the idea that

> In 1797 the grandiose had by no means made the deep invasions into the every-day language of the country that it has since done. Any thing of the sublime, or of the recondite school was a good deal more apt to provoke a smile, than it is to-day—the improvement proceeding, as I have understood through better judges than myself, from the great melioration of mind and manners that is to be traced to the speeches in Congress, and to the profundities of the newspapers (pp. 37–38).

On other occasions, reference is made to the "pretending name of drawing-room" (p. 12), to the widespread creation of "colonels" and "generals" (pp. 478, 480), and to the "half-educated" redundancy of describing New York as a "commercial emporium" (p. 47). In the "old Suffolk" celebrated in *The Sea Lions,* "sixteen men" do *not* turn around to reply if one calls out "Squire" or "Doctor." Grandiloquence is not just an offense against "good, plain, direct, and manly English" (*Ways of the Hour,* p. 178); it is also a means whereby simple things are made to seem more complicated than they are, and false things may be made to seem true, as in the courtroom of Judge Temple. It is the technique of the "confidence man" (probably identified by Cooper with the new generation of Whig politicians), and in this respect at least his polemic is not to be thought of as simply a nostalgic alliance with the ordered social hierarchy of old rural America.

There are, then, at least three aspects of the New England speech profile that Cooper attacks: the conforming of spoken and written, the commitment to euphemism, and the tendency toward grandiloquence. The last of these is not unique to New England, but those among Cooper's characters who sin in this respect often turn out to be Yankees. Against these habits and conventions, Cooper in the later novels tries to set up a counterexample in the language and society of old New York state. The Hudson valley seems to have offered an unusual case of a society in which the old manorial gentry was surviving and even prospering under settler conditions (see D. Ellis, 1967; Pocock, 1975, p. 514). In *The Spy,* Cooper had noted that the hinterland of New York city was more prone than any other part of the country to the "aristocratical notions of blood and alliances" (p. 27) derived from the British model. To point out his own contamination with this world view is to say nothing new; he did, of course, marry into the De Lancey family. But Cooper was never a true aristocrat, never believing in *birth* as the foundation of a social hierarchy. He did believe in a natural hierarchy, with the best at the top, but this is a very different thing. In his New York novels, he is interested (as he is so often elsewhere) in that state as the site of conflict between old and new traditions, between the royalist legacy and the new immigrant ideology. It is thus described in the preface to *Afloat and Ashore:*

> The influence of these two sources of thought is still obvious to the reflecting, giving rise to a double set of social opinions; one of which bears all the characteristics of its New England and puritanical origin, while the other may be said to come of the usages and notions of the middle states, proper (p. viii).

It must be emphasized that Cooper offers no arguments in favor of the royalist tradition; in fact, he speaks scathingly of those who had opposed independence in 1776 without ever losing their place in post-revolutionary high society, or their social influence as committed Anglophiles (pp. 356–57). The Littlepages were "to a man" loyal to the colonies, not to the crown (*The Chainbearer,* p. 12), and Cooper's idea of the "simple American gentleman" (*Home as Found,* p. 210) has nothing to do with worship of things British—quite the opposite.

At the same time, Cooper has no time for the hypocritical (as he sees it), egalitarian rhetoric of the restless middle class and those who were pretending to be at one with them. The polite American style that governs his narrative and is spoken by most of the characters we are to respect (the significant exception of Natty Bumppo has been discussed) is as free from the Yankee dialect as it is from Anglicisms. The rioters in *Lionel Lincoln* (p. 352) speak a "barbarous idiom," but the polite narrative alternative is not to be interpreted as the language of a royalist. In the later novels, as has been said, Cooper is much more interested in the analysis of the relations between different kinds of American English than in any extensive defense of the American against the British standard, a controversy he seems to have come to regard as secondary, albeit still important. The narrator of *The Redskins* comments that he is

> no more for condemning a usage . . . simply because it is English, than I am for approving it simply because it is English. I wish every thing to stand on its own merits (p. 337).

The argument, in other words, needs to be focused on the linguistic condition of America. Similarly, *Satanstoe* suggests that the British-American crux might well be a red herring: "it might be well for us to correct a great many faults into which we have certainly fallen, before we declaim with so much confidence about the purity of our English" (p. 437). Thus, the extended sense of the term *garrison,* used to describe a military work even when unoccupied and explained without adverse comment in *The Pathfinder* (1981, p. 48), occasions in *The Oak Openings,* published just eight years later, a brief dissertation on "the convertible nature of our language" (p. 174), and an adjudication of which innovations should be allowed and which resisted. The address at this point seems to be directed at the American rather than the British reader, though it certainly assures the latter than there is an American writer prepared to exercise a real discrimination in his linguistic patriotism. At the same time, the image of the fashionable fops who form, with Rupert Hardinge, the "English set" in *Afloat and Ashore,* with their "lofty disdain" for all things American, is totally negative. Cooper never ceases to maintain a thorough contempt for the "miserable moral dependence of this country on Great Britain" (pp. 383, 483), wherever he sees it. The criticism of America, and of certain habits and trends in the American language, never crosses the line into Anglophilia.

The language of the middle states was, as we have seen, that advanced as the best national standard in Cooper's travel book of 1837, *Gleanings in Europe: England.* In the Littlepage novels of 1845–46, it is clear that New York state is a frontier area in which the spread of New England speech and society is in tension with the polite New York speech that is also Cooper's narrative and native diction. This struggle is not limited to those Americans who are of British origin, for it involves also the New York Dutch. Andries Coejemans is proud that his faults of speech are all "honest New York mistakes, and no 'New England gipperish' " (*The Chainbearer*, p. 21). *Satanstoe* is full of information on the normalization of New York Dutch into American English phrases, a process of which the word *sleigh* constitutes the most famous example. Like the Scots, the Irish, and the Quakers in other novels, Cooper's Dutch Americans become more Dutch as they become more excited (pp. 59, 439). Mother Doortje's name goes through various metamorphoses in the speech of Littlepage and, more dramatically, Jason Newcome, in a process that implicitly images the takeover of Dutch by English as well as the struggle between the various kinds of English involved. In *The Monikins* (p. 135), the human and monikin speakers agree to use Latin so that no prejudice in favor of either "dialect" is established; in the less completely fictionalized world of nineteenth-century America, no such compromise was possible.[17]

Just as he was in *The Pioneers,* Cooper is aware in the later novels of all the strains and tensions apparent in the pot as its contents are trying to melt. The idea that there already *is* a unified America is not maintained. What is happening is something darker and more troubling than the easy emergence of a common language. This appears also in the shift of emphasis in Cooper's view of the process of naming. Lewis and Clark, as we have seen, were enthusiastic authors of names, but any implacable criticism of their insouciance in this respect must take account of the fact that the great majority of those names have not survived. As explorers they moved too fast and left too little behind them to be able to rechristen the landscape after their own images. Cooper's father was, of course, the namer of a place (Cooperstown), and it is surely unarguable that the uneasier aspects of Judge Temple's relation to Templeton are an echo of some of Cooper's perhaps unconscious intuitions of paternal narcissism (see Railton, 1978, pp. 75–113).

In *The Chronicles of Cooperstown* Cooper tells us (anonymously) that

> The name of "Cooperstown," it is true, appears in one or two papers as early as 1786; but the place was indiscriminately known by this appellation, and that of the "Foot of the Lake," until the year 1791, when it became the county town (1838, p. 26).

The name of the father, in other words, was established at the expense of an impersonal and more natural place name, one that has almost a Native American quality in its fidelity to physical location rather than to human endeavor. Although it would not be convincing to argue for a complete revolt against the father in Cooper's image of Templeton, we can still see in Natty's objections to the settling of the land and the creation of the law an awareness that such acts of naming do serve to exclude as much as they include.

Cooper's views on this subject seem to have become stronger by 1838, with the publication of *Homeward Bound*. Here, the impulse to self-aggrandizement in the naming of places is portrayed quite negatively in the person of Steadfast Dodge. One of Cooper's villains, Dodge boasts that "the practice of naming towns and counties after distinguished citizens" is to be applauded (p. 248). "Dodgetown" does not last long, however. It first becomes "Dodgeborough," then

> a new family coming in that summer, a party was got up to change it to Dodge-ville, a name that was immensely popular, as ville means city in Latin; but it must be owned the people like change, or rotation in names, as well as in office, and they called the place Butterfield Hollow, for a whole month, after the new inhabitant, whose name is Butterfield. He moved away in the fall; and so, after trying Belindy (*Anglice* Belinda), Nineveh, Grand Cairo, and Pumpkin Valley, they made me the offer to restore the ancient name, provided some *addendum* more noble and proper could be found than town, or ville, or borough; it is not yet determined what it shall be, but I believe we shall finally settle down in Dodgeople, or Dodgeopolis (p. 249).

Not only is the namer of the place now an unscrupulous and hypocritical entrepreneur, rather than the basically upright Judge Temple, but the name itself is unstable, subject to all the vacillations of an unstable community. Moreover, although *The Pioneers* was set in a developing society, no one significant actually arrives in Templeton during the course of the novel, except the past owner of the land. Cooper thus achieves the imaginary feat of making the westward migration seem to go backwards, at least in time. By the 1840s, however, the pace seems to have quickened, and the already complex ethics of naming Templeton has come to seem a model of stability and propriety compared to the new traditions. Stewart (1967, p. 235) notes that there were six towns called Jackson in 1813, and forty by 1831, reflecting not just the popularity of the president but also the pace of settlement itself: Van Deusen (1963, p. 6) remarks that between 1830 and 1840 Indiana's population doubled while that of Illinois tripled. The increasing sensitivity to acts of naming in Cooper's later fiction is thus implicitly a response to a process now seen to be running out of control. Whereas Templeton (and Cooperstown) took their names from social circumstances that were already on the ground, things have turned around by the time of *Wyandotté* (1843). Maps and names used to come "after the place"; now, in a frenzy of expansionist ambition, "the former precede the last" (p. 513). In *Afloat and Ashore* (p. 251) the captain commemorates himself and his friends in his imaginary chart, before remarking that it might be "a capital idea to poke in a little patriotism among the names . . . Washington should have a finger in the pie" (p. 257). *The Crater,* which is largely about the discovery of a new world, is also full of reflections on the various options for naming it (pp. 70–71, 124).[18]

We are now in a position to understand a final thematic obsession in Cooper's image of the language: the positive coding of silence, or minimal speech, of which Natty Bumppo was such a prominent exponent. The orgy of naming that is transcribed in the later novels, the grandiloquence of the transplanted New England middle class, and the loud invocations of the authority of the people are all forms of *noise.* Cooper dislikes noise because it is a symptom of change and debate, and most of all of disturbance, whereby every fractious element in the social contract seeks to drown out its rivals. Cooper's thematic affinity is therefore with silence, broken only by the enunciation of a few well-chosen words. The primary image of this condition is to be found in the Native American languages, the subject of the next chapter. But it appears in other forms throughout the novels. Silence speaks for an integrated rather than an aggressive relation of man to nature (although nature itself may contain a principle of aggression). It is the (a)linguistic analogue of a kind of ecological tact in Cooper's heroes; they leave no trace behind them, and create no disturbance. Their modern successors would be the perfect (and impossible) National Park visitors, alive to all things while themselves invisible. Harvey Birch in *The Spy* is almost so, coming and going with the inscrutability of a natural force. Thus also Natty Bumppo. Like Ben Boden (*The Oak Openings*, p. 21), Cooper's heroes exercise "quick sight and long practice," seeing and respecting precisely what is *there* rather than imagining (with the aid of rhetoric) what is not. The "Trackless" is so called because he leaves "little or no trail in his journeys and marches" (*Satanstoe*, p. 337); even Manytongues the interpreter is, paradoxically, "a man of surprisingly few words" (*The Redskins*, p. 326). This Native American quality of silence and invisibility is one that Cooper wishes to reclaim or preserve as essential to the true American character. He comments in *Miles Wallingford* that

> It is lucky for us that the American character inclines to silence and thoughtfulness, in grave emergencies; we are noisy, garrulous, and sputtering, only in our politics (p. 281).

The noisy, the garrulous, and the sputtering are not only breaches of an artistic decorum but also and more crucially images of a basic strife within the social order, so that competition for attention becomes necessary. Natty Bumppo is a wish fulfillment for one aspect of Cooper's moral and ecological intelligence (however at odds it may be with others); so too is his famous *silent* laugh an image of the state of pre-linguistic innocence that Cooper would in one of his voices like to re-establish, turning the historical clock back to a time before the fury and the mire of political strife. Natty and the Indians are a vanishing breed. But there is one microcosmic society that shares with them their basic values, that of sailors in their life at sea. Not accidentally, Cooper's seamen also project the image of a pre-pubertal male society, in which the disruptive challenge of the female (and hence of procreation in general) does not have to be faced. In the life and language of the ship at sea, Cooper finds another workable union of silence and articulation.

We rarely encounter in Cooper's novels the kind of metaphysical speculations on the image of the sea that informs the later writings of, for example, Melville and Conrad.[19] The passage that opens Chapter 15 of *The Red Rover* (pp. 242–43) is very untypical in this respect. More commonly, the sea is just a surface on which human relations are articulated and played out, without itself being a presence in the narrative. It provides the element of threat and danger that keeps the senses operating with the maximum concentration (as does the forest in other novels), but it is not itself the subject of any symbolistic fantasy. Over seas and through forests, Cooper's protagonists perform their elaborate rituals of combat and evasion; in *The Prairie,* the open spaces of the center of the continent are constantly assimilated to the sea through Cooper's habit of referring to the long grass as "the fog," through which the characters have to navigate. The comparison is made explicit on several occasions (e.g., 1832b, pp. 242, 260, 276).

What appeals to Cooper is not so much the sea itself, as some kind of medium for speculative representation, but the human society that is associated with it. The shipboard community is for him the ideal image of society as a whole—and only ideal, given that it contains no women and no complex social organization. The crew of a ship is a model of organic hierarchy: the captain must be in absolute authority, but yet the task of every man is essential to the well-being of all the others. For Cooper, Britain's traditional naval supremacy is to be related to the convention whereby even the son of a Duke does service at sea that would elsewhere be thought "nearly menial" (*The Two Admirals,* p. 294). All sailors are "accustomed to defer to station and authority" (*The Crater,* p. 348), but in the ideal vessel (marred only by the likes of Captain Spike in *Jack Tier*) that deference is rewarded by the experience, efficiency, and concern for all hands of the commander himself. The image of the ship's community is thus a clear alternative to the feeling "fast upspreading in the country that we ought to be all commanders" (*The Two Admirals,* p. v). As the principle of subordination is inflexibly maintained, the sense of common concern becomes all the stronger:

> The close contact in which men are brought with each other, the security that exists for opening the heart and expanding the charities, gets in time to influence the whole character, and a certain degree of frankness and simplicity takes the place of the reserve

and acting that might have been quickened in the same individual, under a different system of schooling (*Jack Tier,* p. 401).

The homoerotic implications developed so dazzlingly by Melville are left latent and unexplored by Cooper, whose ethic is more thoroughly asexual. Cooper is more interested in the harmony of separates than in the force of erotic connections. In this respect, the sea is like the frontier, itself described as a "neutral ground" where pretensions are softened and differences put aside thanks to the sheer effort of merely surviving (*Home as Found,* pp. 187–88). Like the frontier as it is "spoken" by Natty Bumppo, the sea brings out a language of "frankness and simplicity" rather than one of "reserve and acting." Cooper's sea diction is, of course, notoriously technical and specialized. We can hardly be surprised at the " 'long shore' blunders that are to be found in the original editions" of *The Water Witch* as a result of compositorial misreadings (p. vii), when we encounter the kind of language of which the following would be a fair (though extreme) example:

> By lowering the gaff the spanker was imperfectly bent; that is to say, it was bent on the upper leach. The boom was got in under cover of the hurricane-house, and of the bundle of the sail; the out-hauler was bent, the boom replaced, the sail being hoisted with a little and a hurried lacing to the luff (*Homeward Bound,* p. 422).

This passage is intimidating to the average reader, but to the sailor it is totally intelligible and totally precise. Every word refers to an unambiguous thing or describes an unambiguous act. There is no space for rhetorical distortion; it is as exact a language as that employed by Natty Bumppo when he is following a trail. The undecorated speech of "the Straight-tongue" articulates an uncluttered vision, which *imagines* nothing but *sees* all that is there. Cooper's ideal seamen have the same faculties. Hazlitt saw Cooper as a writer in a state of "thraldom to outward impression," one who could "write volumes on a grain of sand or an insect's wing" (Dekker and McWilliams, 1973, p. 158). But what Hazlitt saw as a deadening trait is for Cooper nothing less than a moral imperative, here well explained by H. Daniel Peck:

> Cooper's heroes are characterized by their ability to read carefully, sometimes painstakingly, what is open for all to see but can in fact

be isolated only by the "practised eye." That is, they are distinguished by the power of *observation* rather than by the power of interpretation (1977, p. 21).

Interpretation distorts and divides—its lowest and all too common incarnation is in the newspeak of Steadfast Dodge and his kind. Cooper's ideal of observation records facts and nothing else—there is no room for the vested interests to fill out the meaning of things through the exercise of the imagination.

This is why the language of the sea is proposed as something of an ideal. It is an uncontaminated diction, aiming not at persuasion but at scrupulously precise communication. Persuasion is the obligation of democracy, of course, and the necessary language of a society wherein no one can assume authority. Cooper's recourse to an alternative image of hierarchy, wherein the right to command is absolutely unquestioned, is thus in a sense very undemocratic. But, for Cooper, this contrast is not as absolute as it might seem. The ideal ship's captain earns obedience by merit rather than by birth or assumption, and is at all times sensitive to the needs of those beneath him, without whom indeed he could not himself function. Had the wagon trains had captains, Cooper would have felt better about the prairies.

Despite the aggressive technicality of passages such as the one cited above, the true linguistic expression of the seaman's life is, once again, near-silence, a subsuming of saying by the urgency of doing:

> At no time does the trained seaman ever appear so great, as when he meets sudden misfortunes with the steadiness and quiet which it is a material part of the *morale* of discipline to inculcate (*The Two Admirals,* p. 505).

On board ship it is necessity that enforces silence, given the need for "exertion and activity in the least of its operations" (*The Water Witch,* p. 330). Again:

> Order on board ship is out of the question without coolness, silence and submission. A fussy sailor is always a bad sailor; calmness and quiet being the great requisites for the profession, after the general knowledge is obtained. No really good officer ever makes a noise except when the roar of the elements makes it indispensable, in order to be heard (*Miles Wallingford,* p. 252).

Steadfast Dodge, and Hiram Dolittle, and others like them, could never make worthy sailors; the ship at sea, like the ship of state, would be in Cooper's eyes the better without them. The apparently hyperlinguistic sea diction thus once again hides an ideal of silence, and is thus conformable to the same ideal reproduced elsewhere in Cooper's writings. In meeting sudden misfortune with steadiness and resolve, and above all in silence, the sailor shares an important virtue with another of Cooper's characters whom we must now explore in detail: the Native American.

6

Silence and Poetry:
The Language
of the Native American

It is by now something of a commonplace that we do not look for
any great degree of anthropological disinterest in the representation
of the Native American in the poetry and fiction of the nineteenth
century, or perhaps of any other century. Scholarly and interpretative history by such writers as Pearce (1953), Sheehan (1973),
and Rogin (1975, esp. pp. 113–248) has made us more aware than
ever before that the image of the Indian was far too potent, threatening, and ideologically overcharged to reside for long in the realm
of any dispassionately scientific inquiry. The melodramatic and
negative figure of the Shawnee in Bird's *Nick of the Woods* (1837)
is offered in the spirit of realism, but it is not to be received as
more simply true to life than some of the more Ossianic representations of noble savages that appear in the pages of other contemporary books. Tecumseh had fought with the British in the War of
1812, and certainly seems to have been guilty of what are called
atrocities (see Smelser, 1968, pp. 238–39); but the portrait of his
tribe in Bird's novel draws on far deeper pathologies and ideologies
than can be accounted for even by the pressure of recent history.

It is not surprising that the image of the dispossessed native
should be obsessively and ambivalently attractive to those writing
during a period of unprecedented American expansionism, when the
debate surrounding the policy of Indian removals was in full swing.

But even the earliest narratives and treatises dealing with the native populations of the Americas are marked by perspectives that we now tend to recognize as largely mythological. This is not to say that no exact information of any sort can be derived from these texts; but such information, where it was produced, stood little chance of being received in the spirit of an epistemological innocence.

The traditional representations of the American Indian display the whole range of options evident in the general debate about primitivism that was an important part of European history from at least the sixteenth century onwards. For some, the Native American stood forth as raw material for future civilization; for others, he was a residue of former states of social or pre-social existence that must, whether tragically or fortunately, be destroyed. Jedediah Morse commented proudly that the "civil and religious communities . . . are making joint efforts for the improvement and happiness of Indians, such as were never made in any former period of our history" (1822, p. 84). Joel Barlow, in a passage whose blandly condescending ethnocentricity is only partly explained by his commitment to the Enlightenment ideal of a single human nature, had looked forward to a time when economic and racial assimilation would destroy all marks of difference:

> Yet when their tribes to happy nations rise,
> And earth by culture warms the genial skies,
> A fairer tint and more majestic grace
> Shall flush their features and exalt the race;
> While milder arts, with social joys refined,
> Inspire new beauties in the growing mind.
>   (1970, 2:154)

Jefferson's mandate to Lewis and Clark expresses a different kind of aggression. For him, some degree of anthropological largesse is an important enabling tool in the dissemination of "reason and justice . . . as it may better enable those who endeavor to civilize and instruct them, to adapt their measures to the existing notions and practices of those on whom they are to operate" (Lewis and Clark, 1953, p. 483). Another perspective may be found in a writer like Heckewelder, one of Cooper's major sources, for whom the Native American was already civilized in his own terms, so that subsequent interference could only spoil what was already there.

It is beyond the scope of this study to attempt any detailed account of the range of ideological representations within which the Native American was figured by the writers and anthropologists of the first half of the nineteenth century. The particular question at issue here is that of language, and what is true of the image of the Indian in general is true also of the image of his language. George Philip Krapp (1960, 1:265–67) has rightly remarked that Cooper's transcription of that language is unreal, being too stilted and literary to seem convincing as a facsimile of real speech. To an extent this is undeniable, and Cooper himself had little or no experience of a native population whose very disappearance he is indeed chronicling. But it could be claimed that we would look in vain for any representation of real Indian speech in the period. First, by "real" is meant the *English* spoken by the Indian, which bears no relation to his own language; second, even such apparently factual accounts as that of Logan's speech had been transformed into flourishing literary traditions. Speaking as they were in an alien language, many natives would have tended to use the phrases that they felt were expected of them, so that the whole distinction between real and unreal must have become easily blurred.[1]

It is, then, less useful to try to discriminate between simple models of truth and fiction than to assess the *functions* of various such models. Whatever their ultimate relation to reality, they all articulate various priorities and perspectives, and perhaps thereby work to restructure the very idea of reality, at least for the consciousness if less often in fact. At first sight, no genre might seem more potentially innocent of ideological motivation than that of the treatise on language; but one of the very first of these, Roger Williams' *A Key into the Language of America,* published in 1643, has been recognized as largely "an ironic and critical comment upon European civilization in general and New England in particular" (Williams, 1973, p. 13). Williams describes a world in which there is no crime, where the poor are cared for, and where a populist monarchy maintains order through sachems who never exercise their authority against the will of the people. These motifs and others like them recur time and time again throughout the literature on the Native American, so that the image of his society often seems to come into line with that other image of civic virtue discussed in Chapter 2, the Anglo-Saxon commonwealth. For Heckewelder (and then for Cooper) this social contract is dependent on a respect for natural talent, "a tacit, yet universal submission to the aristocracy of experience, talents, and virtue" (1818, p. 98). This is, of course, exactly the kind of hegemony that Cooper wants for America at large; rule by the best, with an equal opportunity for our natural inequalities to emerge. This is what the testing interactions of the oceans and the forests bring forth; and, in *The Oak Openings* (p. 122), Cooper sees in Indian society a "principle of democracy" quite unlike "that bastard democracy which is coming so much in fashion among ourselves."

What was the language of this democracy? Not that of Steadfast Dodge, certainly. The ideal Native American in Cooper's novels speaks a language composed of silence and poetry. He understands indeed the poetry of silence itself, expressive also in the sounds of the wind in the trees, with which his own minimal articulation is designed to be in the closest possible sympathy. On occasions when speech *is* appropriate, he speaks forth with a metaphorical intensity conventionally associated also with a primitive relation to nature and to the elemental human passions, one the developed world has all too often lost. Poetry and silence are thus closely related in Cooper's model, and by no means in contrast or in tension. In his heroic natives, figures are always *apt* (as they had been for Rousseau and Wordsworth, who had theorized such a language), and silence always decorous; the tact consists in knowing the right occasion for each. But Cooper also transcribes other Indians who have been contaminated or ruined by contact with their conquerors; they speak an inelegant pidgin English unmarked by any evident memories of their own authentic, poetic locutions.

Silence is a cultural convention among Cooper's Indians, even as it is most admirably displayed by his heroic characters. Even at the show-stopping moment in *The Last of the Mohicans* when Natty takes off the head of his bear costume to reveal himself to Magua, "the philosophy of the latter was so far mastered, as to permit him to utter the never-failing—'Hugh!' " (1983, p. 262). Chingachgook says the same at a moment of high danger, "after which, no further expression of surprise or alarm was suffered to escape him" (p. 74). Such cases are ubiquitous in Cooper's frontier novels. This cult of silence, or minimal articulation, is valorized in particular ways, as it is in the language of the sailor and the tracker. It is a sign of inscrutable stoicism, and also of the subservience of expression to function, of word to deed. As for the sailor on the sea, survival in the forest depends on such priorities; while others talk of performing, and miss their chance, the Indian performs in silence. Natty Bumppo of course shares this priority, and "the silent laugh for which he was so remarkable" (1980, p. 154) 'sounds' throughout the Leatherstocking tales. In his ongoing argument with Battius, in *The Prairie,* he retorts: "I know nothing of your words, which hide their meaning in sound" (1832b, p. 230). In *The Pathfinder* we learn that he "prayed often, daily if not hourly—but it was mentally, in his own simple modes of thinking, and without the aid of words at all" (1981, p. 440). Natty is also prone to fits of garrulousness and even pedantry; but this is always in his role as a speaker of English, which is "a language he was apt to use when a little abstracted in mind" (1983, p. 272). As a Delaware speaker and as a principle of nature, whether destroyer or preserver, his articulation is always much more economical.

One step up from silence in Natty's linguistic personality is, as we have seen, the language of simple fact, which others, whether through being blinded by predisposition, interest, fantasy, or sheer lack of backwoodsmanship, are unable to achieve. This too he shares with the Native Americans. Contrasting the ideal purpose of the American press, "to circulate truth," with its actual function as "a means of circulating lies," Cooper notes that the "red men . . . had no 'forked tongues' to make falsehood take the place of truth; or, if such existed, they were not believed" (*The Oak Openings,* p. 196). In native society, a man's real nature corresponds with his apparent nature, and the hypocrite is usually recognized for what he is. This commitment to fact appears not only in the Indian's total oneness with the environment, which he perceives so completely, but also in the habit of *naming* that plays such an important part in Cooper's tales. Native American names are, crucially, *not* arbitrary; they are bestowed in recognition of some special achievement, or because of some particular association. Once again, the names speak for a reality, as Natty makes clear:

I'm an admirator of names, though the Christian fashions fall far below savage customs in this particular. The biggest coward I ever knew was called Lyon; and his wife, Patience, would scold you out of hearing in less time than a hunted deer would run a rod. With an Indian 'tis a matter of conscience; what he calls himself, he generally is—not that Chingachgook, which signifies big sarpent, is really a snake, big or little; but that he understands the windings and turnings of human natur, and is silent, and strikes his enemies when they least expect him (1983, p. 57).

With his "beautiful and unerring sense of justice," and the "entire indifference with which he regarded all distinctions that did not depend on personal merit" (1981, p. 34), such a naming convention is obviously dear to Natty, for it preserves the image of a correspondence between word and fact that the civilized and literate world has long ago lost.[2] It is also what that world most needs, prone as it is to the production of such oxymoronic christenings as that of Steadfast Dodge, along with the personalities that match them. Natty Bumppo himself is admitted into this society of right naming, as he tells us in *The Prairie:*

> I've been called in my time by as many names as there are people among whom I've dwelt. Now, the Delawares nam'd me for my eyes, and I was called after the far-sighted hawk. Then, agin, the settlers of the Otsego hills christened me anew, from the fashion of my leggings; and various have been the names by which I have gone through life (1832b, p. 191).

Various indeed: Hawkeye, Leatherstocking, "La Longue Carabine," Deerslayer, the "Straight-tongue," the Pathfinder, the "Pigeon," among them. Various, and *true.* When Natty is explaining all these to Judith Hutter (*The Deerslayer,* p. 67), he tells her "My names have all come nat'rally." The different names do not cause any confusion or emanate from deceit, as they do in the "confidence man" tradition, because they all relate to the man they designate by some right and recognizable meaning. Roger Williams (1973, p. 96) had made a biblical parallel in noting of the Native Americans that "Obscure and meane persons amongst them have no Names: Nullius numeri, &c. as the Lord Jesus foretells his followers, that their Names should be cast out."

The contrast to this convention of variable but appropriate naming is, of course, provided by the civilized world where people have only one so-called proper name that is in a way quite improper by virtue of its being arbitrary and failing to signify any visible or essential qualities. The primitive naming convention would, however, be impossible in developed society for at least two reasons. First, men's qualities are not clear or constant enough to be so designated; and, second, the social and legal prerequisites of a complex society depend on there being one name only for each person. This is tied in with the conventions governing the inheritance of *property* (so that in one of its senses, "proper" means "own"). Property contracts and obligations depend on a stability of names: one name, one person. Native American culture, on the other hand, was not a property culture, and all legal conflicts were decided by immediate adjudication rather than by recourse to any preestablished written tradition. Thus, an audience before Tamenund replaces the courtroom of Judge Temple. Roy Harvey Pearce (1953, pp. 66–67) has suggested that the American Indian's status as a hunter and gatherer was exaggerated precisely as a way of maximizing his apparent threat to property, then as now the basis of civilized society. (Such exaggerations continue to be put into play to this day, as, for example, in the context of the Hopi-Navajo land disputes, where the Navajo are often imaged as incorrigibly nomadic and therefore less deserving of support.) Countless eighteenth-century treatises on the development of civil society, by such writers as Kames, Millar, and Ferguson, had stressed property as the central element in the evolution of the civilized life. The changes of name to which Natty is subject would be impossible if he were a settler, governed by the conventions of a literate and legalized community. The implications of this contrast are not pursued by Cooper to the point of outright contradiction; but it is implied nevertheless that in losing this flexibility, settled life has lost something of great political value: the self-evident, public manifestation of essential character, simple enough to be inscribed in a name and creative enough to accede to other names as the need arises. This process of loss bears comparison with that of the division of labor itself. As society diversifies, each member is limited to a simpler and simpler job; the name solidifies along with the occupation. In the undivided world in which each man is master of the whole of his existence, the name is free to adapt to the changes in circumstances and associations that the person experiences. Moreover, as large and complex societies come into being, problems of recognition become compounded, and the pressure to establish a fixed name becomes correspondingly more urgent. The reliability of the name takes the place of the reliance on personal acquaintance that is now impossible.

Natty is articulate on the subject of the arrival of new names into the landscape. In *The Deerslayer,* much is made of the lake as an "as yet unchristened sheet of water" (p. 135). His own "silent enjoyment" of the (appropriately designated) Glimmerglass leads him to wonder whether it has yet been formally named:

> If they've not begun to blaze their trees, and set up their compasses, and line off their maps, it's likely they've not bethought them to disturb natur' with a name (p. 43).

And later:

> I'm glad it has no name . . . or, at least, no pale-face name; for their christenings always foretell waste and destruction. No doubt, howsever, the red-skins have their modes of knowing it, and the hunters and trappers, too; they are likely to call the place by something reasonable and resembling (p. 44).

This, thirty-five years later (in composition) and sixty years earlier (in historical time), is the young Natty's verdict on the efforts of Lewis and Clark and their kind. Morse makes a similar point:

> Civilized discoverers more frequently give commemorative names. Uncivilized, or nearly so, almost universally, *descriptive.* Thus modern names are apt to be arbitrary. Ancient ones very generally have an appropriate meaning (1824, p. 48).

No one stopped, of course, to ask whether Jefferson River already had a name.

But in the decades after Lewis and Clark, they often did. For the Indian names of places and persons had great poetic potential, the greater indeed as the actual presence of the original givers of the name was rapidly coming to an end. Webster noted much earlier that

> It is remarkable, that almost all the rivers in America, as well as many places, preserve the names given them by the natives of the country. This is paying a tribute of respect to the Indians, who

formerly possessed these fertile regions; and the names are a kind of history of the savage settlements (1789b, pp. 96–97).

This is indeed an epitaphic concession, one that Cooper echoes in saying of the New York state natives that "In a short time there will be no remains of these extraordinary people . . . but their names" (1983, p. 20). And it is a comfortable one. Even Harry March, who is as ruthless and mercenary an Indian-killer as one could find, allows himself (without any sense of conflict) a romantic indulgence in the preservation of Indian names: "I'm glad they've been compelled to keep the red-men's name, for it would be too hard to rob them of both land and name!" (*The Deerslayer,* p. 45). Stewart (1967, p. 279) has observed that "the romantics of the mid-century and after applied such names, not the explorers and frontiersmen," so that Harry may well be an anachronism in a tale supposedly of the 1740s. Stewart has further discovered that "Seekonk, founded in 1812, was the first Massachusetts town to take an Indian name deliberately: Saugus soon followed in 1815" (p. 276). Lydia Sigourney makes the point:

> Ye say, they have all passed away,
> That noble race and brave,
> That their light canoes have vanished
> From off the crested wave;
> That mid the forest where they roamed
> There rings no hunter's shout;
> But their name is on your waters,
> Ye may not wash it out (1843, p. 258).

Here, the name no longer signifies actual possession so much as the sentimental image of innocence for the mental relief of a conquering race.

We may then suggest that by the time Cooper and his contemporaries were writing their novels and poems the actual presence of the American Indian east of the Mississippi is inversely proportional to the poetic appeal of his vocabulary. Walter Channing's essay of 1815 sets the tone of much of what was to follow:

In their original language we have names of places, and things, which are but feebly rendered by our own, I should say by the English. Their words of description are either derived from incidents, and of which they are framed to convey most exact ideas, or are so formed as to convey their signification in their sounds; and although so ridiculous in their English dress as to be a new cause for English satire and merriment, are in themselves the very language for poetry, for they are made only for expression, and their objects are the very element for poetry (1815, p. 313).

Chastellux, traveling to America in the eighteenth century, had complained of the plain-spoken bluntness of American English, resulting in such trite designations as *blue bird* and *black duck,* and stemming from men's attentions being "employed in objects of utility" with no room or need for a supervening language of poetry (1787, 1:41–42).[3] Many American authors or would-be authors were to repeat the complaint, and Marryat, in his role as disenchanted traveler, rubbed salt in the wounds:

> It is a great pity that the Americans have not adhered more to the Indian names, which are euphonous, and very often musical; but, so far from it, they appear to have had a pleasure in dismissing them altogether. There is a river running into Lake Champlain, near Burlington, formerly called by the Indians Winooski, but this name has been superseded by the settlers, who, by way of improvement, have designated it the Onion River (1839, 2:237).

Marryat was in fact traveling on the spur of the revival of Indian names, a process seemingly unperceived by him. N. P. Willis was very much in favor of native names, to replace the results of "vulgar chance" with the proper and poetic epiphets (see Spencer, 1957, pp. 201–2). Of course, such names were modified to bring them into line with the convenience of English phonetic and poetic conventions. Webster, as part of his general case for the normalization of all foreign words into English, had argued that "the harsh, gutteral sounds of the natives" ought not to be retained:

> Where popular practice has softened and abridged words of this kind, the change has been made in conformity with the genius of our language, which is accommodated to a civilized people; and the orthography ought to be conformed to the practice of speaking (1807b, p. v).

The anonymous author of the essay on "Domestic Literature" in the *Atlantic Magazine* (1, 1824, 130–39) would similarly recommend the prettying up of the unmanageable native phonemes:

He who would employ their machinery, in verse, needs not introduce barbarous names, insusceptible of being euphonised; but may
employ, directly, the personification and its attributes; and, in so
doing, speak the universally intelligible language of poetry (p. 134).

In other words, the *image* of incorporation suggested by the popularity of native names was not at all answered by the facts, to the
degree that the names themselves were doctored before they could
appear in English. The awkwardness of these names in their unmodified forms had been commented on by, among others, Richard
Owen Cambridge, who found them an undecipherable ingredient in
military dispatches (*The World,* no. 102; Dec. 1754, pp. 611–16).
The reports of Lismahago's adventures in North America occasion
similar reflections in Smollett's *Humphry Clinker.* Perhaps the most
famous parody is that by Paulding, in *The Lay of the Scottish
Fiddle:*

> Steady the vessels held their way,
> Coasting along the spacious bay,
> By Hooper's Strait, Micomico,
> Nanticoke, Chicacomico,
> Dam-quarter, Chum, and Hiwassee,
> Cobequid, Shubamaccadie,
> Piankatank, and Pamunkey
> (1814b, pp. 53–54).

And so on for another thirteen lines!
    Although Cooper does employ a large measure of romanticism
in his portrayal of the Native American (of which more later), he
does yet avoid the absurdities of an extreme poeticizing of his language. There are two ways in which this can be accomplished. The
first is to attempt some *exact* transcription of the original language,
with all its awkwardness and difficulty; the other is to forgo all
hopes of such transcription, and to emphasize the necessity of translation. Both these options tend to function as ways of emphasizing
the nonsymmetrical relation of the two cultures thus in contact, and
Cooper uses both.
    The first, however, is less common than the second. Lewis and
Clark's text provides a good example of its problems. Criswell
(1940, p. cxx) notes that there are about sixty-five Indian names
in the journals of the expedition, including translations. Both men,

and Clark especially, seem dedicated to finding some way of transcribing for English readers (or for themselves) the exact sounds of those names. Thus, in a text generally most remarkable for its unliterary qualities, we find such recorded names as *Sahcahgagweâ, âh-hí-e, ti-â-co-mo-shack,* and *Shan-na-tâh-que* (1953, pp. 135, 191, 293, 295). Faced with such prototypes, Cooper often shows himself a modifier rather than a faithful transcriber. In the 1850 preface to *The Last of the Mohicans,* he comments on his famous invention of the name Horicon (for Lake George), pleading that "the French name of the lake was too complicated, the American too commonplace, and the Indian too unpronounceable, for either to be used familiarly in a work of fiction" (1983, p. 8). At the same time, there is in his writings some adherence to the convention of exact transcription (which was always a convention, given that the Indian languages were never written down). *Chingachgook* is hardly a mellifluous name, even if *Uncas* and *Magua* trip comfortably enough off the tongue; so little so, indeed, that the name is mistranscribed on the gravestone, as Oliver reads it. Natty has to correct him— "The name should be set down right, for an Indian's name has always some meaning in it"—as he also corrects his pronunciation of the name of the tribe (1980, p. 452). In *The Prairie* (1832b, pp. 252–53) Cooper records and paraphrases such terms as "the Menahasah, or Long-knives . . . the Washsheomantiqua, or Spaniards . . . the Wahconshecheh (bad spirit)"; and in *The Oak Openings,* Pigeonswing also goes by the name *Waub-ke-newh,* a title of which he is "justly proud" (p. 44). In the same novel, the names *Elkswatawa, Pukeesheno,* and *Meethetaske* are all explained in footnotes (p. 196), and *Kekalamazoo* is explained as "the true Indian word, though the whites have seen fit to omit the first syllable" (p. 445). Similarly, *Michillimackinac* is turned into *Mackinaw* (p. 472), and *Chippewa* into *O-jeb-way,* "as the civilized natives of that nation now tell us it should be spelled" (p. 14).

Of course, there is a certain fastidious one-upmanship in Cooper's fidelity to the native vocabulary on such occasions, but it does also serve as a way of highlighting the *otherness* of the cultures it speaks forth, and thus has its place in what is generally a representation of conflict in Cooper's Indian novels. Cooper points out the "utter confusion that pervades the names" involved in Native American history:

When, however, it is recollected, that the Dutch, the English, and the French, each took a conqueror's liberty in this particular; that the natives themselves not only speak different languages, and even dialects of those languages, but that they are also fond of multiplying their appellations, the difficulty is more a matter of regret than of surprise (1983, p. 3).

Hence the overlapping terms—Wapanachki, Lenni Lenape, Delaware, Mahicanni, Mohican, Mohegan—and the parallel list of epithets for the Mengwe, or Iroquois (pp. 4–5). The mention of the "conqueror's liberty" is an apt one, and many of the novels record variously licentious misreadings of Indian names. That of Chingachgook is the most obvious, and the most fitting in that it occurs on his gravestone, an object that would not even have existed had he been buried according to the customs of his own culture, and which thus commemorates his own condition of deracination. *Mohegan* also, we are later told (1983, p. 2), is a form of "Mohican" that has been "corrupted by the English"; and the title of Cooper's novel itself must be seen as a poeticized word when compared with Jonathan Edwards' (1823) form of the tribal name: *Muhhekaneew*. More comically, but also pathetically, Miantonimoh has his "real name, according to the uses and sounds of his own people," reported as "My Anthony Mow" (*The Wept of Wish-ton-Wish,* (p. 81). Susquesus becomes "Succetush" (*Satanstoe,* p. 383), at the same time as the history of his other, honorific names—Sureflint, the Trackless, the Withered Hemlock, the Upright Onondago—is lost with the passage of time and the change in his fortunes (*The Chainbearer,* p. 114; *The Redskins,* pp. 318, 347). Arbitrary naming is indeed the "conqueror's liberty," refiguring the identity of others according to its own needs and fantasies. Wordsworth, who was acutely conscious of the ethical dynamics of naming things and places, describes the naming of the whip-poor-will in his poem "A Morning Exercise," and tells how

> A simple forest cry
> Becames an echo of man's misery
> (1940–49, 2:124).

Cooper's instances depict not only the naming of nature, but also the naming or renaming of man. Thus Jaaf the servant is "indiscriminately called Yap, or Yop—York Dutch being far from severe" (*The Chainbearer,* p. 35). Those whose names are most open to such modifications are usually those who are at the bottom end of the social ladder. In *Wyandotté,* the play on naming takes on a special significance. While the subtitle of the novel, *The Hutted Knoll,* is explained at the end of the first chapter (pp. 23–24), there is no mention whatever of the main title until about two-thirds of the way through, at which point it is revealed as the former honorific name of the downcast Indian who has previously appeared as "Old Nick" or "Saucy Nick." Wyandotté

> was Nick's loftiest appellation; and a grim but faint smile crossed his visage as he heard it again in the mouth of one who had known him when the sound carried terror to the hearts of his enemies (p. 341).

The subject of the novel is thus at one stroke revealed to be the fate of this hitherto somewhat secondary character, and the process by which he has passed from being Wyandotté to being Nick. As in so many other cases, the crisis in naming is a symptom of the larger crisis in the relations between the races. John Mohegan only recovers his original self in his death song, which his Christian hearers, of course, misunderstand (1980, pp. 420–21). Scalping Peter, who ends as a Christian, is rightly if maliciously described by one of his peers as having "no real name" (*The Oak Openings,* p. 363).

The most familiar technique through which Cooper registers the gap or conflict between the two races, red and white, is the reiterated need for translation and for careful etymological explanation. We need not record every instance; the pattern will be familiar enough to every reader of the frontier novels. Translation is in one sense the opposite of exact transcription; even as it is typographically less alien, it confesses the impossibility of adequately reproducing the other language. The exact implications of this strategy in Cooper's writings are certainly open to argument, and I do not mean to claim that it can only be read as a symptom of his respect for the integrity of Indian cultures and languages. Surely, Cooper makes mention of translation to add to the exotic appeal of his narratives, and it can thus be suspected as contributing to a romantic racism. But it also comes across as an image of the conflict between red and white, and the more clearly so because of the context provided by other such conflicts. In *The Last of the Mohicans,* in which (drawing heavily on Heckewelder) the etymological and anthropological identity of the Indian is perhaps more heavily worked than in any other novel, the very first words that Natty Bumppo speaks are uttered in Delaware (1983, p. 30). The task of translation is continually alluded to throughout the book. The deference to the uniqueness of the native language is certainly "romantic" but also thematically informed by Cooper's general interest in representing aspects of American history that have *not* resulted in the friendly interchange of different tongues. It may not be "possible to translate the comprehensive and melodious language" (p. 389) of Uncas' war song in such a way as to make true sense to an English speaker; this language thereby becomes part of Cooper's mythology of loss. As it moves through history, it becomes the low gutteral moan of John Mohegan, of which Cooper had already written. This point may stand despite the authorial archness at the expense of the reader who has "not studied the North American languages," and despite the fictionalizing convenience of trying to preserve "the idioms and peculiarities of the respective speakers, by way of presenting the pictures in the most graphic forms to the minds of the readers" (*The Deerslayer,* pp. 316, 162). To achieve a proper understanding of the other race's "gifts," as Natty is always begging us to do, we must also put ourselves to some trouble in learning something about their language.

I have already noted the connection between silence and poetry in the representation of the North American languages. The man of the forest is at one with nature; he is either linguistically economical to the point of silence, or he bursts forth with a rhetoric abounding in metaphors and tropes. We have seen some of the reasons why Cooper found the silence so appealing; it now remains to say something more about the appeal of the poetic.

The propensity to high poetry is indeed that part of the image of native speech most open to parody and skepticism; and the likes of Mark Twain and Bret Harte did not miss their opportunity. Once again, it must be stressed that the functions of this language in fictional contexts are at least as important, and perhaps more open to analysis, than its relation to something we might choose to call real language. A fondness for the figurative might indeed have been part of some Indian languages. Heckewelder admits against his own general respect for the Delaware among whom he lived an annoying inclination for high-flown language. He admires their

"natural and simple" eloquence but draws back from their indulgence in metaphors:

> They are to their discourse what feathers and beads are to their
> persons, a gawdy but tasteless ornament. Yet we must not judge
> them too severely on that account. There are other nations besides
> the American Indians who admire this mode of expression (1818,
> p. 125).

At once, Heckewelder's missionary mind sees a barbarism in the
approval of ornament, of which metaphor is the linguistic corollary.
The very suspicion of trinkets and baubles so central to the Prot-
estant mind may tell us something about why so many American
writers were attracted to the subject of eloquent Indians. Here, they
could perhaps indulge the flights of poetical fancy that the avowed
ethics of their own culture (internal to themselves as often as not)
appeared to discourage. Images of the primitive served as counter-
balances to the limitations of the modern, so that the American author found his Homer and his Ossian in the Native American whom
he could afford to celebrate by virtue of his imminent or achieved
disappearance.

Cooper also found his poetry here, though before going on to
examine it something must be said about the inherited and ongoing
debates about the origins and implications of the figurative in the
Native American languages. Roger Williams, in his *Key,* had made
much of the copiousness of the language. Pointing out the difficulties of finding English equivalents for Indian words, he notes
that "their Language is exceeding copious, and they have five or six
words sometimes for one thing" (1973, pp. 90–91). This at once
discounts one traditional explanation for the high incidence of
metaphors in primitive languages: that they are so limited in their
vocabularies that the same terms have to do the job of describing
many different things, by association and transference. Metaphors
thus arise of necessity in the basic task of simple designation and
definition; they come from the poverty of language, rather than
from its richness.[4] Williams' observation preempts such an explanation of the North American language, and in a similar spirit Heckewelder disputes the existence of a sign language: "The Indians do
not gesticulate more when they speak than other nations do" (1818,
p. 115). They use gestures not because they need to supplement an

inadequate vocabulary by ostension or demonstration, but because they believe that "too much talking disgraces a man." In fact, they have "words and phrases sufficient to express every thing" (p. 116) when they need them.

Other commentators carry the case even further, suggesting that the native languages are so rich that they do not need as many generic terms as does the English. Here is Gallatin:

> It must have been the primary object of every language to designate with precision every object and every action, and every modification of which every object or action was susceptible. Specific names would naturally precede generic terms; and, if the Indian languages are often deficient in these, they abound in distinct names for every particular species of tree, for every variety of age, sex, or peculiarity, in certain species of animals, and in degrees of consanguinity, and generally for those subdivisions of the same genus, which in our language are distinguished by attributes which qualify the generic term. Thus, instead of designating the several species of oak by the name of white oak, black oak, swamp oak, &c., the Indians have a distinct name for every species, and, in many languages, no generic term, embracing all the species of oak (1836, p. 181).

It has since become a commonplace in sociolinguistics that societies occupying specialized and limited environments develop highly refined ways of describing differences that members of other cultures might not even notice; hence the Bedouins have many words for the various kinds and sizes of camel, and so forth. What is thematically of interest in Gallatin's account is its direct challenge to the European orthodoxy, aptly represented in John Locke's declaration (1979, p. 409) that "It is impossible, that every particular Thing should have a distinct peculiar Name." He goes on to argue that "it is beyond the Power of humane Capacity to frame and retain distinct *Ideas* of all the particular Things we meet with: every Bird, the Beast Men saw; every Tree, and Plant, that affected the Senses, could not find a place in the most capacious Understanding." Hence we have general ideas and general terms to describe them, enabling us "to consider Things, and discourse of them, as it were in bundles" (p. 420).

Without arguing for or against the absolute or theoretical possibility of a language without *any* general terms, we can yet see the point of the contrast between Locke's formulation and the languages reported by Gallatin. For Locke, general terms are necessary to the *progress* of the mind, since they enable it to expand its perceptions of more and more classes of objects without being hobbled by having to find and retain a different name for every new object. This conceptual or generalizing function of the mind is, for Locke and for his tradition, central to the concept of mind itself. From this perspective, any language showing itself to be more preoccupied with specificities than the Indo-European languages is going to seem primitive, not only in itself but in the opportunities it affords its speakers for "broadening" their minds and becoming civilized.

In thus understanding the ethnocentricity of Locke's language theory in this respect, we can see also the corresponding mythology of a linguistic paradise lost. For the garden of paradise was a *closed* space, one in which the precise nomination of every particular object might have been feasible for the small society within its confines. The image of the individual-specific tendency (for it is only that) in the Native American languages becomes thereby a paradisal image. Like all such images, it carries with it a series of economic, political, and social associations: no exploitation of land or of other people, no divided labor and expansionist commercial economy, and no property. If English in general is a language of general terms, then we may recall Tocqueville's assertion that the English of a democracy in particular is prone to such words, as a means of preserving as much executive ambiguity as is compatible with a minimal degree of honesty (1945, 2:73–74). This could only have added to the appeal of the highly specific native languages for a writer like Cooper. If in principle general terms are to be associated with cultures committed to expanding their territories and increasing their possessions, then this was most spectacularly the case (albeit for different reasons) among the demogogues who were coming to control American political life.

These are the strong interpretations underlying the themes and materials that find their way into Cooper's tales by virtue of his representations of the Native American languages. Of course, they are not there articulated with the exclusivity or the precision I have just myself evidenced. Cooper's manipulation of the paradisal association is usually limited and qualified rather than unambiguous. But in a body of work that is as truly ambivalent as Cooper's seems to me to be, it does not seem out of place to point out the extreme positions to which some of his arguments and instances might tend. When Natty is spoken of as using English when he is *"abstracted* in mind" (1983, p. 272, my italics), we can recognize the image of English as a tongue heavily dependent on abstract terms; when he wants to be really precise, he speaks in Delaware. As we have seen, that language also allows for a practice of continual renomination, since identities are consistently recognizable without the reliance on arbitrary names fixed for all time. The personality itself, in other words, need not be reified as another general idea.

In a way that extends the paradisal ramifications of the images of native languages, many commentators noticed also their syncretic tendency, one that twentieth-century linguists and anthropologists have continued to point out. Gallatin notes "a universal tendency to express in the same word, not only all that modifies or relates to the same object, or action, but both the action and the object; thus concentrating in a single expression a complex idea, or several ideas among which there is a natural connexion" (1836, pp. 164–65). Du Ponceau and Pickering, in their remarks on John Eliot's Indian *Grammar,* make similar points. Pickering notes a *"new* manner of compounding words from various roots, so as to strike the mind at once with a whole mass of ideas" (Eliot, 1822, p. 4), and Du Ponceau enthuses over the way in which

> one single word designates the person who acts, and that which is acted upon. The *substantive* is incorporated with the verb in a similar manner. . . . The mind is lost in the contemplation of the multitude of ideas thus expressed at once by means of a single word (pp. xxi–xxii).

A similar syncretic ambition (though quite differently motivated) was evident in Horne Tooke's attempt to prove that all words used adjectivally and conjunctively originally referred to things; but here, the greatest enthusiasm is more typically focused on the verb (as it was in Webster's later writings). Thus, Du Ponceau:

> The Verb is the triumph of human language. Its fundamental idea is that of existence: *I am, sum.* This abstract sentiment receives shape and body from its combination with the various modifications of being . . . (p. xi).

The language here is significant. Without its *realization* in combination with transitive relations to things (e.g., "I eat apples") or with particular states of feeling ("I am hot"), the verb substantive would be an "abstract sentiment." What is so appealing about the Amerindian languages is, then, that they do not ever present the substantive verb ("I am") as in any way separable from the composite forms in which it occurs. Eliot had noticed this (1822, p. 16), and it was frequently remarked on by those who came after. In his notes to Edwards (1823), Pickering cites Heckewelder's assertion: "I cannot find a single instance in the language, in which the verb *I am* is used by itself, that is to say, uncombined with the idea of the *act* to be done."[5]

The appeal and interest of this syndrome is, then, that in the native languages there is *no ego distinction,* no abstract principle of selfhood that has to be combined with various things in the world that are initially posited as alien to it. The self neither takes its definition from the world (as some materialists claimed) nor imposes itself on it; rather, a composite self-in-world is there from the start. Cardell appealed to the "tenants of the American forest" as proof that pronouns (the articles of selfhood) are not an "original . . . nor an absolutely necessary part of speech" (1825, p. 64), a statement congenial with his theory that the *"idea* of the *mind itself,* as a separate existence, is *inferential"* (p. 55).

The Native American languages are in this respect also languages of paradise; they speak forth a primary, integrated state of being in which the self-other and verb-noun differentiations so prominent in other languages have never come into being. Consequently, they reflect a society in which the anxieties of alienation and exploitation are minimal or even absent. This motif will play an important part in the transcendentalist speculations on language to be discussed in the next chapter. There it will function, applied back to the English language in a gesture of wishful transference, as part of an attempt to bypass or ignore the awkward dialectics of exploitation implicit in the separation of active self from passive world.

No wonder, then, that the Delaware, or one among its subdivisions, was such a frequent candidate for the role of most perfect language. The *Encyclopaedia Americana* noted that it "has been pronounced, by competent judges, the most perfect existing" (1829–33, 6:570). Barton (1797, p. lvi), Heckewelder, and others are confident that it is the parent language of the entire east coast of North America. Du Ponceau waxes especially eloquent:

> Who can say what Homer would have produced if he had had for his instrument the language of the Lenni Lenape? This, however, we may with safety assert: that he would have been able to say more in fewer words, than even in his own admirable Greek (Zeisberger, 1830, pp. 95–96).

The above account provides some of the essential elements of the context in which Cooper takes on the whole question of the poetry of the Native American speech. In a famous review of Schoolcraft's *Travels* and Rawle's *Vindication of Heckewelder* that appeared as an article in *North American Review* (26, 1828, 357–403), Lewis Cass described Heckewelder's book (one of Cooper's primary sources) as "little better than a work of the imagination" (p. 372). He made fun of the "labored conceits" that Cooper himself had picked up from studying art instead of nature (p. 374), and also felt obliged to attack the image of the native languages on linguistic grounds, maintaining that they *do* separate nouns and adjectives, and *do* have the substantive verb (pp. 390–91). Cass' account is an attack on the image of integration and paradisal innocence suggested by the accounts of the languages given by Heckewelder and others like him. John T. Frederick (1956) has argued that Cooper adapted such sources very faithfully into his novels; he finds that "more than three-fourths" of the figures and tropes in the novels appear also in the sources (p. 1009), concluding that Cooper "followed diligently and consistently—faithful always to the spirit and usually to the letter—the most trustworthy firsthand accounts of actual Indian speech which the literature of his time afforded" (p. 1014). In this respect Cooper seems to have done the best he could, given his relative lack of acquaintance with actual Native American speakers. But we can see from Cass' reactions to Heckewelder that these sources were themselves often in contention with each other, and on matters that were in the widest sense moral and political.

Cooper's response to this context seems to include a larger range of interpretations and innuendoes than any simple faith in the poetic alone could produce. There are indeed a number of famous set-pieces, familiar to most readers and all parodists of Cooper, wherein (for example) plain Oliver Edwards becomes "Young Eagle" (1980, p. 87), and every question is answered in reference to the grand forces of nature. Natty Bumppo had acquired the habit of speaking "a poetry that he had unconsciously imbibed by his long association with the Delawares" (1981, p. 58). His first words in *The Prairie* are spoken in the cadences and imagery of an Indian orator (1832b, p. 10). But, as we have seen in our discussion of Cooper's interest in the task of translation, there is as much emphasis on what cannot be captured as there is on the reproduction of native rhetoric. Partly because the "meaning of Indian words is much governed by the emphasis and tones," it is "impossible to describe the music of their language . . . in such a way as to render it intelligible to those whose ears have never listened to its melody" (1983, pp. 56, 200). Even Magua is allowed to comment on the duplicity of the "paleface" language, which has two words for every thing, whereas "a red skin will make the sound of his voice speak for him" (1983, p. 91). The quality of sound is exactly what cannot be transcribed into a written text. As such, Cooper's choosing to emphasize it contributes to the preservation of the otherness of the Indian language and its speakers. As well as indulging in the Ossianic cadences familiar to him from contemporary literature, Cooper thus incorporates a more critical and respectful approach to the imaging of the language.

High poetry is not the only language of Cooper's natives; it is perhaps not even the dominant one, despite the notoriety of some of the set-pieces, such as the speech of Tamenund. In *The Red-skins,* he explains the existence of a "sort of *lingua franca,*" a vocabulary derived from particular native languages but then applied wholesale to all others, "these other tribes using them as English" (p. 148). Thus, ironically enough, an Indian might use the terms "squaw" and "papoose" for the convenience of his English-speaking interlocutor, even though such words have no relation to his own specific language. Modern Native Americans continue to have to put up with such linguistic misconceptions. Cooper's first Indian character, John Mohegan in *The Pioneers,* is already a figure stranded between two cultures, and consequently is far from eloquent. Although he seems to speak high poetry—"The children of Miqoun do not love the sight of blood"—he speaks it in "tolerable English, but in a low, monotonous gutteral tone" (1980, p. 87),

far from the musicality that his creator will recover in the voice of
Uncas in the next frontier novel. Lest we miss the point, further
reference is made to Mohegan's "dull, monotonous tones" (p. 164),
and his death song is itself "a kind of low dirge" (p. 410). There
is poetry in the *words,* but it is offset by the *sounds* of the delivery,
which denote exhaustion and despair.

For the culturally deracinated and schizophrenic Indians of the
later novels, even the poetry has gone. The language in which Nick
explains his double identity is already itself evidence of which half
now best describes him:

> Nick always dry— Wyandotté know no thirst. Nick beggar— ask for
> rum— pray for rum— t'ink of rum— talk of rum— long for rum—
> cry for rum. Wyandotté don't know rum when he see him (*Wyan-
> dotté,* p. 344).

Again, Cooper is following a theme in Heckewelder, whose basic
point is the degenerate present demise of cultures that once were
virtuous and independent (1818, p. 8). And he is adjusting the language accordingly.

The question remains, of course, about the precise import of this
variety in Cooper's imaging of the native languages and their speakers. George Copway, the Chippewa chief, declared that Cooper did
indeed give a true picture of the red man (1983, p. xvi), but we
have seen enough to remain cautious on the adjudication of ultimate truth. As I have said before, the brutal or drunken aborigine
is not to be thought of as any more universally true to circumstances than is the poet of the wilderness. More than an element of
racist condescension is present in the idea that the real Native
American is the drunken and despondent one, whether in 1830 or
in 1984. Even accepting all these reservations about what was real,
however, we are still left with the problem of interpreting the ideological import of Cooper's images. No complete account of this
question can be attempted here, but in so far as it bears on the
representation of the language, some further remarks are in order.

Critics and readers of Cooper have always been faced with the
difficulty of deciding the degree to which his portrayals of the Native American partake of reactionary romance, given that they are
also in part a critical exposure of the misdeeds of the white race.
Many of the heroic Indians in Cooper's canon are also tragic; they

confront a seemingly inevitable extinction, at least as members of a free and uncontaminated culture. Further, many of the novels are retrospective, describing a state of affairs that no longer exists; and both Natty and Chingachgook are imaged as exempt from the privilege of procreation. They live and function in an adolescent world of idealized male companionship for which the prospect of any heterosexual bonding becomes a threat (as in *The Pathfinder* and *The Deerslayer*). In this very simple sense, they have no future. All these elements combine to suggest in Cooper a very strong element of reactionary romanticism, albeit one that remains actively present in American culture. From this perspective, the appeal of the Indian languages and cultures is premised on the fact of their imminent disappearance; the Delawares are most appealing of all because they were the *first* to be dispossessed by the white race (1980, p. 84). Their poetic and polemical effect is the greater to the degree that their extinction has been accomplished, and the question of their potential restoration the slighter. The historical Uncas was a very different figure from Cooper's hero.

This is not, however, the whole story. Cooper's ideologies need more careful handling than this. Although he seems to affirm the doctrine of separatism among the various tribes, the very doctrine that contributed so forcefully to their military inferiority (thus Natty prefers Pawnees to Sioux, and Mohicans to Mingoes), he also explains this as part of the policy of the conquerors, and a result of their very presence. Some of the Delaware fight with the British in 1756, others with the French, so that (in Natty's words) "all the harmony of warfare" (1983, p. 187) is destroyed. Again, while some of Cooper's "bad" Indians are indeed demonic, in the spirit of an all too familiar nineteenth-century convention,—the Iroquois camp resembles an "unhallowed and supernatural arena, in which malicious demons had assembled to enact their bloody and lawless rites" (1983, p. 237)—the malice of the villain Magua is at the same time explained as the result of the lingering memory of an unavenged insult (as is that of Wyandotté in a later novel). It is, in other words, the natural emotion for one brought up within his particular culture and tradition.

The case of *The Pioneers,* again, is typical of the complexity of Cooper's image of the Indian, and the Indian question. The narrative turns upon a principle of cyclic restitution. The Effinghams lost their land, but hardship and poverty served to discipline them and make them worthier possessors than they once were (1980, pp. xxx, 31). In the alliance between Effingham and Indian, Cooper pulls off an incipiently duplicitous play. For much of the novel, Oliver is believed to be the child of John Mohegan, whose rights to the land he does indeed vigorously propound. He applauds when Elizabeth utters her own wish to be of native stock: "for I own that I grieve when I see old Mohegan walking about these lands, like the ghost of one of their ancient possessors, and feel how small is my own right to possess them" (p. 280). This is a safe emotion, of course, given that the pattern of restitution works not for Mohegan but for the benefit of Oliver himself, and for the "Tory" faction from which he emanates. The case for Native American rights thus seems to become sentimentalized, because it is voiced without being *exercised*. When Mohegan dies as the last of his race, it is hard not to conclude that no change in behavior toward actual Indians is being proposed.

This interpretation seems to convict Cooper of a sophisticated form of compliance in the policy of removing and destroying the Native American population. But, despite the novel's setting in a place where the Indian is now (in 1823) no more than a memory, and despite the many contemporary arguments for the necessary extinction of the race, the Indian had *not* disappeared from the landscape in 1823, any more than he had when Edward Curtis photographed the "Vanishing Race," any more than he has today. As a polemical presence, Indian John does have considerable force as a prospective image of what might have been about to happen to the Indians west of the Mississippi, who were not yet displaced or destroyed. Given his moral and personal integrity, in other words, the image of the noble savage had more direct polemical import in 1823 than we might assume if we restrict its allusions to the state of affairs in upper New York. This implication becomes even more obvious in the image of the Pawnees in *The Prairie,* so obviously superior to most of those coming west to threaten them.

As an author writing during the development and implementation of the removal policies, Cooper's sympathy for the predicament of the Indian is thus not merely nostalgic. Rogin (1975, p. 4) has made the telling point that during the years 1824–52 "five of the ten major candidates for President had either won reputations as generals in Indian wars or served as Secretary of War, whose major responsibility in this period was relations with the Indians." Cooper's response to this historical climate is far from merely acquiescent, although it is arguably quite schizophrenic. He does foresee and approve the westward course of empire, in principle. At the same time, he is critically aware of the cruelties and compromises involved along the way, for both red and white races. The "converted" Indians of the later novels, like Scalping Peter and Saucy Nick, are tragically divided beings whose careers necessarily pose awkward questions for the dominant culture to face. They are in no sense prototypes of a positive future. Once again, the image of integration is simply not sustained in Cooper's novels, nor is the image of division one that affords him any moral peace of mind.

Returning to the context of the language, we may then suggest that the range of approaches to the question of native speech and vocabulary also contributes to the relative ideological openness of Cooper's novels. His analysis of the history and future prospects of the Indian within the emerging social contract is free from the extremes of both romanticism and racist bigotry; nor does the presence of a definite degree of the first simply work as a smokescreen for the insinuation of the second. The poetic element in the language is not pursued to the point of absurdity, nor does it exclude other varieties of Indian English. His characters are not called "Colwall" and "Reldor," as are some of those anthologized in Smith's *American Poems* (1793, pp. 287–91). His account of the anthropological identity of the Indian is uncommonly dispassionate and sympathetic, given how many of the tribes had fought with the British in 1776, and had been encouraged by them to remain hostile until well into the 1790s (see Miller, 1963, p. 183). Apart from some remarks on the "oriental images, that the Indians have probably brought with them from the extremes of the other continent" (1983, p. 342; cf. p. 5), he also remains relatively uninvolved in the tangled and popular debate about the origins of the Native Americans—one that often made telling use of the evidence of language. Freneau and Jefferson thought that they might be the descendants of wandering Carthaginians, while others voted for an origin in one of the lost tribes of Israel! Roger Williams (1973, p. 86) noticed verbal affinities with both Hebrew and Greek, and even Madoc the Welshman was a candidate for the role of founding father—among whites, of course (see Sheehan, 1973, pp. 54–65). Cooper avoids endorsing any of these extreme hypotheses, as he avoids also any argument for the desirability of the disappearance of the native languages. Nor does he, as we have seen, support Cardell's view, also that of Dr. Johnson before him, that

> It is with propriety, therefore, that the knowledge of letters is gen-
> erally recognized by philosophic writers, as the first important
> advance in the career of social refinement, and all nations destitute
> of written records characterized as barbarians (1825), p. 10).

Samuel Lorenzo Knapp was very excited at the invention of an alphabet for the Cherokee (1829, pp. 25–29),[6] and at the existence of an epitaph for the Choctaw chief Push-ma-ta-ha:

> This son of the forest had caught something of civilization. His na-
> tion . . . knew something of the value of letters, and began to see
> that there were surer methods of gaining immortality than by trust-
> ing to a misshapen sound, or a short-lived tradition (p. 293).

In counterpoint to this sort of ethnocentric enthusiasm, Cooper of-fers the grave of Chingachgook, a focus of a whole range of ironies and misunderstandings. And Natty, as we have seen, is no believer in the written word. Speaking of his own race, he says:

> It is one of their customs to write in books what they have done
> and seen, instead of telling them in their villages, where the lie can
> be given to the face of a cowardly boaster, and the brave soldier
> can call on his comrades to witness for the truth of his words. In
> consequence of this bad fashion, a man who is too conscientious to
> misspend his days among the women, in learning the names of
> black marks, may never hear of the deeds of his fathers, nor feel a
> pride in striving to outdo them (1983, p. 31).

This is a younger, brasher Natty Bumppo than the one who records (in *The Pioneers*) his pleasure in being mentioned on the grave-stone of a friend. And his misogyny is clearly open to question, as we notice his connection between literacy, civilization, and the feminine, all the things that threaten him. But if Natty is not simply Cooper here, no more is he merely an object of dramatic parody. Cooper knew in 1826, and was to know even better later in his career, that print brings with it the potential for large-scale decep-tion. The image of direct speech in a public forum has, on the contrary, not only a socially bonding function (reading being most commonly done in isolation), but also a built-in verification principle in the knowledge and consciences of one's auditors. (That it also contains the threat of demagoguery and persuasion via the passions is not explored here.) Not all the gifts of the alphabet are positive ones.

Cooper's Native American speakers do, then, embody in their languages various kinds of alternatives to and criticisms of the prevailing tendencies in the dictions and dialects of their conquerors. While they are in this sense polemically exploited, they are yet not reified into any simple image of paradisal discourse, nor cast as instances of a paradise definitively lost. Cooper's liberalism is a complex one, and it is certainly tainted with the shadows of a tragic-romantic paradigm; this will always prevent him from being canonized as any simply passionate or clear-headed exponent of Native American rights. At the same time, and in his treatment of language in particular, he seems to incorporate into his narratives a definite awareness of the claims of otherness and a distinct (and not merely romantic) sense of the integrity of the native cultures. As is the case in his representations of the varieties of American English in *The Pioneers,* and in the Effingham and Littlepage novels, his emphasis is always on conflict and tension; he offers no consoling mythologies of harmony and integration. The tact and scope of his representation of the unassimilated languages of America can best be understood in comparison with much of the other speculative and fictional literatures of the times, and in particular through a comparison with the material to which we now turn: the texts and contexts of the Transcendentalist movement.

7

The Soul of Language:
The Transcendentalist Alternative

It would be entirely possible to read through the many volumes of the collected works of James Fenimore Cooper without realizing that, for about the last fifteen years of his career, a literary and philosophical movement was coming to fruition that would come to be regarded by later critics as the true and essential origin of both American literature and the American self. Cooper's differences with Transcendentalism and its exponents go very deep indeed. He was a New Yorker, whereas Transcendentalism was an outgrowth of New England; and he was a practicing writer of fiction, while the others were mostly philosophers, theologians, and essayists. Beyond these regional and generic distinctions, deep enough to be sure (we have seen that Cooper had little time for the New Englanders of the 1840s especially), there are also profound differences of political intuition and social theory. On a superficial inspection, we might tend to cast Emerson and others like him as liberals in contrast to a posited conservatism in Cooper. The purpose of this chapter is to qualify and threaten that assumption. For Transcendentalism, to the degree that it can be thus summarized, is founded on the paradigm of the universal selfhood, the exemplary ego that subsumes (as it offers to represent) all other egos into its normative modality. It dissolves also any observed or theorized tension between man and nature, now brought into harmony under the benign gaze of an omnipresent God. As such, Transcendentalism avoids or obscures the very questions that Cooper's fictions have been argued to project and analyze—questions about the differences and tensions between the various elements in the social contract (which may be so wide as to be tragically unresolvable), and about the widening gap between the increasing needs of the human community and the integrity of unspoiled nature.

The world that Cooper transcribes is one dominated by strife and division, and for him the ethics of expansionism are complex even to the point of incoherence; the two sides of his consciousness, that which accepts and applauds the territorial ambitions of the United States, and that which sees in them some fundamental moral flaws, simply do not seem at times to fit together. The art that Cooper produces is thus not always an organic art; it is as disjoined and ungainly as the historical conditions it represents. Transcendentalism, on the contrary, is committed both in theory and in performance to the image of wholeness; it is the literary and philosophical correlative of the mythology of manifest destiny. This tradition enabled Walt Whitman, for example, to utter ideas about language which in the context provided by Cooper's work can only appear as expressions of a startling cultural megalomania:

> Names are the turning point of who shall be master.—There is so much virtue in names that a nation which produces its own names, haughtily adheres to them, and subordinates others to them, leads all the rest of the nations of the earth (1904, p. 34).

However simply critical of the British Whitman may be meaning to be, we do not have to read much of his writings to suspect that what he is suggesting is a correspondingly hegemonic role for the American language. He is able to do so in part because of the framework of expectations made normal by his Transcendentalist peers and precursors.

Of course, qualifications must be appended to the extreme contrast I have just put forward. Just as Cooper's writings incorporate in one place the very doctrines they seem to challenge in others, so we can turn to Emerson (for example) and find ample evidence of an outcry against the evils of capitalism that seems to go far beyond anything in Cooper. And Thoreau was famously in dissent from the American war against Mexico. But when all the evidence is assessed, and when all the various lines and filaments flowing through and into Transcendentalism are justified one with another, the system that emerges is, I would argue, to be seen as a healing rather than a vexing energy. That is, it seeks to adjust the tensions and contradictions so flatly reproduced by Cooper into some over-all pattern of harmony, in which the individual mind is persuaded that it is at one with other minds, with nature, and with God.

The terms of this contrast are especially pertinent to an inspection of the language theories, implicit and explicit, of the Transcendentalists and those who drew upon their writings, even if they do not adequately describe Transcendentalism as a whole. Throughout this inquiry I have been following the evolution of two strands in the writings about the American language; they sometimes intersect, but they are often different. One emphasizes the linguistic rights of the new nation and the socially bonding functions of a common speech, as described by Webster. The other, found in Cooper and elsewhere, suggests that such a common language does not and perhaps cannot exist. What is noticeably rare in the various versions of these arguments that we have been reporting (except as a theoretical preamble or enabling gesture) is any speculation about language *itself,* and as a whole. We have heard much about American English, about British English, and about the various kinds of each; but very little about an abstracted entity called "language." It is this approach, by contrast, that massively dominated the Transcendentalist discussions of the subject. Instead of writing of the *kinds* of languages that are effective agents within variously diversified social contracts (whether international or intranational), they write of language (in the singular) as a universal medium shared by all and enabling all to achieve the same access to God and to nature. In a system of doctrines that is, as Transcendentalism is, so completely mediated through the exemplary self and its utterances, the existence of languages as functioning to connect or divide *different* selves becomes so irrelevant as to seem impertinent. Thoreau, who is at least brave enough (in *Walden*) to confront the neighbors, makes of John Field and his Irish family an emblem of the vicious results of wage labor and of an imagination poisoned by the effects of a surplus economy; they are for Thoreau an instance of what happens when the exemplary selfhood fails to take shape. As Field is exiled from a true dialogue with the pastoralized patrician, so he is excluded from the language in which the book itself is written, unless as a grateful pupil: "I trust he does not read this, unless he will improve by it" (1971, p. 208).

Thoreau should not be scorned for dramatizing what so many of his peers ignored altogether. Kant, who was indeed one of the most important philosophical precursors of Transcendentalism, even as his exact ideas were modified by commentary and translation, was too scrupulous and exact a philosopher not to see the need to leave aside various kinds of evidence against the existence of (if not the potential for) a normative human subjectivity. Kant was the effective founder of the model of the synthetic unity of apperception within which the necessary correspondence of mind and world was posited. Also adumbrated therein was the common functioning of all minds by the exercise of the categories of the understanding. Kant ignored the evidence of such states as dreaming and madness as simply not appropriate to the account of the transcendental psychology, as indeed in his (very precise) terms they are not. If we start with the task of explaining how a unified experience is possible, we need not question the absoluteness of its empirical incidence in the world at that time (though not to do so risks the implication that any subject not conforming to the model might be deemed in some sense inhuman). Kant also ignored or deliberately avoided the whole question of the origin and function of *language,* for which he was roundly criticized by Herder among others. For Locke and Hobbes, and for the whole tradition coming after them, language had been a crucial, at times *the* crucial faculty in organizing the categorical intelligence within the human understanding. The place of language had raised extraordinary problems in the expositions of Kant's precursors; by leaving it out of his own deduction of the categories of the understanding, the organizing elements in all human experience, Kant knew that he could fashion a more authoritative model covering all normal minds at all times and places.[1]

In the various Idealist movements that were based on Kant's writings, however, whether in Germany, Britain, or America, we can trace the increasing and in Kantian terms illicit readmission into the system of the very elements Kant had insisted on excluding as the price of establishing the universality of his argument. Among these elements was that of language. In his attempt to relocate the case for epistemological consensus away from language, Kant had been setting his face against the whole tradition of seventeenth and eighteenth century nominalism, which was, in variously loose and precise forms, the major rationalist tradition. Even where its exponents did not suggest, as Hobbes sometimes did, that language alone provides the coherence within experience, they yet frequently recognized a strong correlation or coincidence between the operations of language and the operations of the mind as a whole. Hence it is not surprising that Kant's attempt to exclude such a prominent philosophical obsession from attention should have failed. In the writings of Herder, Fichte, Hegel, Humboldt, and other Germans, language reasserted itself as a topic in serious philosophical argument. The work of the early progenitors of modern linguistics (e.g., Bopp and Rask), as well as the speculations of etymologists like Tooke and Coleridge, further contributed to a context in which to ask questions about the mind involved framing answers that mentioned, and at times privileged, language.

The versions of European metaphysics that informed the development of Transcendentalism in America were not then, in spite of Kant, by any means devoid of philosophies of language. Furthermore, Emerson and his peers grew out of a culture in which the word had always played a central role. The language of the Bible was God's chosen medium for addressing the faithful; the questions of translation that were addressed by some academic theologians (as they were in quite different contexts by Fenimore Cooper) were just as often left aside. God, conveniently, spoke English, even if his figures and tropes required interpretation and discussion.[2]

Cooper's wonders were ultimately those of the visible world; the pantheistic speculations that Natty sometimes gives way to (e.g., in *The Pathfinder*) are not usually incremental to Cooper's major arguments. He mostly prefers that interpretative tensions be decided by worldly patricians rather than by divine philosophers. With the theorists of Transcendentalism, this is no longer the case. For them the visible only has meaning for the enlivened imagination, which must interpret what lies behind it. Active meditation replaces passive beholding. Of great interest to them was Kant's famous distinction between the phenomenal and the noumenal—things as they appear to the senses, and things as they must be thought to exist in themselves. Like the rest of Kant's method, this distinction had, of course, nothing to do with language. But the Transcendentalists were generally concerned to mount a challenge to he long-standing Lockean emphasis on the arbitrary status of words. Instead of seeing them as rationally artificial entities created for the maintenance of the social contract, they sought to describe them as natural emanations of the things they described, and as the divinely ordained and therefore necessary denominations of the world outside the self. Thus language ceased to be, for them, merely phenomenal, and became a medium through which some intuition of the enduring and essential nature of things could be obtained. Language became a means of access to things as they are in themselves, and in despite of how they might appear to contingent human desires and effective purposes.[3]

Those philosophies of language that propose to locate in words or sounds some replication of the actual operations of the physical world have most often been called "realist." Within such models, words are not arbitrarily produced by the imagination, but arise in response to some evident quality in the things they denote. No extreme version of the realist position has ever seemed seriously tenable, except to mystics; obvious objections arise in explaining the denotation of abstract ideas, and from the existence of different words in different languages. Nevertheless, at certain periods in history, and for certain groups of writers, some strong element of realism has been proposed as essential to language. Onomatopoeic words are obviously favored. Tooke's case for the sensible origins of all abstract words has a realist inclination (if no more), and among the writers of the French Enlightenment much stronger claims were made. De Brosses and Gébelin, among others, saw language as composed of elemental sounds derived with varying degrees of mediation from the natural world (see Stam, 1976, pp. 27–28).

Murray Cohen has argued that the seventeenth century witnesses the crucial division in approaches to this subject. With the writings of Locke and of the grammarians of the Port-Royal, the focus shifts from examining the relation of words to things, to exploring that between words and the order of the mind (1977, pp. 21–42). This established that the succeeding generations would be nominalists instead of realists; that is, they would be more concerned with the way in which language might give shape to the world, rather than with its natural emergence from the world of things. This bias re-

mains clear in Hobbes and in Locke, despite the materialist aspects
of their respective epistemologies. The raw materials for meaning
may indeed come through the senses, but what gives them shape
is the conceptualizing intelligence, whether inextricably involved
with language (as for Hobbes), or closely coincident with it (as in
Locke).

But the realist potential in language theory did not disappear. We
might suggest that it would tend to be most appealing to a faction
or generation for whom the avoidance of any strong image of disjunction between the human and the natural worlds becomes a
priority. Histories of literature have always told us that the British
Romantic period was such a generation, its poets such a faction.
But in fact the remarks on language made by Wordsworth and
Shelley, at least, are strongly nominalistic; words have relation to
thoughts and to passions, and are most *real* when they themselves
are authentic. They emphatically do not offer us any intuition of a
state of *things* in the natural world.

I shall not pursue the implications of this misunderstanding here,
except to say that it is an important one, and has played its part in
blinding many readers to the degree to which the Romantics are
analysts of the alienation rather than mere celebrants of the integration of man and nature. When Wordsworth speaks of the "real language of men" he is as far as he could possibly be from what we
have described as a philosophical realism in matters of language.
With Coleridge the case is more complex. His theological and etymological interests do combine to allow him to gesture toward a
reduction through language of the gap between man and nature
(and between man and other men). At the same time, some of his
finest poetry is written as a rebuke to this very fantasy of integration. The tension appears elsewhere in his poetry and thought.[4]

It was of course Coleridge—along with a Coleridgean (mis)read-
ing of Wordsworth—who was of exemplary importance for the
American Transcendentalists. And in them we can trace a strong
re-emergence of the realist potential in language theory. "Theory"
is perhaps too strict a term, since their speculations seldom take the
form of a rigorously argued case; but realism is almost omnipresent
as the aspiration holding together the various ideas about language
that came out of New England after about 1830.

Before turning to these ideas, one point must be made, and made loudly. The languages of Emerson and his contemporaries are notable for their style and vocabulary, as well as for what they say *about* language. The striking informalities, localisms, and Americanisms in Emerson's diction are famous and obvious to all readers, and they go along with a generally avowed commitment to what is democratic, and to the linguistic and cultural rights of America as its own place. Emerson too calls for "an original relation to the universe," and for the expressive resources suiting "new lands, new men, new thoughts" (1903–4, 1:3). He too is impatient with what he spicily calls "the tape-worm of Europe" (6:145). And he writes a language suited to this spirit, as F. O. Matthiessen (1941, pp. 38–40) long ago pointed out. But, as we have had occasion to observe before, this language had by the late 1830s become almost obligatory for all but the most conservative (and the most skeptical and critical) American writers. Consequently, it ceases to be *in itself* a useful yardstick for making the kinds of discrimination in which I am most interested in this chapter. If everyone speaks the language of the common man, then we can no longer look at style as a sure index of political affiliation or allusion (if indeed we ever could). Barlow's Americanisms made their point because of the specific expectations of the readers of the 1790s and 1800s; they registered as genuinely iconoclastic, even though they were in no sense expressions of the colloquial. By the time of Emerson's early publications, we might almost be excused for making the opposite assumption; that the writer who means to startle or disturb will not use the now dominant popular style.

So, if I seem to be ignoring this aspect of Emerson's linguistic profile, it is not because it is not there, but because it has now become less relevant than before. No specific idea of or commitment to the common man can be assumed from the apparent sanctioning of his language. The point is well made by Spencer (1957, p. 183), who notes that although "the Transcendentalists expressed frequent doubts concerning the soundness of the restive populace, they nevertheless consistently clung to the belief that in the speech of their plain countrymen resided a regenerative medium for the indigenous literature which they desired." The author of the essay on "New Poetry," which appeared in *The Dial* (1, 1840–41, 220–32), notes that the tendency of the times is "democratical," offering "a more liberal doctrine of the poetic faculty than our fathers held"; he praises the writer who is "not afraid to write ill" and who has "a great meaning too much at heart to stand for trifles" (p. 227). In this climate of opinion, crudeness itself becomes an aesthetic virtue, and any author who does not project it comes to be seen, with beguiling alacrity, as a conservative or undemocratic spirit. That Walt Whitman's identity as a true man of the people is so often taken for granted has much to do with the studied informality of his style.

I shall not spend time here compiling lists of Emerson's Americanisms, as I did with Cooper's. A cursory inspection suggests, moreover, that they had been for the most part familiarized by earlier writers.[5] The theoretical underpinnings of the Transcendentalists' comments on language are, however, a significant innovation on or redirection of the inherited wisdoms, and they have had a good deal of influence on the subsequently evolving concept of the American identity itself. As I have said, a rigorous theoretical coherence is usually not to be found in the Transcendentalist writings on language; but such tendencies toward coherence that do exist can be all the more persuasive when they occur in contexts where no complete conviction would be credible if it were proposed. This is the case with the realist tendency in language theory, which could not in the nineteenth century ever hope to explain entirely either the origin or the continuing development of words, but which might convince at a more informal level or as the expression of a general emphasis.

In an essay published in 1849 titled "Thoughts, Words, and Things," Henry M. Goodwin asserted that

> *the soul of language and the soul of things are the same*. Things, i.e. sensible objects, are the original, divine words, from which our words are derived. In language, we do but imitate or repeat the creative process of nature, and embody in words the same thoughts which are there embodied in things (1849, p. 286).

He does not, to be sure, assert that words are emanations *of* things, but that words and things share the same soul. In uttering our words we do not so much imitate nature as God's continuing creation *of* nature. This is a gesture very typical of the Transcendentalist version of the realist emphasis. It is relatively rare to find anyone suggesting a direct and determining relation between nature's objects,

or sounds, and the structure of language. Instances do occur, as
when Benjamin Taylor argues for language as deriving from man's
imitation of the sounds of nature:

> The liquid L, flows like the objects to which it is applied. The gut-
> teral C, is hollow like the cave it designates, or the croak and the
> caw that it imitates. The sound *st*, is *st*rong, *st*able, and *st*ubborn,
> as the objects to which it is applied (1842, p. 175).

Onomatopoeia is thus boldly introduced as the core of language:
"between natural and artificial language, there is no intermediate
chasm, or bridgeless gulf to be o'erleaped; but the transition is easy,
and the connection indissoluble" (p. 182).

Thornton's *Cadmus* had not depended on a natural language, but
it did incorporate some aspects of such a model:

> r imitates the snarling of dogs, and we find nations that have no
> dogs that have not the letter r in their languages. The aspirate of r
> indicates the flight of the partridge and some other birds, as well as
> the voice of some locusts: Gutterals imitate the croaking of frogs or
> toads; the stopt vowels and some of their aspirates are generally
> joined to some of the common vowels by animals: *baa*, the sheep—
> *bou*, the dog—*kuu*, the dove . . . (1793, p. 69).

This is the kind of thinking that is behind Thoreau's complicated
natural etymology in *Walden:*

> No wonder that the earth expresses itself outwardly in leaves, it so
> labors with the idea inwardly. The atoms have already learned this
> law, and are pregnant by it. The overhanging leaf sees here its
> prototype. *Internally,* whether in the globe or animal body, it is a
> moist thick *lobe,* a word especially applicable to the liver and lungs
> and the *leaves* of fat (γείβω, *labor, lapsus,* to flow or slip downward,
> a lapsing; λοβος, *globus,* lobe, globe; also lap, flap and many other
> words), *externally,* a dry thin *leaf,* even as the *f* and *v* are a pressed
> and dried *b.* The radicals of *lobe* are *lb,* the soft mass of the *b*
> (single lobed, or b, double lobed), with a liquid *l* behind it pressing
> it forward (1971, p. 306).

And so on. Thoreau is arguing for (or demonstrating, as he might
say) the correspondence between the soul of language and the soul
of things. Sound not only represents sense, but emanates from the
same place as the things it denotes. The atoms of language give

forth the same progeny as the atoms of the natural world, so that language itself becomes a natural energy.

This is the strong statement of the realist emphasis, and, as I have said, it was by no means universally accepted. But it may be kept in mind (and occasionally perceived) as the extreme toward which all realist arguments tend. Horace Bushnell declared that "no theory of sound, as connected with sense, in the names of things, will be found to hold extensively enough to give it any moment" (1849, p. 20). Much more commonly we find a modified or mediated realism, in which the vocabulary and syntax of language may derive in some ultimate way from nature, but not in a directly imitative way. The Lockean argument for the arbitrariness of human speech *is* definitely countered. Bushnell himself proceeds very much in the spirit of Tooke in suggesting the sensible origins of all abstract terms: "all the terms in language, which are devoted to spiritual and intellectual uses, have a physical or outward sign underlying their import" (p. 25). Even grammar is based on a natural order, so that the relations between words duplicate those between things:

> Nature having them in her own bosom, existing there in real grammatical relation, not only gives us the words, but shows us how to frame them into propositions (p. 28).

Nature seems to give the law to language, and not vice versa. But at the same time "the external grammar of creation *answers to* the internal grammar of the soul, and becomes its vehicle" (p. 28, italics mine). As the outer world is spiritualized—"a vast menstruum of thought or intelligence"—so the inner world of self is materialized by being brought into sympathy with what is in nature.[6] Although words are not facsimiles of things, they yet exist in an almost symbiotic relation to them. The relation that had for Locke always remained mechanical now becomes organic.

In a similar spirit, Josiah Gibbs seeks to "awaken attention to the life and energy which pervades language" (1839, p. 167), not by privileging its relation to things but by showing the natural propensity of certain sounds to represent particular ideas and feelings. The vowel *i* expresses "whatever is clear, shrill, bright, or small," while *m* and *n* are "the natural sounds to express refusal" (pp. 169, 171), and so on. The ingenuity of this explanation is that it seems to accept some disjunction between words and things, but reintroduces a natural connection between words and ideas, or feelings. For many theorists in the Lockean tradition, this connection had also been an arbitrary one. Although less emphatically than Taylor or Thoreau, Gibbs too asserts a natural harmony between man and his language, so that the final step back to nature and to things becomes easier to suggest.

Frederic Adams challenges the skeptics as follows:

> Have the words *soothe* and *gripe* no natural meaning at all of their own, aside from arbitrary convention? Does not the word *soothe* actually soothe, once and always, when spoken? . . . Words like the above are in truth the vocal embodiment of the truth for which they stand. They are fresh coins from the mint of the soul (1844, p. 711).

W. G. T. Shedd, one of Coleridge's early editors, makes the same point:

> As well might it be said that there is no vital and natural connection between the feeling and the blush in which it mantles, or the tear in which it finds vent, as that the word—the *"winged* word"—has only an arbitrary and dead relation to the thought (1848, p. 655).

Words possess "manifest propriety" (a telling phrase!), as do all the forms through which thought expresses itself. Goodwin too insists on "an organic and vital relation between thoughts and words, just as there is between soul and body" (1849, p. 274). For him, as for Bushnell, this relation is manifested not in words as individual elements but in the form of the connections between them. But abstract terms do evolve from sensible ones, and in a way that is not arbitrary but dependent on "a real affinity and correspondence between physical and mental phenomena," often evident in the operations of metaphor (pp. 295–96).

Emerson had put forward many of the same ideas about language in "Nature," first published in 1836. The vocabulary of the spiritual life is rooted in the material, indeed, but things also are "emblematic":

> Every natural fact is a symbol of some spiritual fact. Every appearance in nature corresponds to some state of the mind, and that state

of the mind can only be described by presenting that natural appearance as its picture (1903–4, 1:26).

The poet or writer who preserves or re-establishes this relation, who can "fasten words again to visible things," is "a man in alliance with truth and God" (p. 30). By virtue of this reunion of the spiritual and the physical, words seems to become, for Emerson, themselves physical things—deeds, events, and actions:

> Words and deeds are quite indifferent modes of the divine energy. Words are also actions, and actions are a kind of words (3:8).

An unkind commentary might suggest that such a doctrine is perfectly appropriate to the self-conscious predicament of an alienated artistic or intellectual class: only speak, and the words go forth as deeds without any further exertion.[7] It is certainly an attempt to incorporate into a fundamentally subjective and even solipsistic credo some arguable element of the physical and material world—a kind of corrective to an otherwise unfettered idealism. James Marsh, in an essay on "Ancient and Modern Poetry" for the *North American Review* (1822), had noted the absence of such subjectivity in Greek poetry, as compared with the modern:

> In the mind of the modern, all this has changed. . . . Higher interests, and sublimer conceptions, and profounder feelings are awakened, which predominate in their influence upon the imagination over all the objects of the external world, and all the passing events of life (Marsh, 1976, 1:107).

Much of the aesthetic and linguistic theory of the times can be seen as part of a campaign to redirect the imagination back toward the things around it in the material world. But the reactions of Cooper and the Transcendentalists to this inherited problem are clearly very different. Cooper offers an emphatic and unambiguous challenge to the whole tendency to impose upon nature through the exercise of the figuring imagination, and this is reflected in his image of the language. The Transcendentalists, on the other hand, like Hegel in Germany, most often end up, in their very gesture toward the material world, by reinscribing the hegemony and overall priority of the spiritual, which has now simply become a more inclusive category. While purporting to describe a world and a language from which the ego has disappeared, they in fact project a world that is all ego, all self.

This assertion will call for some further explanation. Before pursuing it, further remarks on the relations between words and things as theorized by Emerson and his contemporaries are called for. This relation goes some way toward explaining the popularity of populism in the generation before Whitman.

The hierarchy of linguistic evolution in the Transcendentalist schema generally runs, as we have seen, from the physical to the spiritual; words begin by describing natural things and come later to be applied to abstract mental states. But given the subterranean pulse of the spiritual, these apparent extremes turn out to have been connected all along. This model can also take the form of a social hierarchy, wherein the least abstracted or intellectualized portions of the populace are imaged as being in the closest contact with the original sources of words—only then to have their authority covertly subsumed! This mythology allows Emerson an eloquent rephrasing of the traditionally contested relation between grammar and usage:

> I learn immediately from any speaker how much he has already lived, through the poverty or the splendor of his speech. Life lies behind us as the quarry from whence we get tiles and copestones for the masonry of to-day. This is the way to learn grammar. Colleges and books only copy the language which the field and the work-yard made (1903–4, 1:98).

Jefferson and Webster, it will be recalled, had both formulated this relation in a similar way: common usage should give the law to grammar, and not the other way round. But their reasons for approving this sequence were quite different from Emerson's. They believed in the innate rationalism of the common man, in his instinct for analogy and conformity, which could only be perverted by polite conventions developing at the dictates of fashion. Emerson's formulation is quite different in spirit. It is the vitality and energy of common speech that appeals to him—its passion, rather than its reason. This passion is not in all men, moreover. Emerson projects a Carlylean democratism in which the shared residuum of the language is something created by "each forcible individual in the course of many hundred years," even as that same language can "convey the public sense with more purity and precision than the

wisest individual" (3:230–31). Thus, the exemplary individual cre-
ates the general standard, which then subsumes all lesser individuals; the "people" is created by the best persons, and the "common
language" is the product of the linguistic heroes of the past. The
oligarchy of energy is made up of primitive impulses. The further
back we go in time, the more poetic language becomes, to the point
where "all spiritual facts are represented by natural symbols." This
same poetry is latent in the earthbound orders of Emerson's own
generation:

> this conversion of an outward phenomenon into a type of some-
> what in human life, never loses its power to affect us. It is this
> which gives that piquancy to the conversation of a strong-natured
> farmer or backwoodsman, which all men relish (1:29).

Like many men of his time, Emerson preferred his primitives at the
point where they were about to pass into the civilized state:

> In history, the great moment is, when the savage is just ceasing to
> be a savage, with all his hairy Pelasgic strength directed on his
> opening sense of beauty. . . . Everything good in nature and the
> world is in that moment of transition, when the swarthy juices still
> flow plentifully from nature, but their astringency or acridity is got
> out by ethics and humanity (6:70–71).

Comparing the relation between grammar and usage with that between ethics and the swarthy juices in the above passage, we can
infer that Emerson's worship of primitive vigor was always safely
modified, both in language and in his image of the social order.
Hence, perhaps, the sporadic, impulsive element of surprise in the
appearance of many of his colloquialisms; their effect depends precisely on the hegemony of the norms of syntax and vocabulary they
pretend to subvert. Emerson liked his juices diluted, and language
is the perfect medium for such dilution. What the hairy Pelasgic
speaks forth takes some time to percolate up to the scholar and the
gentleman; it is sifted through a filter of received restraints repos-
ing most firmly among the literate classes, even as such restraints
are themselves the products of formerly primitive energies. Emerson's populism is coincident with a social and verbal hierarchy, and
it is framed within what has become the enabling assumption of
American liberalism; the primitive juices that really deserve to

rise will be proven deserving by virtue of having already risen. The self-made language is made up by self-making men.

Let us now return to what Emerson applauded as the vital power in primitive language, the "conversion of an outward phenomenon into a type of somewhat in human life." The key word here is, of course, *conversion*. From what has already been sold, we may infer the ways in which the Transcendentalists sought to avoid or disguise the potential disruptions of consensus that had worried the British Romantics in their assessments of this process of conversion. For the Transcendentalists, the soul of language is the same as the soul of things, so that no interpretative violence is done by one on the other. Figures of speech and imagination arise congenially and naturally out of a divinely ordained harmony between the human and the material.

The part of speech that most aptly expresses this harmony is the *verb*. We saw in Chapter 2 that Webster moved from what he thought of as a Tookean emphasis on the noun as the original element in language, to an alternative stress on the verb: *"Motion, action,* is, beyond all controversy, the principal source of words" (Webster, 1843, p. 366).[8] A similar affection for the verb exists among writers of Transcendentalist inclination. It is the part of speech most efficiently embodying the union of subject and object, man and nature, as we have seen in the various interpretations of the Native American languages. For Roswell Judson, all verbs are active verbs, and "the verb is the *esse,* the being, the existence, the life, spring and nativity of every sentence" (1831, p. 31). Josiah Gibbs also saw verbs as the originals of nouns: "Substantives and adjectives develop themselves from verbs by regular organic laws. Where a noun appears to be radical, it may be safely assumed that it is derived from a verb" (1857, p. 18). For Gibbs, "essence and activity are the only actualities in the universe" (p. 55).

We have seen in the previous chapter that the Indian languages were the subject of frequent fascination for their apparent ability to unify essence and activity in a single word-concept. From this it was inferred that they were free of the very concept of selfhood, from an ego state prior to or distinct from the oneness of self with an infinite number of experiences in the world. The Transcendentalist writers were trying to suggest very much the same thing about their own language. James Marsh's 1833 translation of Herder's

The Spirit of Hebrew Poetry specifies the ancient Hebrew as very close to the Native American paradigm in this respect (which could only have enhanced the credibility of the "lost tribe of Israel" explanation of their origins). Both languages thus became images of a synthetic perception of man *in* nature. Hebrew verbs are "all action and emotion. Their radical forms combine the representation of a sensuous image with the feeling of the heart" (Marsh, 1976, 3:I, 32). Further:

> with the Hebrew the verb is almost the whole of the language. In other words everything lives and acts. The nouns are derived from verbs, and in a certain sense are still verbs. They are as it were living beings, extracted and moulded, while their radical source itself was in a state of living energy (3:I, 29).

Marsh's translation of Herder's image of the Hebrew is even more vitalistic and rhapsodic than the similar commendations of the Indian languages already surveyed; but the symmetries are obvious. Hebrew names, like Native American names, were also fluent, changing according to circumstances and experiences (see 3:II, 210–11).

For any generation or faction concerned about the ethical complexities of man's relation to other men, or to passive nature, the status of the verb is clearly likely to be a topic of debate in language theory. It is the verb that carries or signifies the element of *doing* that changes the world. The Transcendentalist assumption of the image of synthesis seeks to make nature and all other men partake sympathetically in and even co-create the doings of any one person, poet, or pioneer. The final responsibility for that doing is then no longer to be laid at the feet of the anxious self, as it so often was in (for example) Wordsworth's meditations on the subject.

I now return to an assertion made some time ago: that, while seeming to describe a world from which the self has disappeared, the Transcendentalists in fact project a world that is all self, all ego. The historical facts of the time are notoriously eloquent about the problems of exploitation, interference, and conflict, not only in the westward migration and in the policy of Indian removal that went on during the Jacksonian period, but also in the debates about the effects of industrialization and capitalization that had such an effect on the profile of the Democratic party. All these and other stresses tend to appear in Transcendentalist writings as resolvable into images of benign cooperation. As long as the single self can pretend to speak for all others, no conflicts need arise. In this respect it is not wholly unjust to speak of the language of Transcendentalism as the language of narcissism. Like Coleridge in his "Hymn Before Sun-rise in the Vale of Chamouni," Benjamin Taylor hears in nature "one universal hymn to the great source of light and life" (1842, p. 62). Henry Goodwin can see the poet as simply a finder, not a creator:

> The poet does not bring his thoughts and impose them upon nature, or merely link them to its forms; they are there already, as truly as what are called natural or organic laws. He simply finds them, apprehends them by the power of imagination (1849, p. 289).

Sampson Reed goes as far as to suggest that when the language of things is allowed to emerge, that of words will disappear, "and being as it were resolved into its original elements, will lose itself in nature" (1838, p. 46). In all these cases, that of Coleridge included, we have to wonder whether the natural voices that are described are not in fact the cultured voices of the author's fantasies of integration. At times, the element of self-projection is clearly to be seen in the rhetoric. Here is Reed again:

> The mind will see itself in what it loves and is able to accomplish. Its own works will be its mirror; and when it is present in the natural world, feeling the same spirit which gives life to every object by which it is surrounded, in its very union with nature it will catch a glimpse of itself, like that of pristine beauty united with innocence, at her own native fountain (p. 33).

The language of synthesis and co-creation ("feeling the same spirit") is almost overpowered here by the echoes of the myth of Narcissus. Although the reflecting pool is replaced by the creative fountain, the excess of reflexivity is nonetheless notable. At times, Emerson's prose seems in the same way to echo with a beguiling innocence the more complex and troubled dramatization of narcissism in such poems as Keats' "Endymion" or Shelley's "Epipsychidion." Thus, Emerson's ideal schoolboy will see "that nature is the opposite of the soul, answering to it part for part. One is seal and one is print. Its beauty is the beauty of his own mind. Its laws are the laws of his own mind" (1903–4, 1:87). Unlike Endymion, he will presumably not wake from his dream to discover that the hand he has been kissing is his own!

The somewhat extraordinary conviction at the heart of this kind of writing in Emerson is that we cannot do harm even if we try:

> There is a soul at the centre of nature and over the will of every man, so that none of us can wrong the universe. It has so infused its strong enchantment into nature that we prosper when we accept its advice, and when we struggle to wound its creatures our hands are glued to our sides, or they beat our own breasts (2:139).

Someone must have forgotten to point this out to the buffalo hunters and the soldiers west of the Mississippi, as well as to the crew of *The Pequod*. For Emerson, nothing made by man can have a significant effect on the grand scheme of things. Man's "operations taken together are so insignificant, a little chipping, patching, and washing, that in an impression so grand as that of the world on the human mind, they do not vary the result" (1:5),[9] Perhaps it is this good faith that allows him to confound the rhetoric of passivity with the rhetoric of megalomania:

> Nature is thoroughly mediate. It is made to serve. It receives the dominion of man as meekly as the ass on which the Saviour rode. It offers all its kingdoms to man as the raw material which he may mould into what is useful. Man is never weary of working it up. He forges the subtile and delicate air into wise and melodious words, and gives them wing as angels of persuasion and command. One after another, his victorious thought comes up with and reduces all things, until the world becomes, at least, only a realized will,—the double of the man (1:40).

Emerson, astonishingly, intends or demands no Blakean or Joycean pun on *forging*, no ironic reading of *poesis* as feigning as well as creating. The poet "conforms things to his thoughts," and "impresses his being" on nature: "His imperial muse tosses the creation like a bauble from hand to hand, and uses it to embody any caprice of thought that is uppermost in his mind" (1:52). As so often with Carlyle, the figure in British literature who is in many respects closest to Emerson, we are tempted to inscribe some saving level of irony into such comments; and as with Carlyle, we either fail to find it or are forced to conclude that its apparent qualifications are merely cosmetic, a symptom of embarrassment perhaps but not of any ultimate loss of conviction. No irony is evident in Emerson's affirming that "what is best in literature is the affirming, prophesying, spermatic words of men-making poets. Only that is poetry which cleanses and mans me" (8:294).

In this way Emerson's poet—be he writer, explorer, politician, or manufacturer—occupies a position that is at once absolutely passive, unable to deflect nature from its grander course, and manically active, digging and molding in all directions. The theoretical elucidation of a language shared by man, nature, and God can therefore seem to be little more than an intellectually opportunistic licensing of every expansionist gesture of the new republic and of the culture that legitimates it. Emerson's utterances are various and diverse enough to ensure that he will continue to provide epigraphs for countless incarnations of the *Sierra Club Calendar;* but the logic underlying and holding together these utterances is that of a surprisingly uncritical representation of manifest destiny.

The very balance which, I have suggested, Transcendentalism sought to reintroduce into the relation of subject and object, self and world, seems to be consistently tipped in the direction of a hegemonic ego, even as its enabling arguments presuppose the very absence of such an entity. When Bushnell speaks of "a logos in the forms of things, by which they are prepared to serve as types or images of what is inmost in our souls" (1849, p. 30), we can trace a logic of servitude within that of symmetry. Shedd's Hegelian emphasis, though out of tune with the letter of much contemporary argument, is yet very much in tune with its spirit as it proposes that art, being committed to form, is a poorer thing than spirit, and thus a "passage into the lower sphere of the defined and sensuous" (1848, p. 660).

It must seem to some readers that in the preceding exposition I have moved away from the central topic of this study, that of language. But my contention throughout has been that ideas about language can never be fully understood simply "in themselves," that they are always implicitly or explicitly contextualized by larger and more general arguments and convictions. In the particular case of the Transcendentalists, such an approach is more than usually necessary, given the degree to which their writings have gained acceptance as the founding texts of American literature, to be celebrated rather than analyzed. It might seem unkind to cite against

Emerson (and others like him, with the case of Whitman begging the most obvious attention) his own celebration of contradiction— "With consistency a great soul has simply nothing to do. . . . To be great is to be misunderstood" (2:57–58). But it must be stressed that any writer who feels able to propose such a credo is calling for an extraordinary degree of trust and suspension of disbelief. Consistency may be the preoccupation of an anxious and cautious intelligence, but it is also the mark of one who is concerned to be aware of all the potential implications and results of his thoughts and actions. He seeks by searching for consistency to eliminate some of the deviations that might reside in his system and leave it open to unintended applications. Conservative thinkers, like Burke, have often scorned this ambition as a sign of the subservience of the individual to some narrow and limiting theory; they have contended, as they still do contend, that life is not like that. As an alternative to consistency, however, they all too often propose simply a faith in the reliability of their own judgmental intuitions. When consistency is dismissed, accountability can very easily disappear along with it.

The faith in inconsistency is very much a part of Emerson's general belief in the power of inspiration over reason, and of intuition over demonstration. Nothing valuable can be received from another, everything must arise as if originally from the self: "it is not instruction, but provocation, that I can receive from another soul" (1:127). This notion has a distinguished pedigree and is not itself implausible; but in its Romantic incarnations it tended to come up against the problems caused by different selves not seeing things in the same way (see Simpson, 1979, for an account of this). Emerson's version, however, allows for an uncomfortable degree of complacency about the innocence of one man's self-assertion and self-projection. This is not to deny that he offers also many penetrating criticisms of the course of nineteenth-century American society; he is eloquent about the evils of divided labor and of the greed underlying the commercial economy. But, as in the writings of Mill and Carlyle, these criticisms are both motivated by and subordinated to a desire to uphold the integrity of the individual self. As such they are at best naive accounts of the problems facing a culture coming to be marked by an increasing degree of diversification and dispersal. For such a society, the assumption of organic integrity most often functions as a utopian fantasy or an ideal projection of how things ought to be. When it is proposed as a description of how things really are, it risks becoming part of an obfuscating and mystifying ideology.

In the work of Fenimore Cooper, language is imaged as a symptom (and indeed a cause) of struggle and conflict within the social contract. For the Transcendentalists it is typically a medium that can embrace in harmonious synthesis every human being and every natural object. This transformation is evident also in the changing associations called up by the image of Saxonism. We have seen that for Webster, writing soon after the American and French Revolutions and during the lifetime of the infamous Horne Tooke, the emphasis on the Anglo-Saxon core of the language proved to be something of a political disaster. Conjuring up as he did all sorts of implications of civil disobedience and radical democracy, he managed to offend the conservative factions in his own party, who were not so far removed from the spirit of the Enlightenment as to ignore the potential connections between changing the language and reforming the state.

In the middle of the nineteenth century Saxonism is still alive and well, but in a very different disguise. Now it tends to be enthusiastically approved of as part of the vitalist energy of the democratic American language. For E. L. Rice, "the Saxon was always acting, and always intent upon some object; he was assiduous in his ordinary duties, and a giant in arms" (1846, p. 69). Going back to "the Saxon fountain" (p. 16) is no longer a threat to the republic but a joyous recovery of primitive energy. George Perkins Marsh, who is full of praise for "the primitive Novanglian type" (1843, p. 8), sees the English language and culture as composed of two different elements, the Gothic and the Roman. Each is necessary to the other, and both can subsist in creative harmony; but the Gothic (roughly synonymous with the Saxon) "looks beneath the form, and seeks the in-dwelling, life-giving principle, of which he holds the form to be but the outward expression. . . . To him truth is symbolized by the phenomena of organic life" (p. 15). The Gothic, in other words, is the Transcendentalist element in culture.

William Swinton, whose Whitmanesque rambles may indeed have been partly written by Whitman himself (see Dressman, 1979), and who sees a great and glorious future for the English language in America—"Freely it absorbs whatever is of use to it, absorbs and assimilates it to its own fluid and flexible substance" (1864, p. 12)— sees also a large class of synonyms generated by the coexistence of the two elements of language. Herein the Saxon is "the homely, hearty, common word—with, perchance, a poetic or sentimental sense superadded thereto: while the Latin remains literal—rigid and scientific" (p. 249). The author of the essay on "The Two Tongues" in the *Atlantic Monthly* (6, 1860, 667–74) sees the social implications of the two languages (polite and plebeian), but defends the opposite principle from that adhered to by Webster's earlier critics. He argues that the aristocratic language "dies out in poverty" while the "strong, new, popular word forces its way up, is heard at the bar, gets quoted in the pulpit, slips into the outer ring of good society." The Saxon idioms are "sharp, energetic, incisive, they do the hard labor of speech—that of carrying heavy loads of thought and shaping new ideas" (p. 669). Some sense of the specifically American appeal of this mid-century image of the Saxon may be deduced from the Englishman Matthew Harrison's cooler view of the Saxon heritage. In a book that was reprinted twice in Philadelphia, in 1850 and 1856, he speaks of the Saxons as "fierce and untamed barbarians" speaking a "harsh and monosyllabic" language (1848, p. 64). His desired "judicious admixture" (p. 90) gave, we may assume, considerably more weight to the Greek and Roman legacies than did some of his contemporaries in America.

Within the energetic self-confidence of the Transcendentalist vision, the Anglo-Saxon yoke has turned into a precious possession. Because the individual will is always at one with the general and the divine will, its tendency to create a legacy of social division has been turned aside. In Cooper's world, language and society are presented as mechanical; the parts remain parts, without combining into any grand whole. Language is always made up of different languages in conflict, and they do not resolve themselves into any democratically representative common language. These are precisely the implications that the Transcendentalists avoid or cover over. Reed, it will be recalled, had looked forward to a time when the language of words would be "resolved into its original elements" and would "lose itself in nature"; he complained that as things are we "drown the voice of nature with the discordant jargon of ten thousand dialects" (1838, p. 46). These are the dialects of Cooper's novels, and they speak for interests that are themselves discordant.

Whereas for Goodwin "the men of most thought" use words "chiefly as external symbols, the summits, as it were, of what lies concealed and cannot be expressed" (1849, p. 283), Natty Bumppo says everything he has to say and says it simply, leaving nothing to the potentially distorting imaginations of his audience. For Rowland Hazard, suggestion and allusion are the resources that privilege poetry over prose, enabling it to reach "those recesses of thought and feeling to which terms have not been extended" and communicating thereby "that volatile essence of sentiment, which, rising by its purity above the gross atmosphere of terms, can only be approached by this delicate process" (1857, p. 12). Here, observation is merely the primitive stage in expressive perception, and belongs to the child (p. 64). For Cooper, and most of all for Natty, who indeed is often compared to a child in a gesture that compounds the ambiguities of the novels, observation is everything, the very achievement of descriptive propriety, the denotation of things without the modifying colors of the imagination. As the Transcendentalists are on the point of trying to dissolve the antithesis between words and things, Natty contends, in the text of *The Prairie*, that words never *can* be things, and that the true and recognizable nature of the world should never be altered by mere words. The insistence on the arbitrary nature of words is, of course, appropriate to a fiction that sets out to analyze conflict within a divided society; words are established by consensus, they are subject to change and decay, and also to being contested, as the things they signify are contested. The organicist view of society insists conversely on some version of the realist persuasion in which words belong integrally to the common soul of man and nature. When Natty stands in the middle of a clearing, he does indeed have time for an occasional reflection on the wonders of the created world, but he is more often obliged to notice the flicker of the leaves that might denote the presence of a skulking Mingo about his "sarcumventions." His observational powers are critical to survival in a world where man is divided against man. Emerson, in contrast, experiences in the same situation an onset of cosmic security:

> Standing on the bare ground,—my head bathed by the blithe air and uplifted into infinite space,—all mean egotism vanishes. I become a transparent eyeball; I am nothing; I see all; the currents of the Uni-

versal Being circulate through me; I am part or parcel of God (1903–4, 1:10).

We might decide that we *prefer* Emerson's experience to Natty's; who, after all, wants to be part of a Hobbesian state of nature, and the war of every man against every man? But the contrast must be assessed at another level besides that of aesthetic participation, for the two alternatives are different responses to the dilemmas of mid-century America, and offer quite different prescriptions. When Emersonian man stares at the horizon, he beholds "somewhat as beautiful as his own nature," and he is "never tired" as long as he can "see far enough" (1:8, 16). Natty on the contrary never thinks of his own nature; he registers the glory of God, and then starts looking for suspicious woodsmoke. He implicitly denies the Emersonian assertion that "facts that end in the statement, cannot be all that is true of this brave lodging wherein man is harbored, and wherein all his faculties find appropriate and endless exercise" (1: 61). For Emerson, God himself "does not speak prose, but communicates with us by hints, omens, inference and dark resemblances in objects lying all around us" (8:12). For Natty, the wonders of creation are self-evident, if only we concentrate on looking rather than speculating. Against Thoreau's complaint that "our vision does not penetrate the surface of things," and that no man ignorant of books can have a true idea of what is nobly human (1971, pp. 96, 100–4), Natty shows how complete and wondrous the surface can be, and how much more truth there is outside the book of words and the society of literate men.

A very sophisticated version of the relation of words to things, and one closely coincident with the sort of ethic projected by Natty Bumppo, was proposed by Alexander Bryan Johnson, an English-born American whose principal career was that of a lawyer and banker, but who also found time to publish lectures and treatises on language and epistemology. His *Treatise on Language* was first published in 1836, and its purpose was to correct the habit whereby we interpret "nature by language" instead of "language by nature" (1947, pp. 27–28):

> Every natural existence we deem a mere representative of some word. Language usurps thus, to an astonishing extent, the dignity which truly belongs to creation. I know we usually say that words

are signs of things. Practically, we make things the signs of words
(p. 40).

Although Johnson too is challenging the inherited orthodoxies of
the nominalist tradition, according to which language orders an
otherwise chaotic world, he is too philosophically sophisticated
(and differently motivated) to resort to the organicist fantasies of
so many of the Transcendentalists. He attacks the predominance of
general ideas, those central (for the Lockean tradition) to the
economy of language and thus the progress of Thought. Noting that
language "refers to the groups which nature presents to us, and not
to the individual phenomena of any group," he seeks to encourage
us to be able to "contemplate created existence apart from their
names" (p. 53), precisely the advice given by Natty to Dr. Battius
in *The Prairie*. Because we are not, says Johnson, "accustomed to
subordinate language to the revelation of our senses . . . we invent theories to reconcile the revelation of our senses with the implications of language" (p. 62). Johnson is here touching a chord
that has sounded very loudly indeed in the critical histories deriving
from the work of Michel Foucault in the 1970s, which suggests that
all systems of ordering objects and experiences (especially those
associated with the Enlightenment) are forms of constriction and
limitation. In forcing disparate phenomena into apparently similar
categories, they often discard or dismiss those phenomena that do
not conform to the type (or general idea). They thus restrict not
only the plenitude of the natural world but also the imagination of
the beholder, which is forced into an unnecessarily narrow range of
perceptions. Perception itself, according to this explanation, is a
form of aggression.

Johnson's case against the function of general terms and ideas in
restricting our perception of the particularities of nature again bears
close relation to the way in which, as we have seen, the Native
American languages were represented; that is, as languages in which
general terms played a less important role, even to the point of
absence in certain cases. By removing the mediating effects of general terms, acts and things acted on could be specified in more particular and exact ways. It bothered Borges' Funes the Memorious
that "the dog at three fourteen (seen from the side) should have
the same name as the dog at three fifteen (seen from the front)"

(Borges, 1970, pp. 93–94). In Native American languages, this dog would not have had the same name; or, more exactly, the compound word used to describe it being seen (and replacing the name) would incorporate all this specific information. Tocqueville, it will be further recalled, had pointed out that general terms were the preferred modes of expression in democratic societies, where one is obliged to appear all things to all men. The vaguer the term, the easier it is to specify it opportunistically as the need arises.

Johnson breaks down the names of things in the world (always general terms) into particular constituent qualities or attributes; he argues that many famous philosophical problems (such as that of identity) have only become problems because it is assumed that what is *named* as distinct must *exist* as distinct. For him, words are not things and never will be:

> if you desire to know what the universe truly is, you must dismiss my names, as well as all others, and contemplate the universe externally with your senses, and internally with your consciousness. The information thus obtained is the universe. The moment this information is clothed in language, either articulately or in thought, you are wandering from the substance of the universe to the shadow (pp. 161–62).

If Natty Bumppo had ever learned to write, and to write a philosophical prose, this might have been exactly what he would have said. The silence that ensues here is alinguistic, or prelinguistic; it does not resound, as do the Transcendentalist epiphanies, with any human noise whatsoever. It is because *all* words are arbitrary that the way back to nature involves ignoring them as far as possible. Language has no soul, only layers of fashionable veils and garments to distract the mind and confuse the senses. That which has soul is not in language.

Johnson's theories are therefore a countervoice to those of the Transcendentalists. He stands, with Cooper, in isolation from the orthodoxies that have been so important in the subsequent establishment of the normative American consciousness. In a deservedly famous and influential book, *The American Renaissance,* F. O. Matthiessen bestowed a title on the efforts of Emerson, Thoreau, Hawthorne, Melville, and Whitman. The European Renaissance, as "every schoolboy knows," came after the Dark Ages. We can only infer that for Matthiessen and for subsequent generations of Americanists, the likes of Cooper, Barlow, Webster, and their contemporaries belong in the American Dark Ages. Matthiessen set out to expound the intrinsic qualities and meanings of the literature of the 1850s. Writing in reaction to an already extant tradition of cultural history (most aptly represented by Parrington) for which literature *was* an expression of the social and historical themes of its time, he believed that "you cannot 'use' a work of art unless you have comprehended its meaning" (1941, p. x). Leaving aside the question of the innocence of this distinction between use and comprehension, itself to say the least suspicious, we must insist that to explain the social and historical identity of art is not to use it. Art simply has no identity that is not socially and historically implicated and allusive, though this need not exhaust all that there is to say about it. Matthiessen touched a deep chord in the literary criticism of his time (for which he was not, of course, simply responsible), because he chose to privilege in his renaissance a group of writers among whom the purposive *abstraction* of art from the social and the historical was pursued to a degree unusual among nineteenth-century writers. The consequences of this, for the academy and beyond, are still with us. There is a relative dearth of research and teaching in the early nationalist and Jacksonian periods, because its writers are perceived to be in some essential sense unliterary. That is, they address overtly and uncomfortably the very questions that Emerson (for example) sought, consciously or otherwise, to avoid or disguise. The Transcendentalist paradigm seems to have satisfied the requirements of an academy that needs (for reasons I cannot explore here) a pure, abstract, theoretical literature, one related indeed to the *idea* of the American self and the language it might speak, but one very far removed from any overt representation of the crises of the period in which it came into being.

Of course, the allusions to and reflections of those crises are still there, and can be traced through a range of literary effects from compensatory hyperbole to silence itself; but they can be easily passed over or missed if we remain within the terms of inquiry laid down by the declared priorities of the Transcendentalists and their critics. One of the broader ambitions of this study has been to try to re-enliven the literature of the period between 1776 and 1850 by explaining the degree to which it articulates different questions and priorities from those laid down by Emerson and his kind. If, for example, we follow through the arguments and controversies surrounding the coming into being of an American English, actual and potential, we can see that the initiatives adopted by the Transcendentalists arguably represent a conceptual impoverishment, or at least a purposive and influential redirecting, of a debate that had been central throughout the first seventy-five years of the republic. These were the years in which a nation was coming into being, and a common language explored and contested. The form that these arguments took (as did the literature written around them) was divisive rather than organic; there was remarkably little imaging of America as an ideal democracy of separate selves in which each person magically incorporated the essential elements of all the others. By the time that Whitman wrote *An American Primer,* probably around 1855, the combination of obligatory populism and Emersonian individualism produces an account of the language that is almost embarrassingly glib about its loyalty to common speech. Confident that a "perfect writer" can make words "sing, dance, kiss, do the male and female act, bear children," Whitman's approval of the impolite is carried to the point of romantic excess: "I have pleasure in the use, on fit occasions, of traitor, coward, liar, shyster, skulk, doughface, trickster, mean curse, backslider, thief, impotent, lickspittle" (1904, p. 16). Not only should we suspect the implications of the faith in the equivalence of words to deeds; but also the assertion that the poet's use of the *language* of the common man makes him one. For Whitman, as for Emerson and at times for Thoreau (though never I think for Melville), the self and its language are conceived in the spirit of Coleridge's famous definition of the symbol, "an actual and essential part of that, the whole of which it represents." It "always partakes of the Reality which it renders intelligible; and while it enunciates the whole, abides itself as a living part in that Unity, of which it is the representative" (Coleridge, 1972, pp. 79, 30).

The social and political correlative of such an image is that each member of the community is as important to the whole as any other member. In the nineteenth century this notion tended to function, as it still does, as a consoling mythology softening the implacable inequalities that were more and more noticeable with the increased pace of industrialization. In the face of struggle and alienation, the organic model proposes an ulterior reality based on harmony and integration. Literary criticism's acceptance of this model has resulted in a relative lack of interest in, and indeed perception of, the issues raised by writers like Cooper, that of language among them. The acceptance of the given terms of the American renaissance has contributed also to the continuance of a mythology of exemplary selfhood and cosmic subjectivity. Some of the consequences or analogues of this mythology include the assumption that equal opportunity is a *fact* and that inequality within society does not really exist. To turn back to Cooper, to Webster, and to the Federalist critics whom he offended, is to be forcefully reminded that Americans did not always think and talk this way. What has been lost by establishing the Transcendentalist image of consciousness as *the* authoritative American self is more than just an academically refined concept of what American literature once was; it is an entire social and historical dimension to the perception of politics, language, and experience. What has all too often come to subsist, as it subsisted so uneasily and yet so comfortingly for *some* commentators of the eighteenth and nineteenth centuries, is the assumption that there is, after all, a common language.

Notes

Prologue: 1776

1. Citations of the draft and of subsequent orthographic details are from Jefferson (1950–), 1:315–19. A convenient reprint can be found in Wills (1979), pp. 374–79.
2. The original sheet is reproduced in facsimile in Boyd (1945), plate X.
3. The standard text of this work is in Johnson (1977), pp. 401–55.
4. The first edition was published in Philadelphia by R. Bell on January 10, 1776; the "New Edition" was published by W. and T. Bradford on February 14, 1776.
5. See Boswell (1970), p. 404. Boswell himself planned but never published a dictionary of words "peculiar to Scotland": see Read (1937b), p. 193. Howell (1971), pp. 156–59, notes how many of the superintendents of the English language were themselves Scotsmen, Campbell, Blair, and Kames among them. On the decline of the Scots language during the eighteenth century, see Tulloch (1980), pp. 171–81.

1. Founding Fathers and the Legacies of Language

1. See Anon [?John Adams], 1774. The letter is reprinted in Albert Matthews (1911–13), 257–64.
2. The hypothesis of Adams's authorship has been challenged on stylistic grounds by Heath (1977), p. 42.

3. See Read (1936) and (1938–39) for useful accounts of the British and American debates on the question of an academy.
4. See Mencken (1973), pp. 88–89. McKnight (1925), p. 2, traces some of these myths to Gifford and discredits them accordingly.
5. See Barrell (1983), pp. 115–19. The whole of Barrell's second chapter is relevant and complementary to the present study. See also Cohen (1977), pp. 81–88. For modern versions of the debate about correctness, see Pattison (1984), pp. 155–69.
6. Tudor is cited in *The Monthly Anthology*, 1 (1803–4), 294; see also Mitchill (1804); and Adams in *The Monthly Anthology*, 4 (1807), 143–44, also reprinted in Lewis P. Simpson (1962), p. 61. For an account of the campaign to rename the nation, see Joseph Jones (1934). Jones counted seventeen Fredonias in the United States in 1931.
7. See Witherspoon (1802), 4:458–75. For a useful summary, see Mencken (1973), pp. 5–11.
8. *The Port Folio*, vol. I, no. 31, p. 247.
9. See Wood (1972), especially pp. 59–61, 363–72, 393–429, 483–99.
10. See, e.g., Lynn Hunt (1983), who brings to light the 1797 treatise of Jean François La Harpe on the subject of fanaticism in revolutionary language. In the British context, the sheer size of the print runs for Burke's *Reflections* and Paine's *Rights of Man* is itself indicative of the power of print.
11. I am grateful to Paulson (1983), p. 15, for this particular citation. The first four chapters of Paulson's book are very informative on the relation between language and revolution. For an account of Burke's importance to the English political debate of the 1790s, see Goodwin (1979), pp. 99–135.
12. See Smelser (1968), pp. 53–54 and note. For a good account of the impact of the French Revolution on American political life, see Miller (1963), Chapters 8 and 9.
13. For an account of the relative popularity of the various available grammars, see Baron (1983), Chapters 6 and 7.
14. *Gazette of the United States*, June 4, 1800; cited in Miller (1963), pp. 228–29. The passage is in fact taken over from *The Anti-Jacobin Review*, 2 (1800), iii.

2. Noah Webster

1. See Warfel (1936). For general accounts of Webster's career, see Ellis (1979), Shoemaker (1936), Pyles (1954), pp. 75–96, and Laird (1972), p. 263ff. The information in Mencken (1973) is, as

ever, indispensable; and for a good account of the Federal English project, see Baron (1982), pp. 41–67.

2. See also Webster (1790a), pp. 78–80. This, of course, remains a contentious subject, and one that excites the notice of every British visitor to America. It would be hard to contend, for example, that *tonite* is not a better rendering of the spoken sound than *tonight,* even as the latter contains more etymological information. English remains a language in which the convenience of the average foreigner learning it is inversely proportional to the preferences of educated readers and speakers; but the gap is smaller in the case of American English than in British English.

3. Even Sheridan notes that a greater approximation of the written to the spoken would enhance national solidarity, as he asks

> Whether it would not greatly contribute to put an end to the odious distinction kept up between the subjects of the same king, if a way were opened, by which the attainment of the English tongue in its purity, both in point of phraseology and pronunciation, might be rendered easy to all inhabitants of his Majesty's dominions, whether of South or North Britain: of Ireland, or the other British dependencies? (1780, preface)

Even the metropolis is divided by two distinct dialects, and the fashions set going by Garrick are introducing provincial norms into polite speech (1786, pp. vi, 28–29).

4. Webster, of course, learned much from Johnson: see Sledd and Kolb (1955), pp. 191–204, and Reed (1962). For Webster's relation to Murray, see Webster (1953), p. 374f., and Lyman (1922).

5. I owe this citation to Barrell (1983), p. 170. Spence is in fact quoting approvingly from Sheridan (1761, p. 9), who goes on to criticize the "pedants" for demanding that foreign words retain the marks of their origins, "and wear a perpetual badge of distinction from natives" (pp. 13–14). Sheridan blames a defective alphabet for the failure of all schemes to conform the written to the spoken, a prospect of which he approves. His own initiatives in this direction involved adapting the Greek conventions for marking the quantities of vowels.

6. For a useful summary of these writings, see Wood (1972), pp. 376–83.

7. V. P. Bynack (1984) has argued otherwise, maintaining that control of the language was seen by Webster as a way of restraining the otherwise inevitable cyclic pattern of history. Bynack and Rollins (1976) both stress the importance of Webster's theological convictions for his linguistic policies.

8. On the complexities of this tradition, see Kliger (1952); Robbins (1961); Pocock (1957) and (1975), pp. 333–552; and Bailyn (1967), pp. 22–93.

9. Compare Adam Smith (1976), 1:143–44. The similarity of this model of the polymorphous psyche to that famously invoked by Marx and Engels may be noted. On the subject of the moral benefits of the wilderness, Webster was in agreement with Franklin, who had noted that the "vast quantity of forest land we have yet to clear, and put in order for cultivation, will for a long time keep the body of our nation laborious and frugal" (1806, 2:427). On the persistence of this image of the western "safety valve" into the nineteenth century, see Henry Nash Smith (1978), pp. 201–10.

10. Compare Priestley (1762), p. 220: "A people having a dependence upon, and intercourse with, another people, more considerable than themselves, are in danger of exchanging their language, in time, for that of their powerful and more learned neighbours."

11. Thus, the *American Museum*, 5 (1789), 238–40, recommends the adoption of a national dress to discourage the craze for foreign fashions and the consequent damage to the economy.

12. For the first of these images, see Pocock (1975), pp. 506–52; and Wood (1972), pp. 12–36, 97–107, 128–32. For the second, see Wood (1972), pp. 49–53, 107–24.

13. Johnson is also attacking the association of the primitive with the sublime, as well as the notion of Scotland's already having a civilization of its own! Thornton (1793, pp. 25–26n.) tells the story of a visit to the Hebrides during which he took down a Gaelic poem in phonetic script. The person who later helped him translate it "often lamented the poverty of the English language, which she said was incapable of expressing the sublimity of many of the passages." This is presumably also to be read as a refutation of Johnson.

14. The letter to Barlow is dated November 16, 1798; see Webster (1953), pp. 187–94. For the rebuke of Priestley, see Webster (1800), p. 8. For discussions of Webster's politics, see Rollins (1976) and Southard (1979).

15. *The Monthly Anthology*, 1 (1803–4), 510; 5 (1808), 272; 7 (1809), 247.

16. The 1828 preface repeats the point:

> As to Americanisms, so called, I have not been able to find many words, in respectable use, which can be so denominated. These I have admitted and noted as peculiar to this country. I have fully ascertained that most of the new words charged to the coinage of this country, were first used in England (1831, p. xlvi).

17. Webster's *Letter to Pickering* (1817) makes the same points, stressing that the attribution of neologism is usually "unfounded," but that "new words will be formed and used, if found necessary or convenient, without a licence from Englishmen" (p. 7). He goes on to argue that "new objects, new ideas, and associations of ideas, compel us, either to invent new terms, or to use English words in a new sense. The latter mode is preferable, and has generally been adopted" (p. 8). Webster is noticeably not enthusiastic about forming new words; but rational coinages are allowed, because "a living language must keep pace with improvements in knowledge and with the multiplication of ideas" (p. 28).

18. I am drawing here on the useful summary in Friend (1967), pp. 18–22.

19. For an account of the Society, from which I take this information, see Read (1934).

20. *The Monthly Anthology,* 5 (1808), 272; 8 (1810), 81, 224–25.

21. For a detailed account of Tooke's treatise, and of its popularity, see Aarsleff (1967), pp. 44–114. Aarsleff argues that much of the appeal of Tooke's methods can be attributed to their compatibility with contemporary scientific procedures, chief among them analysis and reduction.

22. See Kliger (1952) for a detailed study of this whole subject.

23. Tooke is being openly criticized by 1828. Although his derivation of conjunctions and prepositions is still endorsed, he is found guilty of the "most material errors" (1831, p. xlii). Somewhat dishonestly, Webster claims to have made no use of his work in the 1828 *Dictionary.* By 1843 he wants to argue for verbs rather than nouns as the "principal source of words" (1843, p. 366), since *"motion"* and *"action"* must have been what "at first most powerfully impressed the human mind." By 1843, America itself was in motion, and actively, westward.

24. "The Norman Yoke," in Hill (1958), pp. 50–122. Webster elsewhere insists on the centrality of the Saxon element in the language; see (1831), p. xxiv; (1839), p. 11; (1843), p. 358.

25. Hill (1958) suggests that the author was Allan Ramsay; Colbourn (1965), p. 31, and Robbins (1961), pp. 363–65, argue for Obadiah Hulme.

26. See Robbins (1961), pp. 363–65, and Colbourn (1965). On the Pennsylvania Constitution, see Wood (1972), pp. 226–37. On Jefferson's Saxonism in general, see Colbourn (1953) and Hauer (1983), who notes (p. 880) that Jefferson wanted the figures of Hengist and Horsa to appear on the Great Seal of the United States!

3. The Liberties of Literature, 1776–1810

1. Quoted in Spiller et al. (1948), 1:169. For a recent account of Freneau's career, see Elliott (1982), pp. 128–70.
2. *DA* identifies the bird as the song sparrow, while *DAE* opts for the more general definition. On Dwight, see, again, Elliott (1982), pp. 54–91.
3. See Anon. (1809–10), p. 28. Parts of the review, by Francis Jeffrey, are reprinted in Ruland (1976), pp. 72–75. On Barlow, see Elliott (1982), pp. 92–127.
4. See Blair (1960), pp. 3–37, for a general account of localisms in fiction and magazine literature before 1830. Krapp (1960), 1:225–73, is helpful, though he deals mostly in the period after 1850.
5. For a summary of the remarks made by British travelers about American English, see Mathews (1935) and Cairns (1922). On eighteenth-century pronunciation differences, see Marckwardt (1980), pp. 79–84. On Irving, see Lease (1981), pp. 13–35.
6. There is, of course, much more to say here, and a challenging case for the force of this book as a critique of American life is made by Robert Ferguson (1984), pp. 150–72.
7. For recent accounts of Brackenridge, see J. Ellis (1979), pp. 73–112; Elliott (1982), pp. 171–217; and Ferguson (1984), pp. 119–28. Ellis is especially sensitive to Brackenridge's image of America as a "set of irreconcilable contradictions and tensions" (p. 101).
8. Criswell (1940) should be consulted for a detailed account of the language of Lewis and Clark. The standard edition of the journals is by Thwaites (Lewis and Clark, 1904–5); selections are reprinted by De Voto (Lewis and Clark, 1953). Both preserve original spellings. I shall identify citations by date of entry.

4. 1812 Overtures and Jacksonian Operas

1. See Smelser (1968), pp. 218, 247–48, 299.
2. See, for example, Spencer (1957), pp. 73–155.
3. *DAE* gives *screech-owl* as first recorded in 1812, though it had been in use in Britain as a general term, not denoting a particular species. It is recorded as such in Bailey and in Entick, and it appears twice in the text of *Tom Jones* (Bk. 10, ch. 3; Bk. 11, ch. 8). On Paulding, see Taylor (1969), pp. 224–59.
4. See Mathews (1931), p. 116; and Lynn (1959), pp. 39–41.

5. For an account of Pickering's book, see Mencken (1973), pp. 49–54.

6. For a description of the Society, see Read (1936); Heath (1977), pp. 28–35; and Baron (1982), pp. 101–15.

7. For Everett's views on the subject of American English, see Read (1939).

8. See also *The Portico,* 1 (1816), 478, which says of Barlow that his "want of excellence, and of popularity, stands as a lasting monument to warn the innovator of his fate."

9. See Charvat (1936), for a bibliography (pp. 206–9) and an account of the various journals and their political persuasions (pp. 164–205); see also McCloskey (1935), and Sedgwick (1935).

10. *Westminster Review,* 2 (1824), 334–46; see Cairns (1922), pp. 10–19, from which I draw here.

11. In fact, Edwin Ray Hunter (1925), p. 169, cites this phrase as used in a Congressional speech of 1846. For a pertinent account of Bryant's career, see Ferguson (1984), pp. 173–95.

12. See Billington (1962) and Remini (1972), pp. 183ff., among others.

13. See Spencer (1957), pp. 86–87; and Bridgman (1966), pp. 44–45.

14. Unless otherwise specified by date, all citations from Cooper's novels are from the Townsend-Darley edition (1859–61).

15. This was reprinted in England by E. H. Barker (1831), a native of Tom Paine's Thetford and an amateur classicist and publisher. Barker's title was tactfully amended to *A Dictionary of the English Language,* and he claims to be printing a revised edition based on manuscript corrections provided by Webster himself. I have not tested this claim against individual entries, but the argumentative and descriptive material that takes up the first hundred or so pages is a direct reprint of 1828, with the addition (pp. lxxxii–c) of Worcester's "Synopsis of words differently pronounced by different Orthopoëists," which is reprinted from the American edition of 1829. I cite from Barker's 1831 text, in which the prefatory material is paginated (it is not in the 1828 first edition). For Webster's debt to Johnson, see Sledd and Kolb (1955), pp. 191–204; on the 1828 *Dictionary,* see Friend (1967), pp. 34–82, who offers a thorough account.

16. On the Americanisms in the *Dictionary,* see Friend (1967), pp. 49–54. Rollins (1976) stresses Christian quietism rather than patriotism as its prevailing tone, and relates this to a new preoccupation with authority and social control on Webster's part.

17. See Pound (1947); Lohrli (1962); and Mencken (1973), p. 302.

18. See Leavitt (1947), pp. 52–62; and Friend (1967), pp. 82–103.

19. See Barnes (1974), from whom I am here drawing.
20. This subject has been studied by Lynn (1959); Bridgman (1966), pp. 40–77; Tanner (1977), pp. 98–103; and Ziff (1982), pp. 181–94. See also Blair and McDavid (1983).
21. For an account of the magazine, see Mott (1930), pp. 677–84.
22. For a reading of Tocqueville as an analyst of Jacksonianism, see Meyers (1957), pp. 24–41.
23. As well as revising spellings and omitting Americanisms, the British editor is obliged to alter stress in accordance with national preferences. Thus *lev'er* and *lócate* (in Webster 1806) become *lĕ'ver* and *lo-cāte* (1856). Perhaps the most remarkable point is that Webster is deemed fit for adoption at all!

5. The Languages of Cooper's Novels

1. For a judicious account of this confusion, see Wilson (1975). Again, all unspecified references will be to the Townsend-Darley edition.
2. For accounts of the themes of the novel, see McWilliams (1972), pp. 48–64, and Taylor (1969), pp. 101–9. On Cooper's sense of language, see Lease (1981), pp. 36–50.
3. The forms *darter, hum,* and *notion* appear in Humphreys' 1815 glossary, but he also gives some alternative transcriptions, such as *calculate, sitch, despud.* Cooper uses *sitch* for Massachusetts speech elsewhere in the novel (e.g., pp. 71–72).
4. Dutch Americans were familiarly known as Germans, but Cooper intends Hartmann for the real thing (pp. 97–98).
5. Her account should be consulted for a summary of Natty's speech habits throughout the five Leatherstocking novels. In line with the differences between the 1823 and 1832 texts of *The Pioneers,* Pound notes that the later novels are more heavily marked by dialect than the earlier ones.
6. Compare Webster (1790c), p. 28.
7. Webster (1806 and 1828) gives *catamount* but defines *panther* (in 1806) as a "spotted" animal. Perhaps this is why one of Cooper's illustrators has portrayed a handsome jaguar (1980, facing p. 309). But Webster makes *panther* synonymous with *puma* in another definition. Buffon's term *cougar,* used in Campbell's *Gertrude of Wyoming,* does not appear in Webster's first two dictionaries. In the obviously plagiarized version of this episode that appears in *Davy*

Crockett's Almanack, 1837, the animal appears as an enormous lynx or bobcat, apparently about the size of a polar bear. Ben Pump would not have solved his problem of definition by further research, it seems!

8. Fearon (1818), p. 97, also notes *roiled* for "vexed."
9. For a good account of the derived aspects of Cooper's tales and their settings, see Nevius (1976).
10. The most commonly accepted derivation of this notorious word is now from the Dutch *Jan Kees,* or "Mr. Average." See Mencken (1973), p. 122.
11. The copy-text and thus the modern authorized text again show the familiar orthographic variants. There is a high degree of instability between *or* and *our,* as well as the occasional *ick* for *ic* (e.g., p. 157), and *er* for *re* (p. 386). Cooper continues to have trouble with *i* before *e,* for example, *neice, acheive* (pp. 500, 534), and uses *visiters* consistently.
12. Dickens' Sam Weller similarly renders *habeas corpus* as "have his carcase" (*Pickwick Papers,* ch. 40), perhaps an echo of Cooper's "have-us corpses" in *The Pilot* (p. 115). But Scott anticipated both writers in his use of this technique: *Old Mortality* has *Jenny-flections* and *wally-de-shamble* (chs. 7, 14).
13. For discussions of Natty's place in the ideologies variously proposed as Cooper's, see, among others, Axelröd (1978), Dekker (1967), House (1965), Kolodny (1975), McWilliams (1972), Pearce (1947), Henry Nash Smith (1978), and Waples (1938).
14. Pickering (1816), p. 73, had attributed this misuse to Pennsylvania speakers, with New Englanders preserving the proper sense. Even Webster (1828) found the extended use "not justified by etymology."
15. See also *The Sea-Lions,* p. 38. Technically, this word is probably not an Americanism, though it had remained more common in the United States than in Britain.
16. See also *Afloat and Ashore,* p. 542; and *Jack Tier,* pp. 35–36, 81–82.
17. On the struggles between Dutch Americans and New Englanders in Cooper's novels, see House (1965), pp. 93–145. In her sensitivity to Cooper's interest in types, House clearly understands and expounds the importance of his analysis of social tensions.
18. For a study of the westward expansion that takes naming as its critical and historical theme, see Fender (1981). See also Kolodny (1975).

19. For Cooper's use of the image of the sea, see Philbrick (1961), and House (1965), pp. 181–203. On Melville and Conrad, see Simpson (1982b), pp. 118–26.

6. Silence and Poetry:
The Language of the Native American

1. For a summary of the attempts at fact, see Wissler (1942). Laird (1972) is especially good on the subject of the representation of Native American languages. The images remain available, of course; hence the figure of the chief in Kesey's *One Flew Over the Cuckoo's Nest,* who has been robbed of speech.
2. Compare Heckewelder (1818), p. 129; "Indians, who have particularly distinguished themselves by their conduct, or by some other meritorious act, or who have been the subject of some remarkable occurrence, have names given to them in allusion to those circumstances."
3. I owe this citation to Baron (1982), p. 15.
4. On this subject, see Sheehan (1973), pp. 108–9. Simms, in *The Yemassee,* subscribes to this view, relating bold figures to the "poverty of language" (1835, p. 100).
5. See also Zeisberger (1830), p. 111.
6. See also Sheehan (1973), pp. 136–41.

7. The Soul of Language:
The Transcendentalist Alternative

1. For a fuller discussion of this subject and its related implications, see Simpson (1984), especially pp. 1–24. For a more complex (and thus corrective) reading of Emerson, see Wilson (1970), pp. 1–31.
2. See Lowance (1980) on the place of the figurative in biblical exegesis; and Gura (1981) on the assimilation of the Puritan tradition into the linguistic debates in nineteenth-century New England. There were, of course, dissenting voices on the question of how and where to seek true meaning, and the rage for allegory was certainly not unanimous: see Lowance (1980), pp. 80, 143, 197.
3. Gura (1981), pp. 15–31, has argued that the Unitarian idea of language was fundamentally Lockean, and was as such the doctrine against which Transcendentalism was in reaction.
4. See Simpson (1979) and (1982a) on the implications of this sub-

ject, so prophetically adumbrated by Hartman (1977).

5. Most of Emerson's initiatives were apparently colloquialisms rather than conscious Americanisms: see Cronin (1954). Thoreau, in his journals, seems to have been more adventurous: see Mencken (1973), p. 78n. For an account of Thoreau on language, see Ziff (1982), pp. 195–210; and Gura (1981), pp. 109–44.

6. For an account of the Transcendentalist stress on the harmony of mind and world, see Crosby (1975), pp. 146–78.

7. Such an inference can be made from the account of Charvat (1968), pp. 49–67, which places Emerson's thought in reaction to the mores of a philistine middle class. See also Anderson (1971), pp. 3–58. For more theoretical discussions of Emerson's view of the relation between words and things, see Matthiessen (1941), pp. 30–44; Gura (1981), pp. 75–105; and Ziff (1982), pp. 31–46.

8. See also (1817), p. 8; (1839), p. 3.

9. Compare Thoreau on the conscience-easing experience of the sublime, in *Walden* (1971), pp. 317–18.

Bibliography

Aarsleff, Hans. *The Study of Language in England, 1780–1860.* Princeton, 1967.

Adams, Frederic A. "The Collocation of Words in the Greek and Latin Languages, Examined in Relation to the Laws of Thought." *Bibliotheca Sacra,* 1 (1844), 708–25.

Adams, John [Humphrey Ploughjogger]. *The Boston Evening Post.* June 20, 1763.

———. *The Boston Gazette,* January 5, 1767.

· Adams, John. 1852: *The Works of John Adams.* Ed. Charles Francis Adams. 10 vols. Boston.

———. 1961: *Diary and Autobiography of John Adams.* Ed. L. H. Butterfield. Cambridge, Mass.

Adams, John Quincy. *Lectures on Rhetoric and Oratory.* 2 vols. (1810). Facsimile ed. Eds. J. Jeffery Auer and Jerald L. Banninga. New York, 1962.

Alexander, Caleb. *The Columbian Dictionary of the English Language.* Boston, 1800.

American Quarterly Review. Ed. Robert Walsh. 15 vols. Philadelphia, 1827–34.

Anderson, Quentin. *The Imperial Self: An Essay in American Literary and Cultural History.* New York, 1971.

Anon. [?Obadiah Hulme]. 1771: *An Historical Essay on the English Constitution.* London.

Anon. [?John Adams]. 1774: "To the Literati of America." *The Royal American Magazine,* 1 (January 1774), 6–7.

274   BIBLIOGRAPHY

Anon. 1787: *The Adventures of Jonathan Corncob, Loyal American Refugee, Written by Himself.* London, 1787; rpt. Boston, 1976.

Anon. 1809–10: Review of Barlow's *Columbiad. The Edinburgh Review,* 15, 24–40.

Anon. 1810: Review of John Quincy Adams, *Lectures on Rhetoric and Oratory. The Port Folio,* n.s. 4, 122–36.

Anon. 1813–14: Review of *Inchiquen* [*sic*] *the Jesuit's Letters. Quarterly Review,* 10, 494–539.

Anon. 1824: "Domestic Literature." *Atlantic Magazine,* 1, 130–39.

Anon. 1860: "The Two Tongues." *Atlantic Monthly,* 6, 667–74.

Anon. 1867: "Inroads upon English." *Blackwood's Magazine,* 102, 399–417.

Austen, Jane. *Sense and Sensibility.* Ed. Tony Tanner. Harmondsworth, Middlesex, 1980.

Axelröd, Allan M. *History and Utopia: A Study of the World View of James Fenimore Cooper.* Norwood, Pa., 1978.

Bailey, Nathan. *Dictionarium Britannicum: Or, a Compleat Etymological English Dictionary, being also an Interpreter of Hard and Technical Words.* London, 1730.

Bailyn, Bernard. *The Ideological Origins of the American Revolution.* Cambridge, Mass., 1967.

Barlow, Joel. 1807: *The Columbiad.* Philadelphia.

———. 1970: *The Works of Joel Barlow.* Eds. William K. Bottorff and Arthur L. Ford. 2 vols. Gainesville, Fla.

Barnes, James J. *Authors, Publishers and Politicians: The Quest for an Anglo-American Copyright Agreement, 1815–54.* London, 1974.

Baron, Dennis E. *Grammar and Good Taste: Reforming the American Language.* New Haven and London, 1982.

Barrell, John. *English Literature in History, 1730–80: An Equal, Wide Survey.* London, 1983.

Barton, Benjamin Smith. *New Views of the Origin of the Tribes and Nations of America.* Philadelphia, 1797.

Beck, Theodoric Romeyn. "Notes on Mr. Pickering's *Vocabulary of Words and Phrases* . . . with Preliminary Observations." *Transactions of the Albany Institute,* 1 (1830), 25–31.

Bentman, Raymond, "Robert Burns' Use of Scottish Diction." In *From Sensibility to Romanticism: Essays Presented to Frederick A. Pottle.* Eds. Harold Bloom and Frederick W. Hilles. New York, 1965, pp. 239–58.

Billington, Ray Allen. *The Far Western Frontier, 1830–1860.* 1956; rpt. New York, 1962.

Bird, Robert Montgomery. *Nick of the Woods; or, the Jibbenainosay. A Tale of Kentucky.* 2 vols. Philadelphia, 1837.

Blair, Walter. *Native American Humor.* 1937; rpt. New York, 1960.

Blair, Walter, and McDavid, Raven I., Jr. *The Mirth of a Nation: America's Great Dialect Humor.* Minneapolis, 1983.

Blake, William. *The Complete Poetry and Prose of William Blake.* Ed. David V. Erdman. Revised ed. Berkeley and Los Angeles, 1982.

Blau, Joseph L., ed. *American Philosophical Addresses, 1700–1900.* New York, 1946.

'Borealis'. "English Language in America." *Southern Literary Messenger,* 2 (January 1836), 110–11.

Borges, Jorge Luis. *Labyrinths: Selected Stories and Other Writings.* Eds. Donald A. Yates and James E. Irby. Harmondsworth, Middlesex, 1970.

Boswell, James. *Life of Johnson.* Ed. R. W. Chapman. Corr. ed. J. D. Fleeman. London, Oxford, New York, 1970.

Boyd, Julian P., Ed. *The Declaration of Independence: The Evolution of the Text as Shown in Facsimiles of Various Drafts by Its Author, Thomas Jefferson.* Princeton, 1945.

Brackenridge, Hugh Henry. *Modern Chivalry; Containing the Adventures of Captain John Farrago, and Teague O'Regan, his Servant.* 4 vols. Philadelphia, 1792–97.

Brackenridge, Hugh Henry, and Freneau, Philip. *A Poem on the Rising Glory of America.* Philadelphia, 1772.

Brenni, Vito J. *American English. A Bibliography.* Philadelphia, 1964.

Bridgman, Richard. *The Colloquial Style in America.* New York, 1966.

Bristed, Charles Astor. "The English Language in America." *Cambridge Essays, Contributed by Members of the University, 1855,* pp. 57–78. London, 1855.

Bristed, John. *The Resources of the United States of America.* New York, 1818.

Brockden Brown, Charles, ed. 1800: *The Monthly Magazine and American Review.* 3 vols. New York.

———, ed. 1801–2: *The American Review and Literary Journal.* 2 vols. New York.

Brown, Solyman. *An Essay on American Poetry, with Several Miscellaneous Pieces.* New Haven, 1818.

Bryant, William Cullen [Anon.]. 1808. *The Embargo, or Sketches of the Times, a Satire. By a Youth of Thirteen.* Boston.

———. 1809: ——— *The Second Edition. Revised and Enlarged. Together with The Spanish Revolution and other Poems.* Boston.

————. 1821: *Poems*. Cambridge, Mass.

————. 1941: "Dictionary of the New York Dialect of the English Tongue." Ed. Cullen Bryant. *American Speech,* 16, 157–58.

Burke, Edmund. *The Works of the Rt. Hon. Edmund Burke.* 12 vols. Boston, 1899.

Bushnell, Horace. "Preliminary Dissertation on the Nature of Language, as Related to Thought and Spirit." Prefaced to *God in Christ: Three Discourses,* pp. 9–97. Hartford, Conn., 1849.

Bynack, V. P. "Noah Webster's Linguistic Thought and the Idea of an American National Culture." *Journal of the History of Ideas,* 45 (1984), 99–114.

Byron, George Gordon, Lord. *"Famous in My Time": Byron's Letters and Journals.* Vol. 2. Ed. Leslie A. Marchand. Cambridge, Mass., 1973.

Cairns, William B. 1898: *On the Development of American Literature from 1815 to 1833, with Especial Reference to Periodicals. Bulletin of the University of Wisconsin.* Philology and Literature Series. Vol. 1, no. 1. Madison.

————. 1922: *British Criticisms of American Writings, 1815–33: A Contribution to the Study of Anglo-American Literary Relationships. University of Wisconsin Studies in Language & Literature.* No. 14. Madison.

Campbell, Archibald [Anon.]. *Lexiphanes, A Dialogue. Imitated from Lucian, and suited to the Present Times. Being an Attempt to Restore our English Tongue to its Ancient Purity. . . .* 2nd ed. London, 1767.

Campbell, George. *The Philosophy of Rhetoric.* 1776; new ed. London, 1850.

Campbell, N. A. "Protection for our Language." *North American Review,* 149 (1889), 127–28.

Campbell, Patrick. *Travels in the Interior Inhabited Parts of North America.* Edinburgh, 1793.

Campbell, Thomas. *The Poetical Works of Thomas Campbell.* Ed. Rev. W. A. Hill. London and New York, n.d.

Candler, Isaac. *A Summary View of America . . . By an Englishman.* London and Edinburgh, 1824.

Cardell, William S. 1821: *American Academy of Language and Belles Lettres. Circular I* (12th July, 1821).

————. 1823: Ibid. *Circular III* (January, 1822).

————. 1825: *Essay on Language, as connected with the Faculties of the Mind, and as applied to Things in Nature and Art.* New York.

————. 1826: *Elements of English Grammar, deduced from Science and Practice, adapted to the Capacity of Learners.* . . . New York.

Carey, Matthew. See *The American Museum.*

Carrol, James. *The American Criterion of the English Language; containing the Elements of Pronunciation; in five sections; for the use of English Schools and Foreigners.* New London, Conn., 1795.

Channing, Walter. "Essay on American Language and Literature." *North American Review,* 1 (1815), 307–14.

Channing, William Ellery. "Remarks on National Literature" (1830). In *The Works of William E. Channing, D.D.,* pp. 124–38. Boston, 1875.

Charvat, William. 1936: *The Origins of American Critical Thought, 1810–35.* Philadelphia & London.

————. 1959: *Literary Publishing in America, 1790–1850.* Philadelphia.

————. 1968: *The Profession of Authorship in America, 1800–1870. The Papers of William Charvat.* Ed. Matthew J. Bruccoli. Columbus, Ohio.

Chastellux, Marquis de. *Travels in North America, in the Years 1780, 1781 and 1782.* 2 vols. London, 1787.

Cobb, Lyman. *A Critical Review of the Orthography of Dr. Webster's Series of Books for Systematick Instruction in the English Language.* New York, 1831.

Cobbett, William. *Cobbett's English Grammar.* With an introduction by H. L. Stephen. London, 1906.

Cogswell, J. G. "Review of Schoolcraft's *Narrative Journal of Travels through the northwestern Region of the United States.*" *North American Review,* 15 (1822), 224–50.

Cohen, Murray. *Sensible Words: Linguistic Practice in England, 1640–1785.* Baltimore and London, 1977.

Colbourn, H. Trevor. 1953: "The Saxon Heritage of Thomas Jefferson." Ph.D. diss., The Johns Hopkins University.

————. 1965: *The Lamp of Experience: Whig History and the Intellectual Origins of the American Revolution.* Chapel Hill.

Coleridge, Samuel Taylor. *Lay Sermons.* Ed. R. J. White. *The Collected Works of Samuel Taylor Coleridge.* Vol. 6. London and Princeton, 1972.

Cooper, James Fenimore. 1831: *The Spy; A Tale of the Neutral Ground.* Revised and corrected. London.

————. 1832a: [Anon.]. *Notions of the Americans: Picked up by a Travelling Bachelor.* 2 vols. 1828; rpt. Philadelphia.

————. 1832b: *The Prairie; A Tale.* Revised and corrected. London.

————. 1834: *A Letter to his Countrymen.* New York.

————. 1838: [Anon.]. *The Chronicles of Cooperstown.* Cooperstown, N.Y.

————. 1859–61: *Cooper's Novels.* Illustrated from Drawings by F. O. C. Darley. 32 vols. New York.

————. 1960–68: *The Letters and Journals of James Fenimore Cooper.* Ed. James Franklin Beard. 6 vols. Cambridge, Mass.

————. 1969: *The American Democrat, or Hints on the Social and Civic Relations of the United States of America.* (1838). Eds. George Dekker and Larry Johnston. Harmondsworth, Middlesex.

————. 1980: *The Pioneers; or the Sources of the Susquehanna. A Descriptive Tale.* Eds. James F. Beard, Lance Schacterle, Kenneth M. Anderson, Jr. Albany, N.Y.

————. 1981: *The Pathfinder, or The Inland Sea.* Ed. Richard Dilworth Rust. Albany, N.Y.

————. 1982: *Gleanings in Europe: England.* Eds. Donald A. Ringe, Kenneth W. Staggs, James P. Elliott, R. D. Madison. Albany, N.Y.

————. 1983: *The Last of the Mohicans. A Narrative of 1757.* Eds. James F. Beard, James A. Sappenfield, E. N. Feltskog. Albany, N.Y.

Cowper, William. *Poems.* 3rd ed. 2 vols. London, 1787.

Craigie, Sir William, and Hulbert, James R. *A Dictionary of American English on Historical Principles.* 4 vols. Chicago, 1938.

Criswell, Elijah Harry. *Lewis and Clark: Linguistic Pioneers.* In *University of Missouri Studies: A Quarterly of Research.* Vol. 15, no. 2 (April 1940). Columbia, Missouri.

Cronin, Morton. "Some Notes on Emerson's Prose Diction." *American Speech,* 29 (1954), 105–13.

Crosby, Donald A. *Horace Bushnell's Theory of Language in the Context of other nineteenth-century Philosophies of Language.* The Hague and Paris, 1975.

Dehon, Theodore. "A Discourse upon the Importance of Literature in our Country." *The Monthly Anthology,* 4 (1807), 465–74.

Dekker, George. *James Fenimore Cooper the Novelist.* London, 1967.

Dekker, George, and McWilliams, John P., eds. *Fenimore Cooper: The Critical Heritage.* London and Boston, 1973.

"Demophilus." *The Genuine Principles of the Ancient Saxon, or English Constitution.* Philadelphia, 1776.

Derrida, Jacques. *Of Grammatology.* Trans. Gayatri Chakravorty Spivak. Baltimore and London, 1976.

Dillard, J. L. *Black English: Its History and Usage in the United States.* 1972. Rpt. New York, 1973.

Dressman, Michael Rowan. "Walt Whitman's Plans for the Perfect Dictionary." In *Studies in the American Renaissance, 1979,* pp. 457–74. Ed. Joel Myerson. Boston, 1979.

Du Ponceau, Peter S. *A Discourse on the Necessity and the Means of Making our National Literature Independent of that of Great Britain.* Philadelphia, 1834.

Dunglison, Robley. "Americanisms." *Virginia Literary Museum,* 1 (1829–30), 417–20; 457–60; 479–80; 497–99; 531–33; 577–79.

Dwight, Timothy. 1785: *The Conquest of Canaan. A Poem, in eleven books.* Hartford, Conn.

———. 1794: *Greenfield Hill. A Poem in Seven Parts.* New York.

———. 1969: *Travels in New England and New York.* Eds. Barbara Miller Soloman and Patricia M. King. 4 vols. Cambridge, Mass.

Edwards, Jonathan. *Observations on the Language of the Muhhekaneew Indians.* New ed., with notes by John Pickering. Boston, 1823.

Eliot, John. *A Grammar of the Massachusetts Indian Language.* With remarks by Peter S. Du Ponceau, and further notes by John Pickering. Boston, 1822.

Eliot, T. S. *American Literature and the American Language.* An Address Delivered at Washington University on June 9, 1953. *Washington University Studies. New Series. Language and Literature,* no. 23. 1953.

Elliott, Emory. *Revolutionary Writers: Literature and Authority in the New Republic, 1725–1810.* Oxford and New York, 1982.

Elliott, John. See Johnson, Samuel, Jr.

Ellis, David Maldwyn. *Landlords and Farmers in the Hudson-Mohawk Region, 1790–1850.* 1946; rpt. New York, 1967.

Ellis, Joseph J. *After the Revolution: Profiles of Early American Culture.* New York and London, 1979.

Elphinston, James. *A Minniature ov Inglish Orthoggraphy.* London, 1795.

Elstob, Elizabeth. *The Rudiments of Grammar for the English-Saxon Tongue, first given in English: with an Apology for the Study of Northern Antiquities.* London, 1715.

Emerson, Ralph Waldo. *The Complete Works of Ralph Waldo Emerson.* Centenary ed. 12 vols. Boston and New York, 1903–4.

Emmons, Richard. *The Fredoniad; or, Independence Preserved. An Epick Poem of the Late War of 1812.* 4 vols. Boston, 1827.

Encyclopaedia Americana. A Popular Dictionary of Arts, Sciences, Literature, History, Politics and Biography. Eds. Francis Lieber and Edward Wigglesworth. 13 vols. Philadelphia, 1829–33.

Entick, John. *Entick's New Spelling Dictionary.* Ed. William Crakelt. London, 1791.

Everett, Edward. Review of "Circulars Addressed to the American Members of the American Academy of Language and Belles Lettres. By the Corresponding Secretary." In *North American Review,* 14 (1822), 350–359.

Fearon, Henry Bradshaw. *Sketches of America. A Narrative of a Journey of five thousand miles through the Eastern and Western States of America.* . . . London, 1818.

Fender, Stephen. *Plotting the Golden West. American Literature and the Rhetoric of the California Trail.* Cambridge, 1981.

Ferguson, Robert A. *Law and Letters in American Culture.* Cambridge, Mass. and London, 1984.

Fielding, Henry. *Tom Jones.* Ed. Sheridan Baker. New York and London, 1973.

Fletcher, Richard M. *The Stylistic Development of Edgar Allan Poe.* The Hague and Paris, 1973.

Fliegelman, Jay. *Prodigals and Pilgrims: The American Revolution Against Patriarchal Authority, 1750–1800.* Cambridge, 1982.

Franklin, Benjamin. *The Complete Works, in Philosophy, Politics and Morals.* 3 vols. London, 1806.

Frederick, John T. "Cooper's Eloquent Indians." *PMLA,* 71 (1956), 1004–17.

Freneau, Philip. *Poems Written and Published During the American Revolutionary War.* 2 vols. Philadelphia, 1809.

Fridén, Georg. *James Fenimore Cooper and Ossian. Essays and Studies on American Language and Literature, Publications of the American Institute in the University of Upsala, VIII.* Cambridge, Mass. and Upsala, 1949.

Friend, Joseph H. *The Development of American Lexicography.* The Hague and Paris, 1967.

Gallatin, Albert. "Synopsis of the Indian Tribes of North America." *Archaeologica Americana. Transactions and Collections of the American Antiquarian Society.* Vol. 2. Cambridge, 1836.

Gates, W. B. "Cooper's Indebtedness to Shakespeare." *PMLA,* 67 (1952), 716–31.

Gibbs, Josiah W. 1839: "On the Natural Significancy of Articulate Sounds." *The American Biblical Repository.* 2nd series, no. 3 (July 1839), 166–74.

————. 1857: *Philological Studies, with English Illustrations.* New Haven.

Godwin, William. *The Enquirer. Reflections on Education, Manners, and Literature. In a series of Essays.* London, 1797.

Goodwin, Albert. *The Friends of Liberty: The English Democratic Movement in the Age of the French Revolution.* London, 1979.

Goodwin, Henry M. "Thoughts, Words, and Things." *Bibliotheca Sacra,* 6 (1849), 271–300.

Griswold, Rufus Wilmot, ed. *The Prose Writers of America, with a Survey of the History, Condition and Prospects of American Literature.* Philadelphia, 1847.

Gura, Philip F. *The Wisdom of Words: Language, Theology and Literature in the New England Renaissance.* Middletown, Conn. 1981.

Hall, Captain Basil, F. R. S. *Travels in North America in the Years 1827 and 1828.* 3rd ed. 3 vols. Edinburgh, 1830.

Harrison, Rev. Matthew. *The Rise, Progress and Present Structure of the English Language.* London, 1848.

Harte, F. Bret. *Condensed Novels and Other Papers.* New York, 1867.

Hartman, Geoffrey. *Wordsworth's Poetry, 1787–1814.* Sixth printing. New Haven and London, 1977.

Hauer, Stanley D. "Thomas Jefferson and the Anglo-Saxon Language." *PMLA,* 98 (1983), 879–98.

Hazard, Rowland G. *Essay on Language, and other Papers.* Ed. E. P. Peabody. Boston, 1857.

Heath, Shirley Brice. "A National Language Academy? Debate in the New Nation." *Linguistics. An International Review,* 189 (1977), 9–43.

Heckewelder, Rev. John. *An Account of the History, Manners, and Customs of the Indian Nations, Who Once Inhabited Pennsylvania and the Neighbouring States.* Philadelphia, 1818.

Henshall, Samuel. *The Saxon and English Languages Reciprocally Illustrative of each other . . . and a New Mode of Radically Studying the Saxon and English Languages.* London, 1798.

Hill, Christopher. "The Norman Yoke." In *Puritanism and Revolution: Studies in the Interpretation of the English Revolution of the Seventeenth Century,* pp. 50–122. London, 1958.

Hobbes, Thomas. *Leviathan.* London and New York. 1973.

Hoerder, Dirk. *Crowd Action in Revolutionary Massachusetts, 1765–80.* New York, San Francisco, London, 1977.

House, Kay Seymour. *Cooper's Americans.* Columbus, Ohio, 1965.

Howell, Wilbur Samuel. *Eighteenth-Century British Logic and Rhetoric.* Princeton, 1971.

Hume, David. *The Letters of David Hume.* Ed. J. Y. T. Greig. 2 vols. Oxford, 1932.

Humphreys, David. 1804: *The Miscellaneous Works of David Humphreys.* New York.

————. ?1815: *The Yankey in England. A Drama, in Five Acts.* By General Humphreys.

Hunt, Lynn. "The Rhetoric of Revolution in France." *History Workshop Journal,* 15 (1983), 78–94.

Hunter, Edwin Ray. "The American Colloquial Idiom, 1830–60." Ph.D. diss., University of Chicago, 1925.

Hustvedt, S. B. "Philippic Freneau." *American Speech,* 4 (1928–29), 1–18.

Ingersoll, Charles Jared [Anon.]. 1810: *Inchiquin, the Jesuit's Letters; During a Late Residence in the United States of America.* . . . New York.

————. 1823: *A Discourse Concerning the Influence of America on the Mind.* Philadelphia.

Irving, Washington. 1968: *Washington Irving's Contributions to "The Corrector."* Ed. Martin Roth. *Minnesota Monographs in the Humanities,* vol. 3. Minneapolis.

————. 1977: *Letters of Jonathan Oldstyle, Gent.; Salmagundi.* Eds. Bruce I. Granger and Martha Hartzog. *The Complete Works of Washington Irving,* vol. 6. Boston.

Jackson, Donald. "The Race to Publish Lewis and Clark." *Pennsylvania Magazine of History and Biography,* LXXXV (1961), 163–77.

Jefferson, Thomas. 1903: *The Writings of Thomas Jefferson.* Eds. Andrew A. Lipscomb and A. E. Bergh. 20 vols. Washington.

————. 1926: *The Commonplace Book of Thomas Jefferson.* Ed. Gilbert Chinard. *Johns Hopkins Studies in Romance Literature & Languages,* extra vol. 2. Baltimore and Paris.

————. 1950– : *The Papers of Thomas Jefferson.* Ed. Julian P. Boyd et al. 20 vols. in progress Princeton.

Johnson, Alexander Bryan. *A Treatise on Language.* Ed. David Rynin. Berkeley and Los Angeles, 1947.

Johnson, Samuel. 1773: *A Dictionary of the English Language, in which the Words are deduced from their Originals, and Illustrated in their Different Significations, by Examples from the Best Writers. To which are prefixed A History of the Language and an English Grammar.* 4th ed. Revised by the author. 2 vols. London.

————. 1957: *Johnson: Poetry and Prose.* Ed. Mona Wilson. 2nd ed. London.

————. 1977: *Political Writings*. Ed. Donald J. Greene. *The Yale Edition of the Works of Samuel Johnson*, vol. 10. New Haven and London.

Johnson, Samuel, Jr. *A School Dictionary*. New Haven, 1798.

Johnson, Samuel, Jr., and Elliott, John. *A Selected, Pronouncing and Accented Dictionary*. Suffield, Conn., 1800.

Jones, Joseph. "Hail, Fredonia!" *American Speech*, 9 (1934), 12–17.

Judson, Roswell. *Two Epistles of Free Stricture, on the American Dictionary of Mr. Webster, on the Hebrew Grammar and Hebrew Chrestomathy of Mr. Stuart, and on the Manual Hebrew Lexicon of Mr. Gibbs*. 2nd ed. New Haven, 1830.

Kime, Wayne R. "Washington Irving and Frontier Speech." *American Speech*, 42 (1967), 5–18.

Kliger, Samuel. *The Goths in England: A Study in Seventeenth and Eighteenth-Century Thought*. Cambridge, Mass., 1952.

Knapp, Samuel Lorenzo. *Lectures on American Literature, with Remarks on some Passages of American History*. New York, 1829.

Kolodny, Annette. *The Lay of the Land: Metaphor as Experience and Literature in American Life and Letters*. Chapel Hill, 1975.

Krapp, George Philip. *The English Language in America*. 1925; rpt. 2 vols. New York, 1960.

Krumpelmann, John T. "Timothy Flint, Contributor of Americanisms, 1826." *American Speech*, 44 (1969), 135–38.

Laird, Charlton. *Language in America*. 1970; rpt. Englewood Cliffs, N.J., 1972.

Lease, Benjamin. *Anglo-American Encounters: England and the Rise of American Literature*. Cambridge, 1981.

Leavitt, Robert Keith. *Noah's Ark: New England Yankees and the Endless Quest*. Springfield, Mass., 1947.

Lenin, V. I. *On Literature and Art*. Moscow, 1970.

Leonard, Sterling Andrus. *The Doctrine of Correctness in English Usage, 1700–1800. University of Wisconsin Studies in Language and Literature*, no. 25. Madison, 1929.

Lewis, Meriwether, and Clark, William. 1904–5: *Original Journals of the Lewis and Clark Expedition, 1804–06*. Ed. Reuben Gold Thwaites. 8 vols. (in 15). New York.

————. 1953: *The Journals of Lewis and Clark*. Ed. Bernard de Voto. Boston.

Locke, John. *An Essay Concerning Human Understanding*. Ed. Peter H. Nidditch. Corr. ed. Oxford, 1979.

Lohrli, Anne. "Dickens' *Household Words* on American English." *American Speech*, 37 (1962), 83–94.

Longfellow, Henry Wadsworth. Review of Sidney's *Defence of Poetry.* *North American Review,* 34 (1832), 56–78.

[Longstreet, Augustus Baldwin]. *Georgia Scenes, Characters, Incidents &c., in the First Half Century of the Republic. By a Native Georgian.* Augusta, 1835.

Low, Donald A., ed. *Robert Burns: The Critical Heritage.* London and Boston, 1974.

Lowance, Mason I., Jr. *The Language of Canaan: Metaphor and Symbol in New England from the Puritans to the Transcendentalists.* Cambridge, Mass., and London, 1980.

Lowell, James Russell. *Meliboeus-Hipponax. The Biglow Papers.* Ed. Homer Wilbur. Cambridge, Mass., 1848.

Lowth, Robert. *A Short Introduction to English Grammar.* London, 1762.

Lyman, Rollo La Verne. *English Grammar in American Schools Before 1850.* Dept. of the Interior, Bureau of Education, *Bulletin* (1921) no. 12. Washington, 1922.

Lynn, Kenneth S. *Mark Twain and Southwestern Humor.* Boston and Toronto, 1959.

McCloskey, John C. "The Campaign of Periodicals after the War of 1812 for National American Literature." *PMLA,* 50 (1935), 262–73.

McDavid, Raven I., Jr., Ed. *An Examination of the Attitudes of the NCTE Toward Language.* National Council of Teachers of English. Research Report no. 4. 1965.

McDowell, Tremaine. "James Fenimore Cooper as Self-Critic." *Studies in Philology,* 27 (1930), 508–16.

McKnight, George H. "Conservatism in American Speech." *American Speech,* 1 (1925), 1–17.

McWilliams, John P., Jr. *Political Justice in a Republic: James Fenimore Cooper's America.* Berkeley, Los Angeles, London, 1972.

Marckwardt, Albert H. *American English.* 2nd ed., rev. J. L. Dillard. Oxford and New York, 1980.

Marryat, Captain Frederick, C. B. *A Diary in America, with Remarks on its Institutions.* 3 vols. London, 1839.

Marsh, George Perkins. *The Goths in England.* A Discourse Delivered at the Anniversary of the Philomathesian Society of Middlebury College, August 15, 1843. Middlebury, Vt., 1843.

Marsh, James. *Selected Works of James Marsh.* 3 vols. Delmar, N.Y., 1976.

Mathews, Mitford M. *1931: The Beginnings of American English. Essays and Comments.* Chicago.

————. 1935: "Notes and Comments upon American English made by British Travelers and Observers, 1770–1850." Ph.D. diss., Harvard University.

————, ed. 1951: *A Dictionary of Americanisms on Historical Principles.* 2 vols. Chicago.

Matthews, Albert. "Early Discussions of Americanisms." *Publications of the Colonial Society of Massachusetts,* 14 (1911–13), 257–64.

Matthews, Brander. *Americanisms and Britticisms, with other Essays on other Isms.* New York, 1892.

Matthiessen, F. O. *American Renaissance: Art and Expression in the Age of Emerson and Whitman.* New York, London, Toronto, 1941.

Mencken, H. L. *The American Language; An Inquiry into the Development of English in the United States.* 4th ed. & two supplements, abridged and revised by Raven I. McDavis, Jr. and David W. Maurer. 1963; 4th printing, New York, 1973.

Meyers, Marvin. *The Jacksonian Persuasion. Politics and Belief.* Stanford, Calif., 1957.

Miller, John C. *The Federalist Era: 1789–1801.* 1960; rpt. New York, Evanston, London, 1963.

Miller, Perry. *Nature's Nation.* Cambridge, Mass., 1967.

Mitchill, Samuel Latham. 1804: *Address to the Fredes, or the People of the United States.* New York, 1804.

————. 1821: *A Discourse on the State and Prospects of American Literature.* Delivered at Schenectady, July 24, 1821, before the New York Alpha of the Phi-Beta-Kappa Society. Albany.

Morse, Jedidiah. 1789: *The American Geography; or, a View of the Present Situation of the United States of America.* Elizabethtown, N.J.

————. 1822: *A Report to the Secretary of War of the United States, on Indian Affairs, comprising a Narrative of a Tour performed in the Summer of 1820.* New Haven.

————. 1824: Ed. *The First Annual Report of the American Society for Promoting the Civilization and General Improvement of the Indian Tribes of the United States.* New Haven.

Mott, Frank Luther. *A History of American Magazines, 1741–1850.* New York and London, 1930.

Murray, Lindley. *An English Grammar: Comprehending the Principles and Rules of the Language, Illustrated by appropriate Exercises, and a Key to the Exercises.* 5th American from the last English edition. Corrected and enlarged. 2 vols. New York, 1823.

Mushkat, Jerome. *Tammany: The Evolution of a Political Machine.* Syracuse, 1971.

Neal, John. 1824–25: ["X.Y.Z."]. "American Writers." In five parts. *Blackwood's Edinburgh Magazine*, 16 (1824), 304–11, 415–28, 560–71; 17 (1825), 48–69, 186–207.

———. 1825: *Brother Jonathan: or, the New Englanders.* 3 vols. Edinburgh.

Neumann, J. H. *American Pronunciation according to Noah Webster (1783).* Excerpt from Ph.D. diss., Columbia University pamphlet, 1924.

Nevius, Blake. *Cooper's Landscapes: An Essay on the Picturesque Vision.* Berkeley, Los Angeles, London, 1976.

North-American Review and Miscellaneous Journal. Boston, 1815–   .

Överland, Orm. *The Making and Meaning of an American Classic: James Fenimore Cooper's "The Prairie."* New York and Oslo, Bergen, Tromsö, 1973.

Paine, Thomas. *Common Sense: Addressed to the Inhabitants of America.* Philadelphia. R. Bell, 1776.

———. New Edition. Philadelphia. W. & T. Bradford, 1776.

Patterson, Paul [Anon.]. *The Playfair Papers, or Brother Jonathan, the Smartest Nation in all Creation.* 3 vols. London, 1841.

Pattison, Robert. *On Literacy: The Politics of the Word from Homer to the Age of Rock.* 1982; rpt. Oxford and New York, 1984.

Paulding, James Kirke. 1812: [Anon.]. *The Diverting History of John Bull and Brother Jonathan.* By Hector Bull Us. New York.

———. 1814a: [Lemuel Lengthy]. "Americanisms." *The Analectic Magazine*, 3, 404–9.

———. 1814b: [Anon.]. *The Lay of the Scottish Fiddle.* 1st American, from the 4th Edinburgh edition. London.

———. 1815: [Anon.]. *The United States and England: being a Reply to the Criticism on Inchiquin's Letters, contained in the Quarterly Review for January, 1814.* New York.

———. 1818: *The Backwoodsman. A Poem.* Philadelphia.

———. 1822: [Anon.]. *A Sketch of Old England, by a New-England Man.* 2 vols. New York.

———. 1823: [Anon.]. *Konigsmarke, The Long Finne.* 3 vols. New York and London.

———. 1825: [Anon.]. *John Bull in America; or the New Munchhausen.* New York.

Paulson, Ronald. *Representations of Revolution, 1789–1820.* New Haven and London, 1983.

Peach, Linden. *British Influence on the Birth of American Literature.* New York, 1982.

Pearce, Roy Harvey. 1947: "The Leatherstocking Tales Re-Examined." *South Atlantic Quarterly,* 46, 524–36.

———. 1953: *The Savages of America: A Study of the Indian and the Idea of Civilization.* Baltimore.

Peck, H. Daniel. *A World By Itself: The Pastoral Moment in Cooper's Fiction.* New Haven and London, 1977.

Philbrick, Thomas L. *James Fenimore Cooper and the Development of American Sea Fiction.* Cambridge, Mass., 1961.

Pickering, John. *A Vocabulary, or Collection of Words and Phrases which have been supposed to be peculiar to the United States of America, to which is prefixed an Essay on the Present State of the English Language in the United States.* Boston, 1816.

Pocock, J. G. A., 1957: *The Ancient Constitution and the Feudal Law: English Historical Thought in the Seventeenth Century.* Cambridge, 1957.

———. 1975: *The Machiavellian Moment: Florentine Political Thought and the Atlantic Republican Tradition.* Princeton.

Pound, Louise. 1927: "The Dialect of Cooper's Leather-Stocking." *American Speech,* 2, 479–88.

———. 1947: "The American Dialect of Charles Dickens." *American Speech,* 22, 124–30.

Price, Richard. *Observations on the Nature of Civil Liberty, the Principles of Government, and the Justice and Policy of the War with America.* London; rpt. Philadelphia, 1776.

Priestley, Joseph. *A Course of Lectures on the Theory of Language and Universal Grammar.* Warrington, 1762.

Pyles, Thomas. *Words and Ways of American English.* London, 1954.

Quirk, Randolph. *The English Language and Images of Matter.* London, 1972.

Railton, Stephen. *Fenimore Cooper: A Study of his Life and Imagination.* Princeton, 1978.

Read, Allen Walker. 1933a: "British Recognition of American Speech in the Eighteenth-Century." *Dialect Notes,* 6, 313–34.

———. 1933b: "Noah Webster as Euphemist." *Dialect Notes,* 6, 385–91.

———. 1934. "The Philological Society of New York, 1788." *American Speech,* 9, 131–36.

———. 1936: "American Projects for an Academy to Regulate Speech." *PMLA,* 51, 1141–79.

————. 1937a: "Bilingualism in the Middle Colonies." *American Speech*, 12, 93–99.

————. 1937b: "Projected English Dictionaries, 1755–1828." *JEGP*, 36, 188–205; 347–66.

————. 1938: "The Assimilation of the Speech of British Immigrants in Colonial America." *JEGP*, 37, 70–79.

————. 1938–39: "Suggestions for an Academy in England in the Latter Half of the Eighteenth Century." *Modern Philology*, 36, 145–56.

————. 1939: "Edward Everett's Attitude Towards American English." *New England Quarterly*, 12, 112–29.

Reed, Joseph W. "Noah Webster's Debt to Samuel Johnson." *American Speech*, 37 (1962), 95–105.

Reed, Sampson. *Observations on the Growth of the Mind, with Remarks on Some other Subjects.* 3rd ed. Boston, 1838.

Remini, Robert Vincent, ed. *The Age of Jackson.* Columbia, S.C., 1972.

Rice, E. L. *Introduction to American Literature; or, the Origin and Development of the English Language, with Gems of Poetry.* Cincinnat [*sic*], 1846.

Robbins, Caroline. *The Eighteenth-Century Commonwealthman. Studies in the Transition, Development and Circumstance of English Liberal Thought from the Restoration of Charles II until the War with the Thirteen Colonies.* Cambridge, Mass., 1961.

Rogin, Michael Paul. *Fathers and Children: Andrew Jackson and the Subjugation of the American Indian.* New York, 1975.

Rollins, Richard M. "Words as Social Control: Noah Webster and the Creation of the American Dictionary." *American Quarterly*, 28 (1976), 415–30.

Ruland, Richard, ed. *The Native Muse. Theories of American Literature from Bradford to Whitman.* Vol. 1. New York, 1976.

Sampson, Geoffrey. *Liberty and Language.* Oxford and New York, 1979.

Schlesinger, Arthur M., Jr. *The Age of Jackson. 1945;* rpt. New York, 1946.

Sedgwick, William Ellery. "The Materials for an American Literature: A Critical Problem of the Early Nineteenth Century." *Harvard Studies and Notes in Philology and Literature*, 17 (1935), 141–62.

Shedd, W. G. T. "The Relation of Language to Thought." *Bibliotheca Sacra*, 5 (1848), 650–63.

Sheehan, Bernard W. *Seeds of Extinction: Jeffersonian Philanthropy and the American Indian.* Chapel Hill, 1973.

Sheridan, Thomas. 1761: *A Dissertation on the Causes of the Difficulties, which occur, in learning the English Tongue. With a Scheme for publishing an English Grammar and Dictionary, upon a Plan entirely new.* London.

————. 1780: *A General Dictionary of the English Language; one main object of which, is, to establish a plain and permanent Standard of Pronunciation.* 2 vols. London.

————. 1786: *Elements of English: Being a new Method of Teaching the Whole Art of Reading, both with regard to Pronunciation and Spelling. Part the First.* London.

Sherman, John. *The Philosophy of Language Illustrated: An Entirely New System of Grammar, wholly divested of Scholastic Rubbish, of traditionary Falsehood and Absurdity, and reduced to Principles of Fact and Common Sense, according to the real Nature, Genius and Idiom of the English Tongue: designed for Colleges, Academies, and District Schools in the United States.* Trenton Falls, N.Y. 1826.

Shoemaker, Ervin C. *Noah Webster, Pioneer of Learning.* New York, 1936.

Shulman, David. "N. P. Willis and the American Language." *American Speech,* 23 (1948), 39–47.

Sigourney, Mrs. L. H. *Select Poems.* 4th ed. Philadelphia, 1843.

Simms, William Gilmore. 1835: *The Yemassee. A Romance of Carolina.* 2 vols. New York.

————. 1962: *Views and Reviews in American Literature, History and Fiction* (1845). Ed. C. Hugh Holman. Cambridge, Mass., 1962.

Simpson, David E. 1979: *Irony and Authority in Romantic Poetry.* London and Totowa, N.J.

————. 1982a: *Wordsworth and the Figurings of the Real.* London and Atlantic Highlands, N.J.

————. 1982b: *Fetishism and Imagination: Dickens, Melville, Conrad.* Baltimore and London.

————, ed. 1984: *German Aesthetic and Literary Criticism: Kant, Fichte, Schelling, Schopenhauer, Hegel.* Cambridge.

Simpson, Lewis P., ed. *The Federalist Literary Mind: Selections from "The Monthly Anthology and Boston Review," 1803–11.* Baton Rouge, 1962.

Sledd, James H. and Kolb, Gwin J. *Dr. Johnson's Dictionary: Essays in the Biography of a Book.* Chicago, 1955.

Smelser, Marshall. *The Democratic Republic, 1801–1815.* New York, 1968.

Smith, Adam. 1976: *An Inquiry into the Nature and Causes of the Wealth of Nations.* Eds. R. H. Campbell, A. S. Skinner, W. B.

Todd. *The Glasgow Edition of the Works and Correspondence of Adam Smith.* 2 vols. Oxford.

——. 1977: *The Correspondence of Adam Smith.* Eds. Ernest Campbell Mossner and Ian Simpson Ross. *The Glasgow Edition of the Works and Correspondence of Adam Smith.* Oxford.

Smith, Elihu Hubbard, ed. *American Poems.* Litchfield, Conn., 1793.

Smith, Henry Nash. *Virgin Land: The American West as Symbol and Myth.* 1970; rpt. Cambridge, Mass. and London, 1978.

Smollett, Tobias. *Humphry Clinker.* Ed. James L. Thorson. New York and London, 1983.

Southard, Bruce. "Noah Webster: America's Forgotten Linguist." *American Speech,* 54 (1979), 12–22.

Spence, Thomas. 1775: *The Grand Repository of the English Language.* Newcastle-upon-Tyne,

——. 1808: *Dhĕ' Impŏrtănt Triăl ŏv Tŏmĭs Spĕns.* London.

Spencer, Benjamin T. *The Quest for Nationality. An American Literary Campaign.* Syracuse, N.Y., 1957.

Spiller, Robert E. "Cooper's Notes on Language." *American Speech,* 4 (1928–29), 294–300.

Spiller, Robert E., Thorp, Willard, Johnson, Thomas H., Canby, Henry Seidel, eds. *Literary History of the United States.* 3 vols. New York. 1948.

Staël, Madame de. *The Influence of Literature upon Society.* Hartford, Conn., 1843.

Stam, James H. *Inquiries into the Origin of Language: The Fate of a Question.* New York, 1976.

Stewart, George R. *Names on the Land. A Historical Account of Place-Naming in the United States.* Rev. ed. Boston, 1967.

Swinton, William. *Rambles Among Words: Their Poetry, History and Wisdom.* Rev. ed. New York, 1864.

Tanner, Tony. *The Reign of Wonder. Naivety and Reality in American Literature.* 1965; rpt. Cambridge, 1977.

Taylor, Benjamin F. *Attractions of Language, or a Popular View of Natural Language, in all its Varied Displays, in the Animate and Inanimate World.* Hamilton, N.Y., 1842.

Taylor, William F. *Cavalier and Yankee: The Old South and American National Character.* 1961; rpt. New York and Evanston, 1969.

The American Museum, or, Repository of Ancient and Modern Fugitive Pieces, &c., Prose and Poetical. Ed. Matthew Carey. 12 vols. Philadelphia, 1787–92.

The Analectic Magazine, containing Selections from foreign Reviews

and Magazines, of such Articles, as are most valuable, curious or entertaining. 14 vols. Philadelphia, 1813–19.

The Dial: A Magazine for Literature, Philosophy, and Religion. Eds. George Ripley, Ralph Waldo Emerson, Margaret Fuller Ossoli. 4 vols. Boston and London, 1840–43.

The Eclectic Review. 10 vols. London, 1805–13.

The Monthly Anthology; or Magazine of Polite Literature. [Title changed in 1804 to *The Monthly Anthology and Boston Review.*] 10 vols. Boston, 1803–11.

The Port Folio. By Oliver Oldschool Esq. [Joseph Dennie] (until 1812). Philadelphia, 1801–27.

The Portico, A Repository of Science and Literature. 5 vols. Baltimore, 1816–18.

The United States Magazine and Democratic Review. Eds. John D. O'Sullivan and S. D. Langtree. 29 vols. Washington [later New York], 1837–51.

Thoreau, Henry David. *Walden.* Ed. J. Lyndon Shanley. *The Works of Henry David Thoreau.* Princeton, 1971.

Thornton, William. *Cadmus; or, a Treatise on the Elements of Written Language.* Philadelphia, 1793.

Tooke, John Horne. *ΕΠΕΑ ΠΤΕΡΟΕΝΤΑ; or the Diversions of Purley.* New edition, revised and corrected by Richard Taylor. 2 vols. London, 1829.

Tocqueville, Alexis de. *Democracy in America.* The Henry Reeve text. Revised by Francis Bowen. Ed. Phillips Bradley. 2 vols. New York, 1945.

Trollope, Mrs. Frances M. *Domestic Manners of the Americans.* London and New York, 1832.

Tulloch, Graham. *The Language of Walter Scott. A Study of his Scottish and Period Language.* London, 1980.

Turner, Sharon. *The History of the Anglo-Saxons, from the Earliest Period to the Norman Conquest.* 7th ed. 3 vols. London, 1852.

Twain, Mark. "Concerning the American Language." *The Stolen White Elephant, &c.* Boston, 1882, pp. 265–69.

Tyler, Royall. 1790: *The Contrast. A Comedy in Five Acts.* Written by a Citizen of the United States. Philadelphia.

———. 1809: *The Yankey in London. Being the First Part of a Series of Letters written by an American Youth, during nine months' Residence in the City of London.* Vol. One. New York.

———. 1968: *The Verse of Royall Tyler.* Ed. Marius B. Péladeau. Charlottesville, Va., 1968.

Van Deusen, Glyndon G. *1828–48: The Jacksonian Era*. New York, 1963.

Walker, John. *A Critical Pronouncing Dictionary and Expositor of the English Language*. . . . London, 1791.

Waln, Robert [Anon.]. *American Bards. A Satire*. Philadelphia, 1820.

Waples, Dorothy. *The Whig Myth of James Fenimore Cooper*. Yale Studies in English, vol. 88. New Haven and London, 1938.

Warfel, Harry. *Noah Webster: Schoolmaster to America*. New York, 1936.

Webster, Noah. 1785: *Sketches of American Policy*. Hartford, Conn.

——. 1789a: *Dissertations on the English Language, with an Essay on a Reformed Mode of Spelling*. Boston.

——. 1789b: *An American Selection of Lessons in Reading and Speaking*. 6th ed. Newport, R.I.

——. 1790a: *Rudiments of English Grammar; being an Introduction to the second Part of the Grammatical Institute of the English Language*. Hartford, Conn.

——. 1790b: *A Collection of Essays and Fugitiv Writings on Moral, Political, Historical and Literary Subjects*. Boston.

——. 1790c: *A Grammatical Institute of the English Language; Part Second, Grammar*. Boston.

——. 1798a: *A Letter to the Governors, Instructors and Trustees of the Universities and Other Seminaries of Learning in the United States, on the Errors of English Grammars*. New York.

——. 1798b: *An Oration Pronounced before the Citizens of New-Haven, on the anniversary of the Independence of the United States, July 4th, 1798*. New Haven.

——. 1800: *Ten Letters to Dr. Joseph Priestly* [sic]. New Haven.

——. 1802: *Miscellaneous Papers on Political and Commercial Subjects*. New York.

——. 1806: *Compendious Dictionary of the English Language, in which Five Thousand Words are added to the number found in the best English Compends*. Hartford and New Haven.

——. 1807a: *A Philosophical and Practical Grammar of the English Language*. New Haven.

——. 1807b: *The American Spelling Book, containing the Rudiments of the English Language, for the use of Schools in the United States*. Rev. ed. Boston.

——. 1817: *A Letter to the Honorable John Pickering, on the subject of his Vocabulary*. Boston.

——. 1823: *Letters to a Young Gentleman commencing his Educa-*

tion; to which is subjoined a brief History of the United States.
New Haven.

———. 1828: *An American Dictionary of the English Language.* 2 vols.
New York.

———. 1830: *A Dictionary of the English Language, abridged from the
American Dictionary, for the use of Primary Schools and the
Counting House.* New York.

———. 1831: *A Dictionary of the English Language.* Rpt. London.
[E. H. Barker]. 2 vols.

———. 1839: *Observations on Language and on the Errors of Class
Books; also, Observations on Commerce.* New Haven.

———. 1843: *A Collection of Papers on Political, Literary and Moral
Subjects.* New York.

———. 1856: *Webster's Pronouncing Dictionary of the English Language.* A new edition. Ed. and rev. P. A. Nuttall. London.

———. 1858: *A Dictionary of the English Language.* Rev. & enlarged
Chauncey A. Goodrich. London.

———. 1953: *The Letters of Noah Webster.* Ed. Harry H. Warfel. New
York.

Whitman, Walt. *An American Primer.* Ed. Horace Traubel. Boston,
1904.

Williams, Roger. *A Key into the Language of America.* Eds. John J.
Teunissen and Evelyn J. Hinz. Detroit, 1973.

Wills, Garry. *Inventing America: Jefferson's Declaration of Independence.* 1978; rpt. New York, 1979.

Wilson, R. Jackson. 1970: *In Quest of Community: Social Philosophy
in the United States, 1860–1920.* 1968; rpt. London, Oxford,
New York.

———. 1975: "Gentlemen Democrats at Home and Abroad: Alexis de
Tocqueville, Samuel F. B. Morse, James Fenimore Cooper." In
Men, Women, and Issues in American History, Volume 1, pp.
133–52. Eds. Howard H. Quint and Milton Cantor. Home-
wood, Ill.

Wissler, Clark. "The American Indian and the American Philosophical
Society." *American Philosophical Society, Proceedings,* 86
(1942), 189–204.

Witherspoon, Rev. John. *The Works of the Rev. John Witherspoon, D.D.,
L.L.D.* 2nd ed. 4 vols. Philadelphia, 1802.

Wood, Gordon S. *The Creation of the American Republic, 1776–1787.*
1969; rpt. New York and London, 1972.

Worcester, Joseph Emerson. 1828: Ed. *Johnson's English Dictionary as*

Improved by Todd, and abridged by Chalmers; with Walker's Pronouncing Dictionary, combined: to which is added, Walker's Key to the classical Pronunciation of Greek, Latin and Scripture Proper Names. Boston.

——. 1830a: *A Comprehensive Pronouncing and Explanatory Dictionary of the English Language, with Pronouncing Vocabularies of Classical and Scripture proper names.* Boston.

——, ed. 1830b: Noah Webster, *An American Dictionary of the English Language, abridged.* 1829; 3rd ed. New York.

——. 1846: *A Universal and Critical Dictionary of the English Language.* Boston.

——. 1853: *A Gross Literary Fraud Exposed; relating to the Publication of Worcester's Dictionary in London.* Boston.

Wordsworth, William. *The Poetical Works of William Wordsworth.* Ed. E. de Selincourt. 5 vols. Oxford, 1940–49.

Worth, Gorham. [Anon.] *American Bards. A Modern Poem.* "West of the Mountains," 1819. [Published in Cincinnati.]

Zeisberger, David. "A Grammar of the Language of the Lenni Lenape or Delaware Indians." Trans. Peter S. Du Ponceau. *Transactions of the American Philosophical Society held at Philadelphia for Promoting Useful Knowledge.* Vol. 3 (n.s.), 65–251. Philadelphia, 1830.

Ziff, Larzer. *Literary Democracy: The Declaration of Cultural Independence in America.* 1981; rpt. Harmondsworth, Middlesex, 1982.

Index